Municipal Environmental Compliance Manual

Edited by
Lisa Dowden
John McNurney

LEWIS PUBLISHERS
Boca Raton   Ann Arbor   London   Tokyo

Library of Congress Cataloging-in-Publication Data

Municipal environmental compliance manual / [edited] by Lisa G. Dowden, John M. McNurney.
     p. cm.
    Includes index.
    ISBN 1-56670-098-1
    1. Environmental law—United States.   2. Municipal corporations—United States.
I. Dowden, Lisa G.   II. McNurney, J. M.
KF3775.M79   1994
344.73\046—dc20
[347.30446]   94-31122
                                                              CIP

© 1995 by CRC Press, Inc.
Lewis Publishers is an imprint of CRC Press

No claim to original U.S. Government works
International Standard Book Number 1-56670-098-1
Library of Congress Card Number 94-31122
Printed in the United States of America 1 2 3 4 5 6 7 8 9 0
Printed on acid-free paper

About the Authors

Lisa G. Dowden
Spiegel & McDiarmid, Washington, DC

Ms. Dowden is a partner in the Washington, DC, law firm of Spiegel & McDiarmid. The firm represents some 400 cities, counties, states, and public agencies in the environmental, energy, communications, and airport fields. Ms. Dowden provides environmental compliance counseling to numerous municipal and public utility clients and has performed environmental compliance assessments for municipalities and utilities across the country. She is responsible, along with John McNurney of R. W. Beck, for the annual updates to the American Public Power Association's *Environmental Compliance Manual for Electric Utilities*, a compliance guide for municipally owned electric utilities. She has written and spoken extensively on hazardous waste, Superfund, and their effects on local government operations. Ms. Dowden is a 1986 graduate of the Harvard Law School and a 1983 graduate of Washington University in St. Louis and serves as a vice chair on the Solid and Hazardous Waste Committee of the American Bar Association's Section on Natural Resources, Energy, and Environmental Law.

John M. McNurney
R. W. Beck, Denver, CO

Mr. McNurney is a Partner and Senior Director of Environmental Services in the Denver office of R. W. Beck, a national engineering firm which specializes in providing engineering and technical analysis to municipalities, local governments, utilities, industry, and regional authorities across the country. Mr. McNurney has provided environmental management services for projects across the U.S. and its territories. His engineering work emphasizes compliance investigations, water resources issues, facility siting, and permitting strategy, and his biological work has included ecosystem analysis and toxicology. In addition to his 24 years of practical experience, he has been a primary instructor for 32 environmental compliance training seminars attended by over 1,300 local government attendees. Mr. McNurney is a graduate of the University of Illinois, with a B.S. in general biology and an M.S. in environmental engineering.

Contributing Authors

Todd W. Filsinger
R. W. Beck, Denver, CO

An executive engineer with the Consulting Services Group, Mr. Filsinger provides management for municipal projects in the areas of acquisition, feasibility, financial evaluation, and integrated resource planning. For a number of environmental compliance assessments, Mr. Filsinger has provided management structure analysis for municipal environmental departments. He holds a B.S. in mechanical engineering from Colorado State University and an M.B.A. from the University of Colorado.

Mark S. Hegedus
Spiegel & McDiarmid, Washington, DC

Mr. Hegedus is an associate with Spiegel & McDiarmid. He counsels and provides updates to municipal and public utility clients on environmental issues ranging from electric and magnetic fields (EMF) to hazardous substance release reporting and community right-to-know. Mr. Hegedus is involved in the legislative arena on Clean Water Act reauthorization issues. Mr. Hegedus is a 1991 graduate of the New York University School of Law and a 1985 graduate of the University of Michigan.

Susanna M. Higgins
R. W. Beck, Denver, CO

Ms. Higgins' experience in environmental planning, biology, property risk assessment, and preparation of environmental documentation has been applied to a variety of projects. Her experience includes preparation of environmental documents for power-generating facilities, mining projects, and oil and gas facilities and analysis of transportation resources, land use, and regulatory compliance. Ms. Higgins received her B.A. in environmental sciences from the University of Colorado.

David A. Kahl
R. W. Beck, Denver, CO

A principal engineer with the Solid Waste Resource Recovery Group at R. W. Beck, Mr. Kahl has experience with a wide variety of solid waste issues. He has conducted studies on the feasibility of composting technologies, curbside collection of recyclable materials, and integrated waste management systems. Mr. Kahl serves on the Board of Directors of Eco-Cycle, a community recycling program in Boulder, CO. He holds a B.A. in English and a B.S. in mechanical engineering from the University of Iowa.

Mark A. Keyworth
R. W. Beck, Denver, CO

Mr. Keyworth specializes in wastewater treatment design evaluation and assessment of sludge disposal options. His experience includes independent engineering review and wastewater monitoring and permitting for municipal wastewater treatment plants, NPDES compliance for a citywide wastewater treatment system, and evaluation and design of effluent toxicity testing to determine compliance with regulations. Mr. Keyworth received a B.S. in microbiology from Colorado State University and an M.S. in environmental engineering from Virginia Polytechnic Institute.

David Kolker
Spiegel & McDiarmid, Washington, DC

David Kolker is a partner with Spiegel & McDiarmid. In the legislative area, Mr. Kolker represents American Communities for Cleanup Equity (ACCE), a national coalition of local governments seeking reform of the Superfund statute as it relates to liability for municipalities. Mr. Kolker also litigates a variety of matters before federal agencies, trial courts, and appellate courts, and has written and taught about local governments and Superfund. Mr. Kolker graduated from Harvard Law School in 1985, and from Yale University in 1980.

Wendy S. Lader
Spiegel & McDiarmid, Washington, DC

Ms. Lader is an associate with Spiegel & McDiarmid. She has provided environmental compliance counseling in numerous areas and participated in municipal environmental compliance assessments. Ms. Lader is a 1992 graduate of the University of Pennsylvania Law School and a 1986 graduate of Harvard University.

Susan K. Lawson
R. W. Beck, Denver, CO

Ms. Lawson is a principal planning analyst specializing in public involvement and multiparty dispute management. Her experience includes technical communications, facilitation, technical education programs, and assistance to government agencies seeking citizen involvement in planning resource management policy and projects. Ms. Lawson serves as an Adjunct Professor in the Environmental Policy and Management Division of University College of the University of Denver. She received a B.A. in linguistics and communication from the University of Montana.

Matthew D. Lee
R. W. Beck, Denver, CO
An engineer with the Environmental Services Group, Mr. Lee specializes in environmental compliance assessment issues for municipalities, utilities, and industry. Prior to joining R. W. Beck he was an investigator for the Environmental Protection Agency, National Enforcement Investigations Center. Mr. Lee holds a B.S. in mechanical engineering from the Colorado School of Mines.

Linda M. Long
R. W. Beck, Denver, CO
A principal engineer, Ms. Long provides a variety of consulting services associated with power generation facilities for government and industry including air quality analyses, air emission performance testing, and the application of air pollution control technologies. She specializes in allowance programs, continuous emissions monitoring, and emissions inventories and estimates. Ms. Long is a graduate of the Colorado School of Mines with a B.S. in chemical engineering.

David R. Meyer
R. W. Beck, Denver, CO
Mr. Meyer is a senior scientist with 15 years of experience in environmental compliance assessments, licensing and permitting, and risk assessment. In addition he has provided waste management and environmental compliance training for municipalities, covering issues such as organizational management, oil/fuels management, and hazardous waste, recordkeeping, and risk communication. He received his B.S. in range-forest management from Colorado State University and is pursuing a master's degree in environmental policy and management at the University of Denver.

William J. Mundt
R. W. Beck, Denver, CO
A senior scientist, Mr. Mundt's background includes geology, meteorology, and hazardous materials technology. He specializes in environmentally related investigations including site assessment evaluations related to property transfer, subsurface geological/hydrogeological evaluation, independent review of CERCLA investigations, baseline environmental studies, and regulatory compliance issues. Mr. Mundt holds a B.S. in geology from Texas Tech University, a B.S. equivalent in meteorology from San Jose State University, and an A.S. in science and certificate in hazardous materials technology from Front Range Community College.

Michael S. Robinson
R. W. Beck, Denver, CO
Mr. Robinson is a senior engineer specializing in air and water quality issues for utilities, municipalities, and industry, including air emissions analysis and design and review of water treatment systems. His experience includes emissions source inventories, evaluation of pollution control technologies, and analysis of economic impacts of potential compliance alternatives. Mr. Robinson holds a B.S. in mechanical engineering from Colorado State University.

Robert J. Schafish
R. W. Beck, Denver, CO
Mr. Schafish is a principal engineer with 25 years of experience in technical analysis of environmental systems for municipalities, utilities, and governmental authorities. His work has included environmental studies assessing environmental impacts and regulatory compliance, development of solid waste management plans and programs, and expert testimony concerning environmental impacts. He holds a B.S. in civil engineering and an M.S. in environmental engineering from Drexel University.

D. Edward Settle
R. W. Beck, Denver, CO
Mr. Settle is a senior engineer specializing in air quality issues for municipalities and industry. He has prepared Prevention of Significant Deterioration (PSD) and minor source construction or operating permit applications for more than 60 sources of air emissions, including dispersion modeling, preparation of emissions inventories, evaluation of best available control technology, and negotiation with regulatory agencies. Mr. Settle also assesses the compliance status of local government and industry clients with major federal and state environmental regulations including requirements associated with air emissions, water discharges, PCBs, hazardous waste, waste oil, and oil releases. Mr. Settle holds a B.S. in chemistry from Bob Jones University and is currently pursuing an M.S. in chemical engineering at the Colorado School of Mines.

James F. Short
R. W. Beck, Denver, CO
A senior engineer, Mr. Short's primary focus is environmental compliance assessments for municipalities and utilities, including practical assessment of environmental contamination and evaluation of remedial and preventative engineering. His related experience includes hazardous waste site remedial investigations, oil spill prevention control and countermeasure (SPCC) plans, risk assessment, and independent engineering. He holds a B.S. in chemical engineering from Oklahoma State University.

Russell F. Smith III
Spiegel & McDiarmid, Washington, DC

Mr. Smith is a senior associate attorney at Spiegel & McDiarmid. His practice includes the representation of clients before administrative agencies and courts and compliance counseling on matters arising under the Clean Water Act and the laws regulating PCBs and pesticides. He also advises clients on insurance coverage for the cleanup of environmental contamination. Mr. Smith is a 1986 graduate of the University of Michigan Law School and a 1980 graduate of Yale University.

Rena I. Steinzor
Spiegel & McDiarmid, Washington, DC

Rena I. Steinzor is of counsel to Spiegel & McDiarmid. She serves as lead counsel to American Communities for Cleanup Equity (ACCE). Ms. Steinzor has published a number of articles on municipal environmental issues, in particular local government liability under Superfund, in several magazines and journals. Before joining the firm, Ms. Steinzor was counsel for the Subcommittee on Commerce, Transportation & Tourism of the Energy and Commerce Committee, U.S. House of Representatives, which was then chaired by James J. Florio (D-N.J.). Ms. Steinzor was the counsel who advised the subcommittee during its consideration of the Superfund Amendments and Reauthorization Act of 1986 and the Asbestos Hazard Emergency Response Act of 1986. Ms. Steinzor is a 1976 graduate of Columbia Law School and a 1971 graduate of the University of Wisconsin.

Scott H. Strauss
Spiegel & McDiarmid, Washington, DC

Scott H. Strauss is a Spiegel & McDiarmid partner who maintains an active energy and environmental practice on behalf of publicly owned entities. In the environmental area Mr. Strauss has worked on numerous issues, including participation in the drafting and enactment of EPA regulations governing the cleanup of hazardous asbestos-containing materials in schools and other public and commercial buildings, and the development of sound regulatory policies to address ratepayer concerns about electric and magnetic fields. Mr. Strauss is a 1981 graduate of the University of Pennsylvania Law School, and received his undergraduate degree from Cornell University in 1978.

Contents

Introduction 1

PART I
HAZARDOUS SUBSTANCES AND WASTES

1. Superfund, *David Kolker and Lisa G. Dowden* 5

2. Hazardous Waste, *Lisa G. Dowden* 19

3. Solid Waste, *Robert J. Schafish, David A. Kahl,*
   Scott S. Strauss, and Lisa G. Dowden 39

4. Emergency Planning and Community Right-to-Know,
   Mark S. Hegedus and Lisa G. Dowden 57

5. Emergency Notifications, *Mark S. Hegedus and Rena I. Steinzor* 69

6. Oil and Fuel Management, *James F. Short,*
   John M. McNurney, and David R. Meyer 81

7. Underground Storage Tanks, *Wendy S. Lader*
   and Rena I. Steinzor 91

8. Pesticides, *Russell F. Smith III and John M. McNurney* 105

9. Asbestos, *Scott H. Strauss* 115

PART II
PERMITS

10. Wastewater and Stormwater Discharges, *Mark A. Keyworth*
    and John M. McNurney 131

11. Municipal Sludge Management: The Other Side of Clean Water,
    Robert J. Schafish 141

12. The Safe Drinking Water Act, *Matthew D. Lee*
    and Susanna M. Higgins 147

13. Air Quality Management, *D. Edward Settle, Michael S. Robinson,*
    and Linda M. Long 157

PART III
COMPLIANCE AND RISK MANAGEMENT ISSUES

14. Establishing Environmental Compliance Programs,
    John M. McNurney and David R. Meyer 181

15. Environmental Compliance:
    Management and Staff Considerations, *Todd W. Filsinger* 191

16. Risk Communication in the Context of Environmental Planning,
    Susan K. Lawson 197

17. Environmental Considerations in Real Estate Transactions,
    William J. Mundt and David R. Meyer 209

18. Insurance, *Russell F. Smith III* 219

Index 229

Introduction

As a local government official, attorney, or employee, you are undoubtedly aware of the ever-proliferating array of federal environmental requirements with which states, municipalities, cities, counties, and towns must comply. Keeping up with the changing requirements and determining how they apply to local government activities can be a full-time job in itself. We have written this book to provide a plain English guide to the federal environmental requirements as they apply to local government activities. The authors who have contributed material to this book are engineers and attorneys who regularly counsel local government clients on environmental compliance. Because we frequently conduct compliance assessments, we have had the opportunity to visit countless municipal facilities and talk with employees about their daily activities. As such, we brought an understanding of the practical workings of many local governments, as well as a thorough grounding in environmental law, to the writing of this book.

The result is an overall picture of the federal environmental requirements applicable to local governments. We have eliminated or vastly restricted discussions of the regulations that do not affect municipal activities, so that you can focus on just those rules that you are likely to encounter. We have sought to avoid legalese and engineering jargon, in order to present the applicable requirements in a readily understandable fashion. The guide also contains practical tips on where to look for environmental risks and potential liabilities in your operations, and compliance advice specifically tailored for municipalities.

Environmental compliance has become an increasingly important concern for local governments, as the risk of environmental liability or fines for noncompliance has grown. The largest dollar exposure any municipality is likely to face would be cleanup or remediation costs under Superfund. These expenditures can easily run into the millions, not counting the amounts spent on legal and engineering services while pursuing the case. Most of the laws and regulations discussed in this book also carry substantial penalties which can reach as high as $25,000 per day per violation for a first-time offense. Subsequent violations carry even stiffer penalties. These fines can be assessed against individuals as well as against their corporate or government employers. The possibility of criminal sanctions is also present, and it has recently become

1

a reality for a few local government officials. Public works department employees and managers have served jail time for falsification of government-required reports and for illegal discharges.

Perhaps the most frightening risk for local government employees with management responsibility is the possibility that they might be held personally liable for an act committed by their employees. Such sanctions are possible where a court finds that a supervisor knew or should have known what an employee was doing. The potential for this type of liability makes it absolutely necessary that local governments develop environmental compliance policies and procedures and provide employees with sufficient training to implement them. A strong compliance program is the best defense against environmental problems, and, if something happens despite your best efforts, a good compliance program can help persuade agency officials to mitigate the penalty. In the worst cases, good compliance programs can be a mitigating factor in criminal sentencing. Not knowing what your employees are doing with respect to the environment is simply too risky, for you and for them, as well as for the city budget. This book contains advice on setting up a compliance program, in addition to information about the applicable federal regulations.

While this guide provides a comprehensive introduction to the federal environmental regulations, as applicable to typical local government activities, you should not assume that it covers every rule applicable to every situation. Most of the regulatory schemes are detailed and complex, and it would be impossible to cover every possible situation in depth. In areas where the requirements are numerous and complex, it was necessary to generalize in order to describe the programs as they apply to local governments. In planning your own compliance programs, there is no substitute for careful study of the requirements and consultation with experts may also be needed to address specific situations. However, this guide should give you a broad, general understanding of the requirements most likely to apply to your facilities, and at least enough information to determine when you are facing environmental risk in a given area. One other caveat is important. This guide covers only federal requirements. Many of the environmental statutes discussed herein provide for the delegation of authority to enforce the program to the individual states, and allows the states to develop their own, more stringent programs. Even where a federal program is in place, a state may sometimes adopt its own regulations on the same subject. It is critically important that you check state and even local requirements before attempting to determine your compliance status.

We hope you find this guide helpful. The authors welcome comments, questions, and suggestions.

Lisa Dowden
Spiegel & McDiarmid
Washington, DC

John McNurney
R.W. Beck
Denver, CO

PART I

Hazardous Substances and Wastes

CHAPTER **1**

Superfund

David Kolker and Lisa G. Dowden

The major federal law imposing liability for the cleanup of hazardous substances is the Comprehensive Environmental Response, Compensation and Liability Act (CERCLA), more commonly known as Superfund (42 U.S.C. § 9601 *et seq.*). The regulations begin at 40 C.F.R. § 300. The Superfund program has two components: (1) a federal fund that is authorized to spend more than $1.5 billion annually through 1994 on the cleanup of the worst hazardous waste sites across the country and (2) a stringent liability scheme to enable the EPA or the states to recover cleanup costs from the parties which are responsible for creating the sites in the first place. Local governments are liable in the same manner as private parties under Superfund.

Because of the risk of liability for costs, Superfund liability is clearly the greatest dollar risk local governments may face in the area of environmental compliance. There are four key ways in which local governments may incur such liability:

- Misuse or improper disposal of hazardous substances by local government employees
- Acquisition of property
- Management of property
- Collection and disposal of solid waste

This chapter will discuss each of these activities. The first section will discuss the nature and scope of the federal Superfund liability scheme. It will explain how the federal cleanup program operates, and when and how sites qualify for federal cleanup funds. The second section will suggest steps that a municipality can take to limit or avoid Superfund liability.

NATURE AND SCOPE OF SUPERFUND'S LIABILITY SCHEME

The Superfund law can impose "strict, joint and several" liability for cleanup costs on all "potentially responsible parties" (PRPs). "Strict" liability is absolute, "no-fault" liability. The concept of negligence is not involved. It does not matter how careful you think you were when you poured the waste out, buried it in the ground, or hired a disposal contractor. It does not even matter if you were following the standard practices of most municipalities at the time. If you sent waste to a site that is causing environmental problems, or if you own or operate such a site, you can be held strictly liable for cleanup costs.

Although strict liability is a very tough standard, the Superfund law does not stop there. The law also makes PRPs "jointly and severally" liable for cleanup costs when the harm caused by the site is "indivisible." From a practical perspective, the concept of "indivisible harm" means that the hazardous wastes at the site have become so intermixed in what is sometimes called a "toxic soup" that it is impossible to separate any one party's wastes from that of another party.

The application of joint and several liability to cases where the harm is indivisible means that the government can ask only a few people who brought hazardous waste to a site to pay the entire cost of cleanup, even if many other people also brought their waste to the facility. It is then up to those few parties to find and sue others responsible for the site in order to get all of those responsible to share the cleanup costs. In short, "joint and several" liability shifts the burden of prosecuting all of the PRPs involved at a Superfund site from the government to a select group of private parties who are chosen by the government as immediate targets for its initial enforcement action.

What you must understand about Superfund liability, and what is also very difficult for many people to accept, is that *it is almost impossible to escape liability once you have been identified correctly as a potentially responsible party at a Superfund site*. You cannot contract away your Superfund liability to another person. Once hazardous substances that you produced are disposed of in an improper fashion, you are liable for cleanup costs for as long as the hazardous substances remain in the environment.

Superfund imposes strict, joint, and several liability on four categories of potentially responsible parties:

> *Past owners and operators.* Anyone who once owned a piece of land or operated a facility where hazardous substances are causing environmental problems is liable under Superfund.
>
> *Present owners and operators.* Anyone who currently owns or operates such land or facilities is also liable.
>
> *Generators of hazardous substances.* Anyone who produced, or "generated," the hazardous substances which were sent to the site and are causing environmental problems.
>
> *Transporters.* Anyone who transported the hazardous substances to the site, if he or she selected the site for disposal.

As you can see, Superfund casts a very broad net. The law defines "facility" (*i.e.*, the site) extremely broadly, to encompass virtually any location where hazardous substances have come to be located. The majority of facilities included in the Superfund program are traditional disposal sites, *e.g.*, landfills, surface impoundments, pits, ponds, and lagoons holding hazardous wastes. However, the law also covers less conventional facilities such as abandoned mine shafts, houses, and even entire towns in which roads were spread with dioxin-laced oils. To complete its extensive coverage, the law applies to some 700 to 800 "hazardous substances" (*i.e.*, chemicals and metals), whether they exist in a pure form or as part of some other chemical mixture.

EPA and the states identify PRPs at a Superfund site by reviewing the facility's disposal records and by examining the actual wastes, drums, equipment carcasses, and similar physical evidence at the site. Documents such as manifests, invoices, and contracts often indicate the identity of generators at the site. Because joint and several liability means that others can be asked to clean up a site that also contains your wastes, PRPs initially identified at a site have an incentive to find and turn in others who may have contributed to the problem.

Once EPA or the states have identified PRPs at a Superfund site, they have two options. First, they can decide to clean up the site using federal funds and sue PRPs after the fact to "recover" these amounts. This type of action is called a *cost recovery* or *Section 107 enforcement action*. Second, the government has the authority to seek a court order asking PRPs to perform the cleanup on their own. This type of suit is called a *cleanup* or *Section 106 enforcement action*. In such cases, PRPs can be asked to do the work themselves or to pay up front to have it done by private contractors.

The federal Superfund law allows EPA to delegate its enforcement authority to the state in which the site is located. The law also requires the states to come up with a matching share of cleanup costs before federal money will be committed to the cleanup effort. Most states have therefore enacted their own state superfund laws, which provide for the funding to meet this matching share requirement, and generally also contain parallel liability provisions. State laws may contain requirements and liability rules that are different from the rules discussed in this chapter, but the federal Superfund law is clearly the general framework for such rules.

HOW THE FEDERAL CLEANUP PROGRAM OPERATES

If your municipality becomes involved as a PRP at a Superfund site, it is extremely important for you to understand how the program operates so that you can take immediate steps to protect your municipality from extensive liability. Superfund cases typically involve a great deal of maneuvering among

PRPs trying to minimize their respective shares of cleanup costs. A PRP who does not understand the program cannot participate skillfully in such maneuvering and can end up paying a disproportionate share of costs.

The first step in the Superfund process is to identify sites that are eligible for federal cleanup funding. As explained above, Superfund liability applies to a whole range of facilities and parties. However, federal cleanup funds are available only for sites that are included on the National Priorities List (NPL). In short, your site does not have to be on the NPL for you to be sued for cleanup costs, but it is significantly more likely that you will be sued if it is on the NPL.

To select sites for the NPL, the EPA first compiles a list of all the facilities that could be covered by the program. Over the years, the EPA has compiled a list of some 38,000 facilities. The computerized database that contains this list is known as the Comprehensive Environmental Response, Compensation and Liability Information System (CERCLIS). Once a facility is placed on this comprehensive list, it is subjected to an evaluation process to see if it is causing significant environmental or human health problems and should therefore be included on the NPL. After the evaluation, the worst sites are proposed for listing and, after a comment period lasting several months, are then included on the NPL.

At the moment, there are over 1,200 sites on the NPL. The EPA estimates that the NPL will grow to some 2,000 sites when all known facilities have been evaluated. The General Accounting Office, Congress' independent investigative agency, estimates that the NPL could include 4,000 sites before the EPA is finished evaluating the nation's worst facilities.

Once a facility is placed on the NPL, the EPA or the state begins the process of identifying and notifying PRPs, and investigating how cleanup should be conducted. A Remedial Investigation and Feasibility Study (RI/FS) is prepared which explains in detail what the problems are at the site and discusses options for addressing them. These studies are major efforts that can take more than a year to complete and can cost millions of dollars. Next, the EPA prepares a Record of Decision (ROD) which contains its final decision on which cleanup approach should be followed. After the ROD has been issued, engineers and construction companies are hired to design and implement the remedy. Following design of the remedy, construction contractors are selected to actually implement the chosen approach. The average cost of a Superfund cleanup is close to $30 million, although there are some huge sites that are expected to cost hundreds of millions of dollars to remedy.

HOW TO PROTECT YOUR MUNICIPALITY
FROM SUPERFUND LIABILITY

There are two kinds of steps you can take to protect your municipality from Superfund liability: defensive steps to get the best result after a problem has occurred and preventive steps to avoid future problems.

DEFENSIVE STEPS TO LIMIT YOUR SUPERFUND LIABILITY

The best way to deal with Superfund's drastic liability scheme is to try to prevent such problems from arising. However, once you are involved in a Superfund case, there are several steps you can take to assure the best possible outcome for your municipality.

Participation in the Superfund Settlement Process

Superfund cases can involve literally hundreds of potentially responsible parties. There have been instances of meetings of hundreds of lawyers in hotel ballrooms to argue about the respective liability of their clients. Once a group of potentially responsible parties at a Superfund site receives "notice letters" that it may be liable for cleanup costs, private industry PRPs typically organize what are called "steering committees" to manage the group's defense to the case, and to formulate any settlement offers the group chooses to make to the EPA or the state. Steering committees also coordinate PRP comments on the studies done by the EPA and the state to define the cleanup actions — studies that directly determine the cost of cleanup. Seats on the steering committee are usually sought by those who have the most to lose at the site because they sent the largest quantities of the worst wastes.

When you receive a notice letter that your municipality has been identified as a PRP at a Superfund site, you have two basic alternatives: (1) you can take a passive role in the case and wait to see whether a settlement is reached or (2) you can take an active role in the case and participate during all stages of the proceedings. If your municipality sent a very small quantity of waste to the site, it may not be cost effective to hire a lawyer to participate in the PRP steering committee or comment on the EPA's cleanup plans. On the other hand, if you do not participate in these activities, you will be forced to live with the results arranged by others. One solution to the dilemma of whether to participate actively in a Superfund case is to organize a group of similarly situated small municipalities which can share the costs of representation during all stages of the proceedings.

EPA's Interim Superfund Municipal Settlement Policy

In December 1989, the EPA issued an interim policy on how municipalities will be included in the Superfund settlement process. The Interim Policy on CERCLA Settlements Involving Municipalities or Municipal Wastes does not create any enforceable rights and is intended only for the guidance of EPA personnel who are responsible for Superfund settlement proceedings. Nonetheless, the Interim Policy is important to municipalities who are planning defensive strategies once they become involved in a Superfund case involving municipal solid waste disposal.

The Interim Policy states that, while municipalities are not exempt from Superfund liability, wastes from households will generally not be included by the EPA in the Superfund settlement process. The Interim Policy provides that, when a municipality generates or transports *municipal solid waste (MSW)*, it will generally not be identified as a PRP unless the EPA either obtains site-specific information that the MSW contains a hazardous substance and the EPA has reason to believe that the hazardous substance is derived from a commercial, institutional, or industrial process or activity. The same policy applies to municipalities who contribute to a Superfund site as generators or transporters of sewage sludge.

The Interim Policy recognizes that there are certain settlement provisions which may be particularly suitable for some municipal PRPs. These provisions include delayed payments, payment schedules over several years, and in-kind contributions (such as cleanup facility operation and maintenance, use of municipal trucks and equipment, or the use of the municipality's sewage treatment plant). These settlement provisions are not always available to municipal PRPs, but may be used where the municipality demonstrates to the EPA that the provisions would be appropriate.

The Interim Policy applies only to how the federal government will exercise its own enforcement authority, so it does not prevent private parties targeted by the government from suing MSW generators as "third-party" defendants. In recent years, hundreds of municipalities have been sued this way because of their role in helping dispose of their citizens' household trash. Although the EPA and Congress have considered various proposals to limit or cap municipal liability at MSW sites, no measure has been adopted as this guide goes to press.

Superfund's De Minimis Settlement Option

One last consideration to keep in mind in deciding how to protect your municipality once you have become involved in a case is that Superfund contains some special settlement provisions designed to help small participants. These special rules, known as the *de minimis* settlement provisions, authorize the EPA and the states to allow those who have contributed small volumes of relatively low toxic waste to "cash out" of the case early, thereby saving the large transactional costs (*e.g.*, attorney's fees) that are typically involved in defending a lawsuit. Under these provisions, you can write the government a check for a fixed amount and walk away from further involvement with the site — although you normally must pay a "premium" for the privilege of permanently ending your involvement. If you receive a Superfund notice letter, you should ask your attorney to look into the *de minimis* option.

PREVENTIVE STEPS TO LIMIT YOUR SUPERFUND LIABILITY

Preventive steps involve careful investigations before you enter into any transaction that could give rise to future Superfund liability, and a local government seeking to protect itself should begin its search in its own backyard. There are a wide variety of municipal activities that can give rise to staggering future liability. Because it is difficult for most local governments, regardless of their size, to address all or most of these problems simultaneously, the best place to start is a comprehensive liability assessment which will give you some sense both of the areas that need the most work and the solutions that are most readily available. Such an assessment can be done by in-house staff or outside consultants. The most important predicate for an effective assessment is to make a firm institutional commitment that you will promptly address the worst problems revealed by the assessment. The chapter on developing a compliance program contains more information on assessments.

Even before you begin the process of comprehensively assessing your municipality's operations, you can focus on areas where preventive steps are of the utmost importance: hazardous substances, property management, solid waste, and property acquisition.

HAZARDOUS SUBSTANCES

Perhaps the most obvious, but frequently overlooked source of potential Superfund risk arises from unintentional contamination of your own property. The chapters on hazardous waste and community right-to-know identify many city operations that use chemical products. If local government employees spill or dispose of these products on municipal property, contamination and releases to the environment may result. The way to counter this type of risk is to make certain that your city, county, or town has eliminated or minimized the use of hazardous substances wherever possible and that employees are trained in the proper use, storage, and disposal of the remaining substances and in emergency response.

A common type of transaction that can lead to Superfund liability is an arrangement with an outside company for the disposal of hazardous wastes your municipality has generated. If anything goes wrong at the disposal site after you sent your wastes there, you can become enmeshed in a Superfund case. It is therefore crucial that you do everything you can to avoid sending your wastes to questionable disposal facilities.

Local governments can reduce their disposal contracting risks by investigating vendors and establishing strong contracts.

The four key steps to selecting a reliable vendor include:

1. Preparing an effective request for proposals (RFP)
2. Assessing qualifications of the vendors
3. A site visit
4. Negotiation of a contract

In order to prepare an effective RFP, it is important to realize that the goal of the selection process is not to select merely the lowest bidder, but the lowest *qualified* bidder. The consequences of selecting an untrustworthy disposal company are so great that it would be foolhardy to try to cut corners by hiring a suspiciously low bidder. There is really no inexpensive way to perform waste disposal services in accordance with EPA regulations. Therefore, a bidder who comes in suspiciously lower than the other respondents to an RFP may be a very risky choice.

Investigation of the vendor is also necessary because the protective contract language and indemnification clauses discussed below cannot help you if the vendor becomes bankrupt. Local governments must determine which vendors are best able to stand behind their promises.

The RFP should clearly spell out what your city wants the vendor to do. Explain what types and amounts of wastes that you produce, what types of disposal are acceptable, and indicate up front that there will be certain required contract provisions for the job, including an indemnification provision requiring the vendor to indemnify your local government in the case of environmental liability assessed due to transport, treatment, storage, or disposal of your waste.

You should request detailed information about each company that submits a bid. The companies should be directed to answer each question in writing, rather than referring to their brochures. The required data should include at least four types of information. First, you will want detailed financial information about the company and any parent company who purportedly stands behind or guarantees it; second, since liability for violations of the environmental laws can be incurred whether or not anyone was negligent in handling your wastes, you need to know whether the vendor has insurance to cover all forms of environmental liability, negligent or not, including Superfund cleanups and groundwater contamination. Ask the company to submit actual insurance policies, since the specific language of the exclusions can be important.

Third, you should find out exactly what each company intends to do with your waste in a step-by-step fashion. How often will they pick it up? What will they do with it? Where will they take it? How many times will the waste be moved before final destruction or disposal? Does the vendor use subcontractors? If so, you need the same information about them that you are requesting from the vendor.

Fourth, you should determine whether the vendor has ever been cited by federal or state officials for violations of any environmental law. Ask them to list each such violation and explain what they did to resolve the problem.

Once you have received answers to the RFP, it is time to assess the qualifications of each of the responding vendors. This is a vital step. Someone must review the financial information each company has submitted, and check to see how stable it is. You should hire a contractor who will still be around in a few years. If a company is suggesting that a parent company stands behind it, it is important to get a letter to this effect.

There should be a review of the insurance policies. The policies should cover all forms of environmental harm. At first glance, it may seem like a good thing if a company offers to indemnify you for the company's own negligence. It is important to understand that, where the environmental laws are concerned, indemnification for negligence is not enough. If wastes from your facilities are found in a Superfund site and traced back, your local government is strictly liable, whether or not it or the contractor was negligent in handling the wastes. You should obtain the same level of strict liability protection from your contractors.

The reviewer should investigate each company's enforcement record. It is not enough to rely on the summaries of enforcement action provided in the responses to the RFP. Someone should call the agencies and try to talk to whoever is responsible for inspecting each disposal site. These people can often provide good information. No environmental agency personnel will go out on a limb and tell a member of the public that a particular facility is safe or recommend that anyone send wastes there. However, if a particular official thinks that a facility is *not* safe, even if it has not been cited officially, he may indicate this. It is not realistic to search for a company with a perfectly clean environmental record. All the major companies have slipped on occasion. On the other hand, there is a big difference between a company that has been cited for some minor recordkeeping violations and a company that is facing major penalties for groundwater contamination.

Once the process has eliminated unsuitable vendors and selected a top contender, the reviewer should visit the disposal site or recycling operation. The reviewer should see the whole site. If the waste storage area is off limits that day for some reason, that is not a good sign. If the reviewer shows up unexpectedly and the vendor does not want to allow admittance, that is also a bad sign. The reviewer wants to learn how the city can be sure that each shipment of waste has been properly disposed of or destroyed. Important indications include whether the operation looks neat and well run, whether protective clothing is properly used, and whether employees are willing to answer all questions.

After you select a contractor, you will need to negotiate the contract. You can work from the vendor's standard contract, but it will probably need some changes to protect the city adequately. The heart of any good disposal contract is the indemnification clause, and all such contracts should include an indemnification clause requiring the vendor to indemnify you for environmental damage caused by the waste. The vendor may offer you indemnify for his acts of negligence or for his violation of any law, but as is discussed above, this is not enough. It is possible to incur Superfund liability without ever being negligent or violating the law.

Try to get a contract provision allowing you to withhold 10 to 20 percent of the payment until after you have received the certificate of destruction telling you the wastes have been disposed. Vendors do not like this provision, but it gives them incentive to honor the contract terms on disposal.

Most disposal contracts have a provision allowing the disposal company to reject your waste if it does not conform to the description you have provided.

Indeed, most contracts go further and exempt the disposal company of all liability associated with nonconforming waste. Because of the liability risks, it is a good idea to have the right of rejection limited to a defined period (say 30 days). The aim is to require the disposal company to tell you up front whether it will exercise its rejection right, and to require it thereafter to assume responsibility for the waste as if it had conformed to the specifications.

In addition, all contracts should have a clause establishing that written terms on receipts, invoices, bills of lading, or other documents used to implement the contract cannot vary the terms of the contract. This clause helps eliminate the problem of companies that demand that your employees sign some document that has not been reviewed by the city's attorney at the time they pick up the wastes. It is very important that all disposal or recycling contracts be reviewed by your attorney.

PROPERTY MANAGEMENT

Some local governments rent property to others. The most common example would be the tenants at a municipal airport, but many local governments also have community or economic redevelopment programs which can include a variety of rental enterprises. If any of your tenants use hazardous substances in their operations (a common problem at airports, for example), the tenants could contaminate your property through improper handling or disposal just as your own employees can. Protective measures include screening your tenants, imposing lease restrictions, developing rules for the handling of hazardous substances, conducting periodic inspections of tenant property, providing tenant training, and employing indemnification clauses in tenant leases.

SOLID WASTE

This chapter has already mentioned some of the Superfund problems that can arise when a local government collects and disposes of solid waste or operates a landfill. Preventive measures might include a contract apportioning liability with your landfill or with other entities that use it, assurances that your landfill meets the new federal requirements, and measures to reduce hazardous substances in your own waste stream. These measures can include visual inspection of waste, ordinances restricting the type of substances that can be disposed, household hazardous waste and used oil collection days, and community education.

PROPERTY ACQUISITION

Equally important in preventing Superfund liability is avoiding a situation in which your municipality purchases land or other facilities that are already contaminated. As the current owner of such property, you become liable for cleanup of this contamination even if you did not own the property at the time the wastes were originally dumped. Superfund gives local governments some special protections in this area. If your municipality acquires the property "involuntarily," *e.g.*, because the former owner did not pay his or her local property taxes, or if you purchase the land without knowing (or having reason to know) of the problems and then take immediate steps to mitigate them once you discover them, you may be able to defend yourself in a Superfund liability case. However, these defenses have not been well developed by the courts and are difficult to invoke effectively. The best bet for protecting your municipality from Superfund liability is to *carefully assess the state of property before you buy it.*

Property Purchase Audits

Local governments are beginning to realize that one of their greatest exposures to future Superfund liability is the inadvertent purchase of contaminated property. This section will explain why it is wise to audit land and facilities before you buy them. Specific information about auditing and how it should be done can be found in Chapter 17. Local governments with large and specialized environmental departments can routinely conduct their own audits. However, the average municipality attempting to institute an audit program for the first time will need to obtain the services of an expert. Experts can help you examine and evaluate the property and negotiate appropriate protection for your municipality.

While it may seem safest to cancel the purchase if environmental problems are uncovered in an audit, that option may not always be available. Instead, you may want to negotiate a sales contract that (1) reduces the purchase price to account for the contamination, (2) requires cleanup before transfer of title, or (3) indemnifies you in case of any future problems.

In some cases, if you discover major environmental problems, go through with the purchase anyway, and become the owner (and operator) of the land, you may have an obligation to inform the government of the situation. The best strategy in such a situation is to have some idea of how you plan to go about remedying the situation when you contact the government. If you do not go through with the purchase, federal law does not require you to notify the government of a problem discovered during the audit, but you should check state law to ensure that it does not contain such a requirement.

Also, you should be very wary of offers to give you free or inexpensive property, whether alone or in the context of a larger transaction. When massive pollution problems are discovered later, the cleanup costs can dwarf the superficial benefits of the transaction.

Lastly, your caution should extend to transactions where your local government acquires less than full ownership rights in a piece of property. For instance, acquiring leasehold rights, easements, rights-of-way or dedicated property for road building, flood control, or the provision of other public facilities could be enough for courts to consider your local government an owner or operator of the property under Superfund. Ownership or operation of the public facilities themselves (such as sewer pipes) can also pose Superfund risks if hazardous substances are placed in the pipes by others.

Why Audit: The Limited Superfund Defenses

If your municipality acquires property by escheat, through any other involuntary transfer or acquisition, or through the exercise of eminent domain authority, you are not liable as a past or present owner under Superfund. If you need to obtain some property, you should check into this alternative. However, you should keep in mind that, in order to escape liability under this provision, you need to show that you did not "cause or contribute" to a release of hazardous substances. This requirement could mean that you have to take immediate steps to mitigate or stop the problem. You could also remain liable under state law for damage to personal property or health. In short, becoming the owner of contaminated property can cause major headaches for your municipality, even if Superfund limits liability because you obtained the property via an involuntary transfer or through the exercise of eminent domain. In addition, the contamination may limit your use of the property, since you must avoid causing any further releases, and may also make it very difficult to sell or dispose of the property.

Property purchase audits also allow developers and lenders to take advantage of a very limited defense under Superfund known as the *innocent landowner* defense. To assert the defense successfully, the property owner must be able to prove both of the following:

> At the time it purchased the land, it *did not know* and *had no reason* to know that any hazardous substance was disposed of on, in, or at the facility.
> At the time of the acquisition, the defendant undertook all *appropriate* inquiry into the previous ownership and uses of the property. This appropriate inquiry must be conducted in a manner *consistent with good commercial practice.*

The law says that in deciding whether the purchaser has made appropriate inquiry and therefore is entitled to the defense, the courts should take into account any *specialized knowledge or experience* of the purchaser, as well as *commonly known or reasonably ascertainable information* about the property. The courts should also consider whether the presence of contamination can be detected by *appropriate* inspection.

Lastly, courts may consider the relationship between the purchase price and the value of the property if uncontaminated. If someone pays a very low price for what would appear to be valuable real estate in the absence of pollution problems, the courts may decide the purchaser knew the land was polluted and deny the defense.

At this stage in the development of the law, it is far from clear what "appropriate" means or what is considered "good" commercial practice. So far, the courts have tended to place a high burden on the person trying to assert this defense. For example, if the buyer should have known of the contamination, genuine ignorance of the problem will not be a sufficient defense. In the face of this trend in the law, your best course of action is to hire an expert who has followed developments in this emerging field carefully and can help you determine how to conduct an adequate audit.

It is also critical to remember that this defense does not relieve you from having to exercise due care after the property is acquired. Courts have held, for example, that the failure to exercise such care can mean that the contamination is not solely the result of another party, thereby making the innocent landowner defense inapplicable.

Whether You Must Notify the Government

Superfund contains an ongoing requirement that facility owners or operators notify the government of a release of a hazardous substance at their facilities. There are severe civil and criminal penalties for failing to report. "Release" means that the hazardous substance is getting out into the environment (air, soil, or water). The list of potential Superfund sites kept by the EPA was originally compiled in large part on the basis of such owner/operator notifications. More detailed information about the Superfund reporting requirements can be found in Chapter 5.

Do not make the mistake of thinking that the releases covered by the Superfund notification requirements are all future accidents. Any ongoing environmental contamination, no matter how long it has persisted, is also covered. In general, you should notify the government as soon as you become aware that a release is occurring that is covered by these requirements. For emergencies or sudden accidents, notification is required immediately. There are no precise time limits established for reporting ongoing releases that are suddenly discovered by a facility owner or operator, but you should avoid delaying the report to the point where the government could get the impression that you are dragging your feet with these crucial requirements.

It is very risky not to report. It can also be very unpleasant to report if you do not handle your contacts with government agencies correctly. If your site gets caught up in the Superfund cleanup process, you can rapidly lose control and suffer expensive, time-consuming negotiations with the government. Your best bet is (1) to be as clear as possible about the problem and how you plan to remedy it and (2) to obtain qualified representation before you approach the agency in question.

CONCLUSION

In summary, property purchase audits, good disposal contracts, and effective property management are the keys to avoiding Superfund liability.

CHAPTER 2

Hazardous Waste

Lisa G. Dowden

This chapter discusses local government compliance with the laws regulating the generation and disposal of hazardous waste. Hazardous waste is regulated under a federal law called the Resource Conservation and Recovery Act (RCRA), 42 U.S.C. § 6901 *et seq.* and the regulations issued under RCRA, which can be found at 40 C.F.R. § 260 *et seq.* RCRA regulates hazardous waste from "cradle to grave." In other words, there are regulations addressing the proper management of hazardous waste from the moment it is produced (or "generated") until its final disposal. In fact, if waste is improperly disposed and causes contamination, there are even regulations that can be said to extend "beyond the grave."

Under RCRA, states may adopt their own hazardous waste programs and, if the program is approved by the EPA, that state takes over responsibility for enforcing RCRA requirements. State programs may be more stringent than the federal program, but they may not be more lenient. The EPA enforces RCRA in states and territories without approved programs.

The most important thing to understand about hazardous waste is that, once your local government has generated hazardous waste, it is responsible for that waste forever. It doesn't matter what types of contracts you sign or how many people handle the waste after it leaves your municipality. If the waste causes contamination anywhere, the government *always* has the option of requiring the generator (your city, county, or town) to pay for cleanup. This is not to say that other individuals or companies (such as your disposal company) might not also have to bear part of the burden. They probably will, and you can even take steps to require them to indemnify you if they mishandle your waste. However, if those other companies are out of business or bankrupt or just make a less attractive target, the government always retains the ability to make the generator pay the full cost of clean up for its wastes. (In fact, under Superfund, you could end up paying to clean up other people's waste as well. See Chapter 1 for more information.) As you can see, if your local government disposes of its hazardous waste improperly, that waste can come back to haunt you years later, with budget-busting financial responsibility. In addition to the cleanup costs, you will probably also have to pay to dispose of the waste all over again. That is why it is important to see to it that your waste is disposed of properly in the first place.

Many local governments do not think of themselves as hazardous waste generators. After all, municipalities tend not to be in the chemical production business, and you may not think that your local government generates any hazardous waste. Chances are, however, that municipal personnel do use commercial chemical products and, when those products are used up or spilled, they generally have to be thrown away. It is those discarded chemical products that may constitute hazardous waste. If your local government operates a vehicle maintenance garage, a streets department, a parks department, an electric utility, or wastewater or drinking water treatment plants, chances are good that it generates some hazardous waste. Local governments are also in the relatively unique position of having to deal with so-called "found" waste. This special problem will be addressed at the end of this chapter. If your local government does generate hazardous waste, it will need a successful compliance program. Such a program will include not only ensuring proper disposal (though this is the "big-ticket" item where the liability exposure is greatest) but also complying with the numerous regulations the EPA has enacted to regulate the management and storage of hazardous waste before the disposal company hauls it away. Compliance with these regulations is important too, because the potential fines for up to $25,000 per day per violation are not inconsequential.

When analyzing your local government's hazardous waste compliance, you need to keep in mind three overriding goals of a successful compliance program:

1. Know what wastes you generate.
2. Minimize waste generation.
3. Manage and dispose of waste safely and in compliance with the law.

This chapter will address each of these goals in turn.

STEP ONE: KNOW YOUR WASTES

Until you know what hazardous wastes your local government generates, you cannot even begin to assess your compliance with the law. It is every generator's responsibility to determine whether or not its activities have produced (or generated) a hazardous waste, and it is the generator's responsibility to identify that waste. *If you illegally dispose of a hazardous waste because you do not know it is hazardous, you will be fined, and may have to pay cleanup costs.* The first task, therefore, is to gather information. At this point, you may be wondering where to look for hazardous waste generation in your city, county, or town. Bear in mind that virtually all of the hazardous waste generated by a municipality will consist of commercial chemical products that are either spilled or used and thrown away. Chemical products that may be covered under the hazardous waste law include paint, solvents, degreasers, cleaners, and pesticides (as explained in Chapter 8; "pesticides" is a generic term that includes herbicides, insecticides, and rodenticides as well as traditional pesticides).

Accordingly, you should focus your attention on municipal facilities where such chemical products are used. Vehicle maintenance facilities almost always have some hazardous waste generation. Streets departments that engage in street and sign painting are also likely candidates. Your parks department is probably a sure bet for pesticide usage. The laboratories in wastewater treatment and drinking water treatment plants are likely to have chemicals on hand. You should also check your police and fire departments. Confiscated drug lab chemicals often contain extremely hazardous waste that must be disposed of after it is no longer needed as evidence. If your local government operates an electric utility, it is also likely to be a source of hazardous waste. Don't forget the building maintenance personnel. The employees charged with cleaning up and maintaining buildings often handle some of the strongest chemical products around.

How will you recognize hazardous waste? The regulations describe a wide range of material that constitutes hazardous waste. The first rule, which may seem obvious but is often overlooked, is that the material must be a waste, *i.e.*, something that you or your employees are throwing away. As long as you have a use for the paint, solvents, pesticide, etc. that are sitting in the purchasing warehouse, the substances are not considered hazardous waste. (These materials may be covered under other laws. See Chapters 4 and 8.) One way to minimize hazardous waste, therefore, is to use up chemical products for their intended purpose. Note: do not overuse such products in order to get rid of them. Applying pesticides in accordance with the instructions on the container label is legal, but increasing the concentration above recommended levels in order to use up the product (or for any other reason) may constitute illegal disposal of a hazardous waste, in addition to a violation of the pesticides law.

Your next step in the identification process will be to determine which wastes meet EPA requirements. There are two kinds of hazardous wastes controlled by the EPA. These are "listed" hazardous wastes and "characteristic" hazardous wastes. Listed wastes are simply wastes that the EPA has placed on one of four hazardous waste lists. Characteristic wastes are hazardous because they exhibit one of four hazardous properties. For instance, they may explode easily.

LISTED WASTES

The EPA's lists of hazardous wastes are lengthy and complex. The lists most likely to involve local governments are those that list commercial chemical products that are hazardous wastes if discarded. Most commercial chemical products are listed at 40 C.F.R. § 261.33(e) and (f). However, the list at 40 C.F.R. § 261.31 includes spent (used) solvents and discarded, unused formulations containing, among other things, pentachlorophenol. It is very important that hazardous waste personnel be familiar with the four lists. Most discarded commercial chemical products are regulated under RCRA if their generic name is one of the substances on the lists or if one of the substances on the lists is the product's sole active ingredient. Although it may seem illogical, a product is not regulated under RCRA if it contains more than one active ingredient unless the product also exhibits a characteristic. Before attempting to take advantage of this apparent loophole in the statute, bear in mind that products containing more than one active ingredient may not be RCRA hazardous wastes, but could still cause you to incur liability under Superfund and related statutes if you spill them or dispose of them improperly. Further, if you take these wastes to a landfill that manages them improperly, you may not be protected from Superfund liability just because the products are not "technically" hazardous wastes.

There are at least two important exceptions to this "sole active ingredient" loophole. First, the spent solvents listed at 40 C.F.R. § 261.31 include all mixtures and blends that contain a total of 10 percent or more (by volume, before use) of any one of the listed solvents. Since spent solvents are frequently a product of municipal operations, this listing is often a critical one. Second, the listing of formulations containing pentachlorophenol is important, since wood preservatives and some herbicides contain this chemical. Local government personnel will need to read the labels for products they use to identify their ingredients and to determine which regulations apply.

Wastes that the tables identify as "acutely hazardous" are even more dangerous than wastes on the other EPA lists, and they are subject to extra regulations. If you generate more than one kilogram of an acutely hazardous waste during a calendar month, that waste is subject to the full range of RCRA regulations. The acutely hazardous substances most likely to be used by local governments include some of the stronger pesticides, herbicides, and solvents. If you are a conditionally exempt generator (explained below), use of an acutely hazardous substance can make you subject to many additional regulations. Therefore, we suggest that you avoid this problem by substituting products that are not on the acutely hazardous list.

You can find the complete EPA lists at 40 C.F.R. §§ 261.31, 261.32, and 261.33(e) and (f). Bear in mind that the EPA changes the lists from time to time, so you should always look for the most recent version of the lists. If you are unsure of how to use the lists, you should get help from qualified professionals. Whenever you have a substance that *you know* is dangerous to human health or the environment, you should treat the substance as a hazardous waste.

Bear in mind that the EPA lists do not cover chemicals listed as hazardous by the states. Many of the state-administered RCRA programs have much stricter requirements than the EPA, and list more chemicals as well. You must comply with both the EPA requirements and your state requirements.

CHARACTERISTIC WASTES

The other type of hazardous waste is a *characteristic waste*. These wastes are hazardous because they have a characteristic or property that makes them dangerous. The four characteristics are ignitability, corrosivity, reactivity, and toxicity.

Ignitability means that the waste catches fire easily, and burns persistently when it does so. *Corrosivity* means that a substance eats away metal. *Reactivity* means that a substance is unstable and subject to violent change. In other words, it explodes. Any substance that reacts violently with water, forms potentially explosive mixtures with water, or that releases toxic gases, vapors, or fumes when mixed with water is reactive. *Toxicity* is a relatively new characteristic, which replaced the former "EP toxicity" characteristic, and measures the presence of certain toxic constituents in a substance. These toxic constituents and their maximum allowable concentrations are listed in a table at 40 C.F.R. § 261.24. The test is explained in detail in Appendix 2 of 40 C.F.R. Part 261. In simple terms, the test (known as the Toxicity Characteristic Leaching Procedure or TCLP) extracts leachate from the waste and tests it for the presence of the toxic constituents. All four of these characteristics can be identified through specific approved tests.

If a waste exhibits *any one* of these four characteristics, it is a hazardous waste subject to regulation under RCRA. However, it should not be necessary for city personnel to perform these tests. You may be familiar enough with a substance to know that it exhibits a characteristic. Manufacturers, material safety data sheets, and product labels may also give enough information to decide that a waste is a characteristic waste. If you do run tests, you must test a representative sample of each waste using approved EPA methods. Testing can be complex, and you must follow EPA sampling methods and testing standards.

Remember that the regulations do not specifically require that you test your wastes. They only require you to identify your wastes. To the extent you can identify listed or characteristic wastes without testing, you can avoid the complex requirements associated with testing. One source of information on commercial chemical products that you intend to discard is the RCRA/Superfund Hotline. You can call the EPA Hotline at 1-800-424-9346 (703-412-9810 in the District of Columbia) and tell the operator the name of your commercial product. The Hotline should be able to give you advice on whether the product is a hazardous waste. Write a memo to your files noting the (1) date, (2) time, (3) person you spoke with, and (4) advice you received.

Other sources of information on chemical products include the National Resources Defense Counsel (NRDC) Toxic Substances Hotline at 1-800-648-6732 and the Chemical Referral Service Hotline at 1-800-262-8200. The Chemical Referral Service is provided by the National Chemical Manufacturers Association. They can provide you with the address and phone number of the manufacturer of your product. You do not have to identify yourself when calling any of the hotlines described above.

You must have some idea of what the substance is. Shipping and storage requirements vary depending on the type of hazard the substance presents (for instance, if it is corrosive or explosive), and you must be able to choose a disposal facility that can handle the waste. You also have to be able to give the transporter enough information to handle an accident or spill along the way. If all else fails, you can send a sample to a lab for testing.

If you do test wastes, you must keep written records of any test results, waste analyses, or other determinations for at least three years from the date when the waste was last sent to an off-site disposal facility (five years for land-banned wastes). Written records are also very valuable in proving to the EPA that you have complied with the requirement that you identify your wastes.

LAND-BANNED WASTES

Some types of hazardous wastes may not be disposed in or on land. Wastes subject to this prohibition are said to be "land banned." Such wastes may be subject to EPA "treatment standards" before they can be disposed in or on land. Both listed and characteristic wastes are covered by the land ban. For generators of hazardous waste, the land ban means that you may need to put more time and effort into finding appropriate *treatment, storage, and disposal (TSD)* facilities for your hazardous wastes. Generators are also responsible for making certifications about the nature and regulatory status of their land-banned wastes to TSD facilities and to the EPA.

It is the responsibility of the generator to determine whether it has generated a land-banned waste. Since generators are already required to use testing or their own knowledge of their wastes to determine whether they have generated hazardous wastes, all you have to do is add another step to the waste identification process described above. You will need to check any hazardous wastes generated at your facility against the lists of wastes for which treatment standards, land ban prohibitions, or landfill disposal restrictions have been established.

You must keep records of the test results or other information you used to identify land-banned wastes for *five years.* Note that the five-year requirement is different from the three-year record retention requirement for other generator records. In general, when dealing with a land-banned waste, you should assume that all related records should be kept for five years instead of three. However, as noted elsewhere, the authors recommend that you keep all of your records indefinitely in any case. When you send your hazardous wastes to a TSD facility, you must also provide, in writing, *with each shipment of waste,* information related to the waste and a certification that your waste complies with any applicable treatment standards. Usually, the disposal company can provide you with the appropriate certification forms, although you remain responsible for filling them out correctly.

While the regulations pertaining to the identification of listed and characteristic wastes can be complex, you will not have every type of hazardous substance at your facility. It is more likely that you will find that you have a few limited types of hazardous waste that you generate on a regular basis and, once you have determined the procedures for handling them, you can process them in a routine manner.

STEP TWO: MINIMIZE WASTE GENERATION

Disposing of hazardous waste safely can be extremely expensive, and compliance with the regulations on storing waste for disposal can be time consuming for municipal personnel, thereby leading to more expense. Moreover, the regulatory controls increase as you produce more waste, or as you produce more toxic waste. As a result, the more waste your local government generates, the more expenses it will incur. As you can see, the regulatory scheme is set up to discourage facilities from generating hazardous waste. One way to minimize your hazardous waste compliance expenses is to minimize your generation of hazardous waste. There are two good reasons for you to have a waste minimization plan. First, as mentioned previously, it can reduce your costs. Second, depending on how much waste a facility generates in a calendar month, it may be required by law. In fact, if your city already disposes of hazardous waste at a TSD, municipal personnel may already be signing hazardous waste manifests that certify that you have a waste minimization program in place. It is definitely in your municipality's interest to ensure that those representations are true. The EPA has issued a guidance document setting forth the criteria by which it will evaluate required hazardous waste minimization plans. This section discusses waste minimization and the rules for determining how much waste your facilities generate.

How can you reduce waste generation? The method is simple. Use commercial chemical products as little as possible and always choose the least toxic product available that will get the job done. Implementation of a waste-minimization program could require employee training, changes in work practices, and changes in product purchasing. For instance, can the municipality substitute latex paint for enamel paint or manual parks maintenance for herbicides? You may be able to substitute products that are not listed as hazardous wastes for products that are listed, and thus reduce hazardous waste volume. If your local government does all its buying through a central purchasing department, you will have to educate these employees about purchasing environmentally safe products. Chemical product purchases are one area where accepting the lowest bid may cost more down the line. The environmental status of such products should be part of any bid specifications.

As mentioned above, one reason to minimize the volume and toxicity of the hazardous wastes you generate is because facilities that generate greater amounts of waste, or more toxic waste, must comply with more regulations than those facilities that are able to minimize waste generation. It is important to know the rules for determining how much waste you generate. The system creates three categories of waste generation: conditionally exempt generators, small quantity generators, and large quantity generators. Which category you are in depends on how much waste you generate.

- Generators that produce no more than 100 kg of hazardous waste during a calendar month are conditionally exempt from many RCRA regulations.
- Small generators that produce between 100 kg and 1,000 kg during a calendar month are exempt from some RCRA regulations.
- Any generator producing 1,000 kg per month or more is subject to all the RCRA regulations.

You may not average your monthly production. For instance, suppose you usually produce less than 100 kg of waste in a month and are therefore conditionally exempt from most of the regulations. If you produce over 100 kg in any one month, *all* of your waste for that month is subject to the regulations for generators who produce 100 to 1,000 kg of waste per month. You should therefore plan to comply with the regulations applicable to the highest quantity of waste you are likely to generate in a month.

If you produce more than 1 kg of acutely hazardous waste in a calendar month, that acutely hazardous waste is subject to all RCRA regulations, regardless of what quantity of hazardous waste you produce.

You may be wondering how to tell how much waste you have produced. To be completely accurate, you will have to weigh it or get information about the weight per gallon from the manufacturer. However, as a rule of thumb, one half of a 55-gallon drum can trigger the limit. Approximately five drums can meet or exceed the 1,000 kg large quantity generator level.

When counting your wastes, you should be aware of the rules described below concerning EPA identification numbers. If one municipal department is generating wastes on a piece of property contiguous with (next to) another municipal department that also generates hazardous wastes, the EPA will treat the entire area as *one site* for the purposes of issuing an I.D. number and counting wastes. For example, if you produce 60 kg of hazardous waste in a calendar month in vehicle maintenance, and the neighboring streets department produces 60 kg, those wastes are combined and considered as one site, and both departments must comply with small quantity generator requirements, even though the two departments would be conditionally exempt if considered separately. If a public street runs between two sites, they are not contiguous. Even if the municipal departments at a single location usually conduct separate operations, they must cooperate for the purpose of coordinating a hazardous waste program. For some local governments, this will require changes in the way various departments are organized or work together.

The regulatory structure also requires facilities that are *not* on contiguous pieces of property to have separate EPA I.D. numbers and to satisfy their own quantity cutoffs. Therefore, you will need a separate I.D. number and waste handling procedures for each site where your local government expects to generate over 100 kg of waste in a calendar month. You cannot freely transport waste in excess of that quantity between your noncontiguous municipal operations.

You must count all hazardous wastes when you are making your monthly determinations. Wastes that you treat and recycle or reclaim on site may have to be counted in the monthly totals. You do not have to count used oil burned for energy recovery (in an industrial boiler, for instance), or recycled, as long as the oil is not contaminated with hazardous wastes. Certain types of used oil filters are also exempt from the hazardous waste requirements. See Chapter 6 for more information.

You do not have to count empty containers because they are not hazardous waste. The residues of hazardous waste in empty containers are also exempt and are not counted. Although it may sound strange, you have to know what the waste is before you can tell if the container is empty. Once the waste is identified, you will know if you are dealing with a *hazardous waste* or an *acutely hazardous waste*.

If you are dealing with a *hazardous waste*, the container is empty if all the waste that can be removed has been removed. Use the normal method for emptying a container of the type you have, *e.g.*, pouring, pumping, etc. Also, no more than one inch of material may remain on the bottom of the container or on the liner. Your container is also considered empty if less than 3 percent by weight of the total capacity is left (for containers of 110 gallons or less) or less than 0.3 percent of the total capacity (for containers larger than 110 gallons).

If you are dealing with an *acutely hazardous waste*, such as some pesticides, the container must be triple rinsed with a solvent capable of removing the product before it can be considered empty. Talk to the manufacturer of the chemical for information on what kind of solvent will work. Remember that the used solvent may also be a hazardous waste. Unless the container is triple rinsed, the acutely hazardous residue remains subject to regulation. You may dispose of your empty containers with your ordinary, nonhazardous solid wastes.

Wastes that are discharged directly into a publicly owned treatment works (sewers) are exempt as long as they have been properly pretreated according to federal pretreatment standards. For a discussion of pretreatment standards, refer to Chapter 10.

Do not increase your waste count by mixing hazardous wastes with nonhazardous wastes. The reason you do not want to mix different types of wastes is that mixing a hazardous waste with a nonhazardous waste can make the entire mixture a hazardous waste. Furthermore, mixing wastes generally constitutes "treatment," which means you might need a permit from the EPA.

Once you have determined the monthly total of the wastes you generate, decide what category of regulatory requirements apply to you. The category you are in, and the regulations you face, depend on whether you are a

- Conditionally exempt generator (no more than 100 kg/month)
- Small quantity generator (100 to 999 kg/month)
- Large quantity generator (1,000 kg or more/month)

STEP THREE: MANAGE AND DISPOSE OF WASTE SAFELY AND IN COMPLIANCE WITH THE LAW

Once you have established your generator category at each facility where you generate hazardous waste you must make certain your waste is being properly handled and disposed of in accordance with the regulations applicable to that generator category. The following discussion is intended to lay out the broad types of regulations that exist, rather than to describe such regulations in detail. You may need expert advice to set up a hazardous waste program that is responsive to your situation.

Before setting up a program, however, you need to consider where you will be managing and storing your wastes prior to disposal. Large- and small-quantity generators must follow specific regulations when storing wastes, but you need to consider how to set up their waste identification and storage areas to prevent spills. If you do not have a special area set aside for waste management, you will never be able to control your hazardous wastes effectively.

Your waste management area should be indoors, with an impermeable floor with curbs or other arrangements to prevent spilled waste from escaping into the environment. This area should not drain into sewers or navigable waters. It should not be near heat sources which could cause explosions. It should be well away from the property line in case wastes do escape.

You will need a waste management area at each facility where you will be generating over 100 kg during a calendar month. Whichever category applies to your facilities, you will need to address the following types of regulations:

1. EPA I.D. numbers
2. Waste storage and handling procedures
3. Preparedness for and prevention of emergency situations
4. Employee training
5. Disposal options
6. Records and reports
7. Waste minimization

Table 1   Hazardous Waste Storage and Disposal Requirements

Requirements	Conditionally Exempt Generators	Small-Quantity Generators	Large-Quantity Generators
Waste identification	Yes	Yes	Yes
Hazardous waste generation	Less than 100 kg in a calendar month	100–1,000 kg in a calendar month	Over 1,000 kg in a calendar month
Acutely hazardous waste	Less than 1 kg in a calendar month	Less than 1 kg in a calendar month	Over 1 kg in a calendar month
Accumulation time	No limit	180 days	90 days
Accumulation amount	100 kg	6,000 kg	No limit
EPA I.D. number required	No	Yes	Yes
Compliance with "preparedness and prevention" regulations	No[a]	Yes	Yes
Compliance with contingency plan regulations required	No	No, but an emergency coordinator is required and employees must know how to respond in an emergency	Yes
Provide employee hazardous waste training	No	No, but you must make certain employees are familiar with waste-handling procedures	Yes
Manifests required	No, but using common carrier or sending to TSD requires it	Yes (except for certain contractual recycling agreements)	Yes
Exception reports	No	Yes	Yes
Biennial reports	No	No	Yes
Waste minimization	No[a]	Yes	Yes
Disposal Options			
TSD	Yes	Yes	Yes
Interim status facility	Yes	Yes	Yes
State permitted TSD	Yes	Yes	Yes
State or municipal solid waste facility	Yes	No	No
Beneficial reclamation facility	Yes	No	No

[a] While these requirements do not *necessarily* apply, conditionally exempt generators would be well advised to keep records and to use common sense to prevent accidents.

REQUIREMENTS FOR CONDITIONALLY EXEMPT GENERATORS

A "conditionally exempt" generator producing no more than 100 kg of hazardous waste during a calendar month is exempt from the RCRA regulations, as long as he complies with the following conditions.

Even as a conditionally exempt generator, you are still responsible for determining when you have generated hazardous waste. You must identify your waste as a listed waste or determine whether it is a characteristic waste through appropriate testing or your knowledge of the waste. Although the three-year recordkeeping requirement for tests and analyses of wastes does not technically apply to conditionally exempt generators, it is to your advantage to keep those records. Compliance does you no good if you cannot prove it. Records are the only way to prove that you have been following the requirement that you identify your wastes.

If you accumulate more than one kilogram of acutely hazardous waste in a calendar month, those wastes are subject to full RCRA regulation. Full RCRA regulation is also triggered if you accumulate more than 100 kg of residue, contaminated soil, waste, or debris from cleaning up a spill of acutely hazardous waste on land or water.

As a conditionally exempt generator, you are allowed to accumulate hazardous waste on site without an EPA I.D. number. However, if you accumulate more than 1 kg of acutely hazardous wastes, or if you exceed 1,000 kg of hazardous waste on site at any time, you become subject to the rules for small-quantity generators and you must dispose of the waste in accordance with those rules within 180 days of the date when your quantity exceeds these levels.

Although there are no specific requirements for waste handling or storage procedures, emergency plans or employee training, it is prudent for conditionally exempt generators to implement some of the concepts described below for large- and small-quantity generators in order to prevent contamination or injury.

Disposal Options

As long as your wastes do not exceed the amounts allowed for conditionally exempt generators, you may dispose of them in several ways. As a conditionally exempt generator, you have more choices than a small-quantity generator or a fully regulated generator. You may treat and dispose of hazardous waste in an on-site facility. However, unless you are a TSD, on-site disposal is a dangerous option. Mismanagement of hazardous waste could lead to contamination and civil and criminal liability.

As an alternative, you may send the wastes to a TSD facility which has a permit issued under RCRA or to an interim facility with permit pending. You may send the waste to a TSD facility with a state permit granted under an EPA-approved hazardous waste plan. You may also select a state-licensed facility which accepts municipal or industrial solid waste. While this last option is less expensive and may seem attractive, a permitted hazardous waste TSD facility should have facilities that can more effectively control your wastes. You may run a greater risk of Superfund liability at a municipal site. Finally, you may send your wastes to a facility that beneficially uses or legitimately recycles or reclaims the waste.

Finally, if you are using a common carrier to transport the waste off site, bear in mind that, even if the RCRA transport requirements do not technically apply to you, the Department of Transportation (DOT) regulations regarding the transport of hazardous substances do apply to everyone. For instance, the DOT regulations require that a vehicle containing *any* amount of hazardous wastes be placarded according to the regulations. They also require paperwork similar to an EPA manifest.

Records and Reports

No annual or biennial documents are required of conditionally exempt generators, at least under federal law. You should keep manifests or other disposal documents related to your waste, however.

REQUIREMENTS FOR SMALL QUANTITY GENERATORS

The "small quantity" generator produces between 100 and 1,000 kg of hazardous waste during a calendar month. Small-quantity generators are exempt from some regulatory requirements, but they must comply with regulations for the storage, transportation, and disposal of hazardous wastes.

EPA Identification Numbers

You will need an EPA identification number before you can transport or dispose of your waste. No transporter or disposal facility may accept hazardous waste from a generator without such a number, and you may not offer your hazardous wastes to transporters or disposal facilities that lack EPA numbers. If you do not have a number, you may apply to the EPA for one, using EPA Form 8700-12.

You must have a separate EPA identification number for each individual site where you generate hazardous wastes. A site is separate if it is not located on a piece of property contiguous with (next to) one of your other sites. If a public street runs between two sites, they are not contiguous. Contiguous sites under the same ownership are treated as one site, no matter how separately you may run your operations. Your generator status may be higher if one municipally owned piece of property generates hazardous waste next to another municipally owned facility which also generates hazardous wastes.

Alternatively, if you are sending a crew out from the Public Works Department to paint a highway bridge or from the Parks Department to apply pesticides at a golf course and they generate hazardous waste (paint or pesticides, in this case) at a location that is separate from your generation facility, you will need to apply for a separate hazardous waste permit if that crew will be generating over 100 kg of hazardous waste or over 1 kg of acutely hazardous waste. *We cannot emphasize enough the importance of eliminating acutely hazardous wastes from your operations wherever possible.* The extra regulatory problems you will incur are often too great to make use of such substances worthwhile. It is unlikely that you would generate sufficient wastes on any one repair job to require on EPA I.D. number. If you do, however, you will need to set up facilities to test and manage waste at the maintenance site. You cannot freely transport your wastes back to your main facility for management and disposal. Your maintenance site cannot "dispose" of its wastes by sending them to your main facility unless your main facility is permitted as a TSD facility under RCRA or a state program.

On jobs where you expect to generate less than 100 kg of waste in a calendar month, you would be a conditionally exempt generator and would not need an EPA I.D. number. Conditionally exempt generators may dispose of their waste at TSDs or at a state-permitted municipal or industrial solid waste landfill.

Waste Storage and Handling Procedures

A small-quantity generator may accumulate wastes on site for 180 days without becoming a TSD. One extension is possible. If you must transport waste over 200 miles for disposal, you may accumulate waste for 270 days. If you keep it any longer, you are considered the operator of a storage facility and must comply with the extensive RCRA requirements which apply to TSD facilities. The amount of accumulated waste may not exceed 6,000 kg at any one time.

If you accumulate more than one kg of *acutely hazardous waste* during a calendar month, that waste is subject to all the RCRA regulations that apply to large generators. Again we suggest that you avoid acutely hazardous wastes whenever possible.

As a small-quantity generator, you are required to store wastes awaiting disposal in containers (such as 55-gallon drums) or tanks in a storage area that meets certain requirements. Your containers or tanks must also meet regulatory guidelines, and you will have to comply with specific labeling and recordkeeping requirements, which may include inspecting the waste storage areas on a weekly or even a daily basis. The storage facilities must also meet regulatory standards.

Preparedness and Prevention

The regulations specify what small-quantity generators must do in order to maintain and operate their hazardous waste facilities to minimize the chance of fire, explosion, or accident which could lead to unplanned releases of chemicals into the environment. Each facility must have certain types of emergency equipment for responding to spills and fires. Each facility must make arrangements, as appropriate, with the local police, fire departments, and state and local emergency response teams for responding to fires, spills, or other likely emergencies. In addition, each facility must have an emergency response coordinator prepared to respond to emergency situations.

Employee Training

You will have to train your employees to manage the wastes and to respond properly in the event of an emergency. Although a formal training program is not required, you must ensure that all employees are trained to handle wastes safely and prepared for emergencies.

Disposal Options

Except for certain types of recycling or reclamation contracts, small-quantity generators must send all hazardous waste to permitted TSDs. Chapter 1 has a discussion on selecting reliable disposal facilities in order to minimize future liability.

Records and Reports

Recordkeeping is a very important generator function, because records are not only required, but can be an effective way of proving your compliance efforts. As mentioned above, all generators must document how they identify each shipment of hazardous waste and maintain those records for three years (five years for land-banned wastes).

You are also required to keep your hazardous waste manifests (described below) and other disposal-related documents for three years. Because of the possibility of Superfund liability, and because of the problem of land-banned wastes which extend record retention requirements to five years, we recommend keeping all your hazardous waste records indefinitely. Records can be invaluable for demonstrating compliance or limiting your liability in Superfund situations.

A third category of records is the "exception report." When you ship hazardous waste to a TSD, the facility is required to send back a copy of the manifest within 30 days. If you do not receive the copy, you must notify the EPA within 60 days by sending it a copy of the original manifest and an indication of the problem. Exception reports should also be maintained for three (or five) years. Other records may not be specifically required, but are useful to prove compliance with regulatory requirements. These may include records of daily or weekly inspections or other required activities which otherwise would not be documented.

Waste Minimization

Small-quantity generators who sign manifests for off-site waste disposal simultaneously sign a certification stating that they have made good faith efforts to minimize hazardous waste generation. Although no specific steps are currently mandated to achieve a "good faith effort," a written hazardous waste minimization plan should be a first step to satisfying this requirement.

REQUIREMENTS FOR LARGE QUANTITY GENERATORS

Generators that produce over 1,000 kg of hazardous waste during a calendar month must follow all RCRA generator regulations.

EPA I.D. Numbers

Like small-quantity generators, large-quantity generators must have EPA I.D. numbers for each site where hazardous waste is generated in amounts equal to or greater than 100 kg/month.

Storage and Handling Procedures

Perhaps the most important of the additional requirements for large-quantity generators is that you may only accumulate waste on site for 90 days, with a possible 30-day extension for uncontrollable and unforeseen circumstances. Like small-quantity generators, large-quantity generators may store their wastes in containers or in tanks. Although container storage is subject to the same requirements (such as labeling and inspection), the tank regulations are much more complex. In fact, the tank regulations can be very expensive to implement, since they require secondary containment, tank testing and monitoring. We generally do not recommend that municipal large-quantity generators attempt to use tank storage.

Preparedness and Prevention

Additional requirements for large-quantity generators include detailed, written contingency plans and explicit emergency procedures. Preparedness includes having special emergency equipment, plans, and arrangements with local emergency response personnel such as the police and fire departments and hospitals. Each facility also must have emergency coordinators prepared to respond to emergencies.

Employee Training

Large-quantity generators are required to implement formal training programs to provide employees handling hazardous waste with classroom or on-the-job instruction. Generators can implement these programs in-house or send employees to outside programs. Employee training must be carefully documented and regularly refreshed, and new employees cannot handle hazardous wastes until they have received the training.

Disposal Options

Large-quantity generators must send their hazardous wastes to TSDs. See Chapter 1 for information on selecting reliable disposal contractors.

Records and Reports

Large-quantity generators must keep the same records on how they identify their wastes which all other generators are required to keep. You must also retain your manifests and other disposal documents for three years (five years for land-banned wastes).

Exception reports are slightly more involved for large-quantity generators. Large-quantity generators who have not received a signed copy of the manifest from the disposal facility within 35 days after the waste was accepted by the initial transporter must contact either the transporter or the TSD facility to determine the status of the waste. If you have not received the manifest from the TSD facility within 45 days, you must file the exception report with EPA, including a copy of the unconfirmed manifest and a cover letter describing the efforts you made to locate the waste.

Large-quantity generators must prepare a report in even-numbered years recording all wastes shipped off site, and naming the disposal facilities and transporters used. You must use EPA Form 8700-13A for the biennial report. Essentially, it requires all the manifest information from each waste shipment from your facility. You must also document what efforts you are making to reduce the quantity and toxicity of the wastes you generate and you must describe, using specific quantities, the progress you have made. You must submit the report to your EPA regional administrator by March 1 of each even-numbered year. Copies are required to be maintained for three years, but, as with all records, we suggest that you keep them indefinitely.

Waste Minimization

A large-quantity generator's signature on a hazardous waste manifest certifies that the generator has a hazardous waste minimization program in place. A written plan to reduce the volume and/or toxicity of the waste produced is an important part of such a program. The plan should show that the program has management support, tracks and allocates costs accurately, and produces and measures results. Municipal plans will probably start with chemical inventories and product substitutions.

TRANSPORTATION AND PACKAGING

Both large- and small-quantity generators (and conditionally exempt generators using permitted TSD disposal facilities) must use the hazardous waste manifest system when arranging to transport wastes off site for disposal. The "manifest" required by the EPA is simply a paperwork system that tracks a hazardous waste through the transportation and disposal process. As a generator, you are responsible for identifying the waste and properly preparing it for shipment. The manifest tells the transporter, the treatment facility, and the government that you have done this. The manifest requirements are a good guide to the steps you must take in preparing and packaging your waste.

The manifest can be obtained from the EPA. It is EPA Form 8700-22. There is also an EPA Form 8700-22A. This second form is used simply for extra pages if you use up all the room on the first form in answering any of the questions. The form asks for information required by federal law and has a shaded area for you to record information that may be required by state law. You should check the manifest requirements for the state receiving the waste and for your home state, in that order. The recipient state or your home state may require you to use different manifest forms.

In order to complete the form, you will need to include the name, mailing address, site address, phone number, and EPA identification number for your facility and every transporter and disposal company that will handle any waste in this shipment. Once you have identified yourself, the transporters and the recipient, you must include information about the wastes. The Department of Transportation (DOT) regulates the transportation of hazardous substances by common carrier. Any substance that qualifies as a hazardous waste under EPA regulations is a hazardous substance regulated by DOT, even if you are not shipping the wastes across state lines. This section does not attempt to explain the DOT tables and regulations. They are very complex. You should seek expert advice if you are unsure about using them.

Often, your disposal facility may pick up your wastes in an appropriately placarded (marked) vehicle and it will tell you how to package the wastes. Even so, you are responsible for following the DOT rules and for making sure that your transporter does also.

The manifest also requires you to identify the quantity of waste being shipped and the type of containers being used. There is room to include special information about the waste if there is anything unusual that people should know about it or if you want to add special instructions in case the waste cannot go to the designated facility. You should check with your state (and the state of the disposal facility) for any state-required information that you must also include on the manifest.

Once you have properly packaged the waste and labeled, marked, and placarded it according to the DOT regulations, you can give it to the transporter along with enough extra copies of the manifest so that each company that handles the waste along its route can have one. Do not forget to sign the manifest. The disposal facility is required to send you a signed copy of the manifest when it receives the waste.

FOUND WASTE

Local governments are perhaps uniquely subject to the problem of "found" waste. Found waste is waste that was accidentally or deliberately left on a street or public right-of-way, vacant lot, or city facility, often in the middle of the night. Since the waste may present a hazard for the public, local governments must often assume responsibility for the waste, thus becoming the "generator" for disposal purposes. There is little that can be done to prevent midnight dumping, but your city should have a policy for dealing with the results.

Local government employees discovering found waste should immediately notify the fire department. Hazmat teams are usually in the best position to identify the waste. The employee discovering the waste should stay until the fire department arrives (to keep the public away) but should not try to move the waste under most circumstances. The fire department can try to identify the waste, and should also look for information about the dumper. Most local governments arrange an "emergency response" service as part of their hazardous waste disposal contract, and call upon this service to get rid of the found waste. Remember that, if found waste is dumped at a facility where you already generate hazardous waste, it could change the facility's generator status for the month. For other locations, you may be able to get a provisional ID number for one-time disposal under your state program.

CONCLUSION

As you can see, the hazardous waste requirements are complex, and as we explain in Chapter 1, mistakes can cost your city, county, or town a great deal in fines or cleanup costs. The hazardous waste laws are designed to give facilities an incentive to generate as little hazardous waste as possible. You may need expert assistance to actually set up and implement your local government's hazardous waste program.

CHAPTER **3**

Solid Waste

*Robert J. Schafish, David A. Kahl, Scott S. Strauss,
and Lisa G. Dowden*

This chapter discusses the requirements applicable to solid waste collection and disposal. It begins with a survey of the various solid waste management alternatives and compliance issues and concludes with a discussion of the federal regulations for municipal solid waste landfills. Today, many states require local and regional governments to deal aggressively with their trash, either through broad-based solid waste management plans or through targeted programs focusing on specific elements of the waste stream. Many such laws have been put in place in recent years, in anticipation of tougher federal requirements and in response to increasing public pressure. These laws feature:

- *Waste reduction goals* ranging from 25 to 50 percent of the solid waste stream.
- *Disposal bans* designed to keep materials out of landfills. Most commonly banned materials are yard waste, lead-acid batteries, used motor oil, and tires.
- *Minimum content requirements*, establishing targets for post-consumer recycled content in products such as newsprint, office paper, and some plastic products.
- *Government purchasing bid preferences* for products containing recycled materials.
- *Deposits or advance disposal fees* on such products as batteries, tires, appliances, and beverage containers.

On the federal level, modifications to the Resource Conservation and Recovery Act (RCRA) — specifically Subtitle D, the Solid Waste Disposal Act — may eventually address many of these same issues. However, it could be some time before the full regulatory picture emerges since the EPA's current regulations deal only with landfills.

At the very least, the new landfill post-closure management requirement and new facility construction standards make existing landfills a resource to husband carefully through aggressive waste reduction programs.

1-56670-098-1/95/$0.00+$.50
© 1995 by CRC Press, Inc.

Many local governments operate their own landfills, and even those that do not often collect and transport residential and commercial solid waste or arrange for private contractors to do so. Municipalities are also often responsible for operating recycling programs. This chapter will discuss the various solid waste disposal and recycling options available to local governments and the federal environmental requirements that may affect them, and will conclude with a description of the federal regulations pertaining to municipal solid waste landfills. These regulations are of interest not only to entities operating landfills, but also to local governments that contract with municipal solid waste landfills.

SOLID WASTE MANAGEMENT ALTERNATIVES

Modern solid waste management offers many options, spanning a wide range of technologies, regulations, and environmental consequences. While one option — recycling, for example — may be more politically palatable than another — such as landfilling — no one approach is inherently better or worse than any other. Indeed, the best solution is probably a combination of several approaches, depending on the prevailing economic, geographic, environmental, and political conditions in a given community. The trend in solid waste management planning is toward an "integrated assessment" approach, considering a wide range of alternatives. An integrated approach is essential for developing workable, long-term, cost-effective solutions to solid waste management.

State and local governments using the integrated assessment approach typically consider solid waste management alternatives in the following categories:

- Reducing waste at the source — keeping materials from becoming trash in the first place.
- Reusing or recycling useful commodities.
- Composting leaves, brush, and grass clippings (or other components of garbage).
- Incineration with energy recovery (waste-to-energy).
- Landfilling.

An integrated solid waste management plan considers most or all of these categories. However, every solid waste management method has unique implementation, construction, and operating requirements, and each must be considered in light of local conditions.

SOURCE REDUCTION

Source reduction means lowering the potential for waste at its origin — manufacturer or consumer — to reduce the quantity and toxicity of materials entering the waste stream. It is grounded in two principles, *i.e.*, conserving resources and reducing waste. Source reduction relieves the pressure on waste collection, processing, and disposal systems.

RECYCLING

Recycling is a method of solid waste management whereby materials that would otherwise become waste are separated, collected, processed, and reconfigured into new and reusable products. Commonly recycled materials include paper, metals, glass, and plastics.

COMPOSTING

Composting is the biological decomposition and stabilization of organic matter. Composting occurs when organic wastes naturally decompose over time and produce a biologically stable end product. This is the same process that has been producing humus (organic topsoil) in forests for millennia. Composting yard waste, alone or in combination with sludge, diverts a bulky waste from landfills and yields products suited to a number of uses.

Depending on their complexity and technology, recycling centers, transfer stations, materials recovery facilities, compost facilities, and waste-to-energy facilities are usually subject to a variety of local zoning ordinances in addition to state and federal air and water quality standards. (Refer to Chapters 10 and 13.) In addition, if hazardous materials are handled, such facilities must comply with the regulations described in the hazardous waste chapter. Compost products must meet quality standards which vary from state to state, although national compost quality standards are under development.

WASTE-TO-ENERGY SYSTEMS

At the end of 1993 there were 138 waste-to-energy (WTE) facilities in the U.S. which burned over 26 million tons of solid waste annually, or approximately 13 percent of the total solid waste generated that year. Additional WTE facilities are in advanced planning stages or under construction.

Two primary categories of WTE technologies are in use today: mass-burn systems and refuse-derived fuel (RDF) systems. Mass-burn facilities burn municipal solid waste with little or no preprocessing except for removal of bulky, unprocessable items such as large tree branches, refrigerators and "white goods", and other materials too large or undesirable for combustion. RDF plants use a variety of retrieval and size reduction equipment to remove noncombustible items and to produce material of uniform size and consistency for burning.

Both mass-burn and RDF plants generate air pollutants in the form of heavy metals, dioxins, furans, acid gases, and nitrogen oxide. Federal and state air quality standards require all facilities to install sophisticated pollution-control devices such as scrubbers and baghouses to control the release of these highly toxic substances. New and existing solid waste incinerators — including those burning refuse-derived fuel — must limit emissions of air pollutants. The EPA's rules for municipal waste combustors (MWCs) are described in Chapter 13. The EPA includes both waste-to-energy plants and incinerators with no energy recovery system in the MWC category. The rules for municipal incinerators are still developing. The best strategy for municipalities with incinerators is to recognize that future air emission requirements are likely to require significant expenditures to bring existing facilities up to standards.

WTE facilities require a reliable source of water for makeup to boilers, cooling, and other plant uses. While boiler water travels through a closed-loop system and thus poses little hazard, cooling water is typically sent to cooling towers or evaporation ponds, where pollutants can be concentrated. Water used to quench incinerator ash can also become contaminated and must be treated before it can be discharged. Even simple stormwater runoff must be collected and treated. All WTE facilities must comply with federal and state standards for discharge of wastewater and must receive a state and/or federal permit for the discharge. See Chapter 10 for further information.

Ash is an inevitable by-product of every incineration technology. Because ash resulting from combustion of MSW typically contains pollutants such as certain heavy metals, many states require segregating this ash in special ash monofills. The ash must be tested to determine if it meets the criteria for classification as a hazardous waste. Incinerators that receive and burn only household waste and nonhazardous waste from commercial and industrial sources were previously excluded from this requirement. The United States Supreme Court issued a ruling on May 2, 1994, holding that municipal incinerator ash is not exempt from the hazardous waste requirements of RCRA. It is expected that this decision will motivate municipalities to reduce the toxicity and the amounts of ash produced at their incinerators.

LANDFILLS

Landfills pose two major environmental threats: airborne and waterborne contaminant release. Airborne contaminants include fugitive dust or gases released or vented from the site. Landfill gases can migrate to remote locations, causing toxicity and explosion hazards. While most landfill emissions consist of methane and carbon dioxide generated during decomposition, volatile chemicals may also be released. There is also some evidence that methane may act as a carrier for PCBs and carcinogens.

Landfill leachate (liquid releases caused by rainfall, for example) contains a variety of organic and inorganic contaminants. Improperly (or illegally) discarded products such as paint thinner, inks, motor oil, or batteries can release toxic compounds such as benzene, toluene, trichloroethylene, cadmium, and lead. Other materials, including some plastics, can release polyvinyl chloride. Without effective landfill liners and leachate collection systems — now required for most landfills by new EPA rules — these by-products can contaminate soil and groundwater.

Although pathogenic organisms such as bacteria, viruses, and parasites die off in time, their presence in municipal solid waste and thus in landfills can raise public health issues.

LEGAL REQUIREMENTS FOR SOLID WASTE LANDFILLS

Any discussion of the federal requirements applicable to solid waste landfills must take account of the much more serious Superfund liability which may arise for local governments engaging in solid waste activities. Whether your municipality owns or operates a landfill, collects solid waste, or arranges for private haulers to do so, your city could incur massive Superfund liability if its trash is present at a Superfund site. More information on Superfund and how it works is presented in Chapter 1. Keep in mind, however, that the main reason you should be concerned about the landfill requirements discussed in this chapter is not the relatively small penalties assessed for violations (although the penalties can be expensive and criminal violations can lead to jail sentences). The reason to be concerned about landfill requirements is that compliance with the requirements can help prevent contamination, and could help shield your local government from devastating Superfund liability.

The regulations probably have affected (or will affect) most municipal governments in one of two ways. If you own or operate a solid waste landfill, you must comply with the regulations, or close. If you do not own or operate a landfill but do collect or arrange for the collection of solid waste, the landfill you use may have closed, or increased tipping fees to raise revenue to comply with the regulations. EPA regulations govern the minimum federal criteria for the location, design, operation, closure, and post-closure care of municipal solid waste (MSW) landfills. These regulations were issued under Subtitle D of the Resource Conservation and Recovery Act (RCRA), and are found at 40 C.F.R. §§ 257 and 258.

These regulations require MSW landfill owners and operators to conduct environmental monitoring, take corrective action to clean up any releases of environmental contamination into groundwater, and provide financial assurances sufficient to guarantee all costs associated with properly operating and closing the landfill. With the exception of a few provisions, most MSW landfill owners and operators had until October 9, 1993, to bring their operations into compliance.

However, the EPA extended that deadline until April 9, 1994, for landfills that:

- Accept 100 tons of waste per day (tpd) or less.
- Are located in states that submitted timely applications for approval of state solid waste programs, or on tribal lands.
- Are not listed on the Superfund National Priorities List.

The EPA believes that many small municipal landfills fall into this category.

Some 20 percent of the sites on the EPA's Superfund National Priorities List (NPL), which includes the 1,200 worst hazardous waste sites eligible for federal cleanup money, are *municipal landfills*, a broad category that includes virtually every landfill that once accepted municipal solid waste. The costs of cleaning up such facilities will probably run into several billions of dollars, and a large share of such costs may ultimately be paid by local governments, including those that owned and operated the sites and those that sent wastes to the sites. The EPA estimates that the vast majority of the approximately 300 municipal landfills on the NPL (in fact, all but nine) accepted significant quantities of industrial hazardous waste along with the considerably more benign municipal solid waste that was also sent to these facilities.

Local governments should ask any consultant, vendor, or fellow local government under consideration for a future solid waste venture about involvement as a potentially responsible party (PRP) at a municipal Superfund site. The consultant, vendor, or fellow local government's potential liability for a Superfund site may just be bad luck or it could be a disturbing sign of both a lack of competence and potential future financial instability.

One way to reduce costs of landfill operation is to regionalize waste disposal: EPA data indicate that a small, 10-ton per day facility costs $55 per ton to operate, while a 1,500-ton per day facility costs $16 per ton. In addition, local governments might consider the possibility of entering into a siting agreement or *host community contract* with a private operator, which can be structured to protect a community's environment as well as its financial resources. Such private/public collaborations may be solid waste management's wave of the future.

In sum, solid waste management will be one of the most significant environmental and fiscal issues facing local governments over the next decade. Local governments are expected to have front-line responsibility for developing and operating safe, affordable waste management programs, with some state or federal technical assistance and oversight (but no funds). Regardless of the perspective from which your community approaches this issue, your final goal should be the same: environmentally sound management of solid waste in accordance with EPA and state regulations, at the lowest possible cost.

This book only addresses federal regulations. States can obtain authority to create their own landfill requirements, so you must also check state law on these matters. In addition, there may be relevant local zoning or health laws that can affect landfill siting and operation. The EPA enforces the requirements in states that have not adopted approved solid waste programs.

COVERAGE OF EXISTING AND NEW MUNICIPAL SOLID WASTE LANDFILLS

In general, the regulations apply to MSW landfill units that received wastes after October 9, 1991. An MSW landfill unit is defined by the EPA as a discrete area of land or an excavation that receives nonhazardous solid waste, including household, commercial and industrial trash, nonhazardous sludge, and small-quantity generator waste. (A landfill that takes *only* sewage sludge is not covered by these regulations.) Approximately 80 percent of all MSW landfills are owned by local governments.

The extent to which the regulations apply to a particular landfill depends upon when it began or ceased receiving wastes, and the extent to which waste has actually been deposited in specific "units" of the facility as of the October 9, 1993 (or April 9, 1994) effective date. The rules can be summarized as follows:

- MSW landfill units that stopped receiving wastes prior to October 9, 1991, are not subject to any of the regulatory requirements.
- Landfill units that stop receiving wastes between October 9, 1991, and October 9, 1993 (the effective date of the regulations — April 9, 1994, for small landfills meeting the criteria), are required only to install, upon closure, a final cover system designed to minimize infiltration and erosion. Certain very small landfills in arid or remote locations may continue receiving waste until October 9, 1995, and still fall within this group.
- "Existing" landfill units, *i.e.*, those that have waste in them and are still receiving waste as of the October 9, 1993 (or April 9, 1994) effective date, must comply with all regulatory requirements except those relating to landfill design and certain of the location restrictions.
- "New" landfill units, which first receive wastes on or after October 9, 1993, must comply with all regulatory requirements. New landfills include horizontal expansions of existing landfill units (so-called "lateral expansions") that have not received wastes as of October 9, 1993.

The EPA originally exempted owners or operators of certain "small landfills" (whether new, existing, or lateral expansions) from the design, groundwater monitoring, and corrective action portions of the regulation. To qualify for the exemption: (1) the landfill had to receive less than 20 tons per day of solid waste (on an annual average); (2) there could be no evidence of groundwater contamination from the landfill; and (3) the landfill had to *either* serve a community that, due to extreme climatic conditions, lacks access to a regional facility for at least three consecutive months per year, *or* had to be so isolated that residents have no practicable waste disposal alternative, *and* the area had to experience 25 inches or less of precipitation annually (so there was little likelihood of groundwater contamination). However, the exemption from the groundwater monitoring requirements was challenged in court and struck down, so now landfills that fall into this category must comply with the groundwater monitoring requirements, or close, by October 9, 1995. The other exemptions still apply.

LOCATION RESTRICTIONS

EPA's regulations do not try to direct where MSW landfills should be sited, but they are explicit on where they should *not* go, absent special demonstrations. There are six kinds of restricted locations that cannot be used as landfill sites absent special demonstrations: (1) around airports; (2) in floodplains; (3) in wetlands; (4) on or around fault lines; (5) in seismic impact zones; and (6) in any other unstable areas such as places prone to mine subsidence. If you are required to show compliance with any of these restrictions, the demonstration must be placed in the facility's operating record and the director of the state's solid waste permit program must be so notified.

All six of these restrictions apply to new MSW landfills and lateral (*i.e.*, horizontal) expansions of existing landfills. Only the airport, floodplain, and unstable areas restrictions apply to existing MSW landfills (or vertical expansions of existing units). Existing landfills that cannot make the requisite demonstrations must close within five years (by October 9, 1996). The regulations allow states with approved plans to extend the five-year deadline for up to two more years if there is no practicable alternative to operation of the existing landfill, and there is no threat of substantial risk to human health or the environment.

If your community is planning to site a landfill in the next few years, you will need to analyze the proposed sites with these new siting criteria in mind. Some states may impose additional siting requirements that also will need to be considered.

DESIGN SPECIFICATIONS

EPA's landfill design regulations are applicable to new MSW landfill units and lateral expansions of existing units. The regulations do not apply to existing MSW landfill units (or vertical expansions of existing units). The EPA's view is that retrofitting liners and leachate collection systems onto existing units is impractical, possibly environmentally hazardous, and disruptive to landfill operations.

The design standard that you will be required to meet depends upon whether or not you are building or horizontally expanding a facility in a state with an approved solid waste program. In states without approved programs, all landfills must be built in accordance with a *uniform design*, although the regulations permit a would-be landfill builder in a state without an approved plan to petition for relief from the requirement that it must use the uniform design. The uniform design requirements include a composite liner and a leachate collection system.

States with approved programs are not bound by the uniform design, and can approve a landfill design based on consideration of site-specific factors, including hydrogeologic characteristics of the facility and surrounding land, area climatic factors, and volume and physical characteristics of the leachate. State flexibility is limited by the requirement that all approved designs must ensure that concentrations of the 24 chemicals listed in Table 1 of the regulation (including arsenic, benzene, lead, mercury, and silver) will not exceed each substance's maximum contaminant level (MCL) in the uppermost aquifer (the one closest to the surface) at the relevant point of compliance. The point of compliance is determined by each state depending on the site situation. The MCLs are set by the EPA as drinking water standards under the Safe Drinking Water Act; the EPA plans to update the list as new MCLs are promulgated.

Although states need consider only the Table 1 chemicals in ruling upon proposed designs, the groundwater monitoring and corrective action requirements address a comprehensive set of "Appendix II constituents." As explained below, the regulation requires that, whenever monitoring results indicate a statistically significant level of any Appendix II constituent exceeding the groundwater protection standard, the owner or operator must initiate an assessment of potential corrective actions and must implement a selected remedy. The EPA believes that this back-up monitoring system will ensure the use of designs that are protective of human health and the environment.

LANDFILL OPERATION

The EPA has included in the regulations detailed procedures governing day-to-day operation, which will apply to both new and existing landfill units.

Technically, MSW landfills can, and do, receive wastes that are hazardous. These hazardous wastes may be found in household trash (*e.g.*, paint thinner, nail polish remover, cleaning solvents) and in industrial waste generated and disposed of in sufficiently small quantities that it is exempt under the hazardous waste disposal requirements of RCRA.

The EPA requires owners or operators of *all* MSW landfills to implement a program at the facility for detecting and preventing the disposal of regulated hazardous wastes and polychlorinated biphenyl (PCB) wastes. This program must include random inspections of incoming loads (unless other measures, such as source controls, are taken to ensure that hazardous wastes are being excluded), inspection records (which would be maintained in the operating record), training of personnel to recognize hazardous or PCB wastes, and notification to appropriate state or EPA personnel if regulated hazardous wastes or PCB wastes are found at the landfill.

The random inspections of waste loads referred to in the regulations are not envisioned as quick checks; instead, the EPA suggests that the loads be discharged at a location near or adjacent to actual landfilling operations and be visually inspected for indications that containers may hold hazardous waste. However, random inspections need not be conducted if other measures are taken to avoid the receipt of hazardous waste, such as institution of a source control restriction, *e.g.*, a requirement that only household wastes are received at the landfill. Personnel conducting inspections should be trained to identify all potential sources of regulated hazardous waste or PCB waste. The EPA suggests that, at a minimum, training should be given to supervisors, spotters, designated inspectors, equipment operators, and weigh station attendants or, in other words, anyone coming into contact with an incoming load. The focus of the training would be to teach identification of containers and labels typically used in hazardous waste disposal.

The owner or operator of an MSW landfill can refuse to accept waste it identifies as hazardous and require the transporter to remove it. However, any waste deposited in the landfill becomes the responsibility of the owner or operator. If the owner or operator discovers regulated hazardous waste at the landfill, the owner or operator must ensure that the wastes are treated, stored, or disposed of in accordance with RCRA and applicable state requirements. As stated earlier, the owner or operator must also notify the state or EPA of the discovery of regulated hazardous wastes.

Cover Material Requirements

In keeping with the accepted practice at most landfills, under the new rule all MSW landfill owners or operators must cover disposed solid waste with six inches of earthen material at the end of each operating day (or more frequently, if necessary), to control rats, flies, other pests, odors, and blowing litter. The director of an approved state program can permit the use of an alternative cover material of an alternative thickness, if sufficiently protective, or may waive the cover requirement entirely where climatic conditions make compliance "impractical."

Disease Vector Control

Consistent with the rules currently in effect, the regulations require that all MSW landfill owners or operators prevent or control on-site "disease vectors" (*e.g.*, flies, mosquitos, and rats), using techniques appropriate for the protection of human health and the environment.

Explosive Gases Control

Methane is a gas produced by the decomposition of solid waste, especially household waste. When concentrated in structures, it is highly explosive. Because of fatal accidents resulting from the buildup of exploding toxic methane vapors, the EPA sets limits for methane concentration, and also requires routine testing of methane levels in landfill unit facilities and below the landfill's surface to ensure that methane levels do not become dangerous. Landfill operators are not required to test for other gases. The methane levels must be tested at least quarterly, although within that limit the type and frequency of monitoring can vary depending upon site-specific factors.

If the minimum levels are exceeded, steps must be taken to correct the gas explosion risk. First, landfill owners and operators must immediately notify the state and take all steps necessary to protect human health. These steps could include evacuation and ventilation of the buildings. The EPA also requires that the owner or operator submit a remediation plan to the state within 60 days of detecting high levels of methane. The plan must describe the nature and extent of the problem and a proposed remedy. Possible remedies for high methane levels could include installing interceptor gas collection trenches and venting in facility structures, as well as withdrawing subsurface gas. Once the plan is placed in the facility's operating record, it should be implemented and the state should be notified of its implementation.

Air Criteria

EPA rules prohibit the open burning of solid waste. The only exception to this blanket prohibition is the infrequent burning of such wastes as agricultural and silvicultural wastes, land clearing debris, diseased trees, or debris from emergency cleanup operations. "Agricultural waste" does *not* include waste pesticides or empty pesticide containers.

Each MSW landfill is also required to comply with the appropriate state implementation plan (SIP) under the Clean Air Act. See Chapter 13 for further discussion of requirements related to solid waste landfills.

Access

The EPA's regulations require all MSW landfill owners and operators to control public access. In the EPA's view, access control is necessary to protect against illegal dumping of hazardous wastes and direct public exposure to solid waste, and is a key element in preventing landfill injuries or death. The EPA suggests that these goals be achieved by installing natural or artificial barriers and posting signs.

Run-On/Run-Off Control Systems

The regulations require all MSW landfill owners and operators to design and construct controls both for run-on and run-off (*e.g.*, rain water, leachate, or other liquids). For run-on control, the system must prevent flow onto the active portion of the landfill during the peak discharge of a 25-year storm, *i.e.*, a storm likely to occur, on the average, every 25 years. To control run-off, the system must collect and control at least the water volume resulting from a 24-hour, 25-year storm from the active portion of the landfill. Once collected, run-off must be handled according to the regulations concerning surface water, described below. The purpose of run-off control is to prevent erosion, surface discharge of wastes, and the creation of leachate by percolation of water through the landfill. The EPA does not specify how such control systems must be designed.

Surface Water Requirements

The regulations attempt to prevent solid waste activities from adversely affecting the quality of surface waters. First, MSW landfills may not cause an unpermitted point source discharge into waters of the U.S., including wetlands, in violation of the Clean Water Act. Second, they may not cause a nonpoint source discharge of pollutants into waters of the U.S., including wetlands, in violation of any requirement of an area- or statewide water quality management plan that has been approved by the EPA under the Clean Water Act. Unpermitted dredge and fill operations also violate the Clean Water Act.

Liquids Restriction

The regulations prohibit disposal in an MSW landfill of bulk or uncontained liquid wastes, unless the liquid is household waste (not including septic waste). Liquid waste in containers is also prohibited, unless the containers are of the size typically found in household waste, are designed to hold liquids for use other than storage (*e.g.*, batteries) or in fact do hold household waste. Liquid restrictions are necessary because the disposal of liquids into a landfill can be a significant source of leachate.

To the extent there is some unavoidable amount of liquid in the landfill, either in the form of leachate or "gas condensate" (liquid generated as a result of gas recovery processes at the unit), that liquid can be "recirculated" within the landfill, if the landfill has been designed with a composite liner and leachate collection system in accordance with the EPA's uniform design.

Recordkeeping

The regulations contain stringent requirements concerning the need for and contents of an MSW landfill "operating record," that is, there must be a single location in which each MSW landfill owner or operator must keep on hand information including inspection records; notification procedures; gas monitoring results; closure and post-closure plans; monitoring, testing, and analytical data; location restriction demonstrations; and cost estimates and financial documentation. The data must be available to the state upon request.

CLOSURE/POST-CLOSURE CARE

The regulations include minimum requirements concerning the closure and post-closure care of all MSW landfills. Closure and post-closure planning and implementation add significant costs to the operation of an MSW landfill, as a result of environmental monitoring, remedial work where necessary, and careful final cover placement and maintenance. Significantly, financial assurance must be given for all foreseeable costs associated with closing the landfill, maintaining and monitoring it for 30 years after it is closed, and for cleaning up any groundwater contamination that may occur.

Closure

The regulations direct owners and operators of both new and existing landfills to prepare and obtain state approval of a written closure plan. The closure plan describes the activities that will be undertaken to close each MSW landfill unit. Once a plan is approved, a copy of it must be kept at the facility or some other place by the owner or operator. The closure plan is important, since it forms the basis for enforcing closure performance standards and for determining the necessary amount of financial assurance.

The central closure requirement is the installation of a "final cover," which must be designed to minimize landfill infiltration and erosion. The EPA's regulation sets minimum thickness levels for the cover layer, though the director of an approved state may allow an equally protective alternative cover design.

Typically, closure activities must begin no later than 30 days after final receipt of waste at each landfill unit and closure activities must be completed within 180 days after they begin. Both time periods may be extended by the state. After closure is completed, the landfill owner or operator must provide certification to the state. Once the certification has been approved, the landfill owner or operator is released from the requirement that it provide financial assurance for closure costs.

Post-Closure

A landfill is supposed to be closed in such a way that it needs only limited maintenance, and will result in minimal leachate and gas formation. Despite perfect closure, there is still a long-term risk of environmental releases at landfills. To address this possibility, the EPA requires significant post-closure care.

The regulations require that post-closure care be conducted for 30 years, though approved states may shorten or lengthen this period. During these 30 years, operators must conduct routine maintenance to maintain the integrity and effectiveness of the landfill's final cover (which is subject to erosion or subsidence damage), and continue leachate management (by maintaining and operating the leachate collection system), groundwater monitoring, and gas monitoring.

The owner or operator must also prepare a written post-closure care plan that describes the nature and extent of planned monitoring and maintenance activities. This plan should also include identification of a person to contact about the closed facility and a description of planned future uses of the property. No future use is permitted if it will disturb the final cover, the waste containment systems, or the monitoring systems, unless the state determines that the use will not harm human health or the environment.

A copy of the post-closure care plan must be kept by the owner or operator and it must be updated until certification of completion by the state. After an

MSW landfill is closed, the owner or operator must make a record of the property's former use as a landfill on the deed of the property itself and note any future use restrictions.

GROUNDWATER MONITORING AND CORRECTIVE ACTION

Both new and existing MSW landfills are required to assess the hydrogeology under the landfill units and to monitor and report on groundwater quality. Groundwater monitoring must continue through post-closure care. The regulations require installation of groundwater monitoring wells and specify placement, sampling, and analysis procedures. The major provisions are briefly reviewed below.

MSW landfills are exempt from the monitoring requirements if they are able to demonstrate, with site-specific data and a certification by a qualified groundwater scientist, that there is no potential for migration of hazardous constituents from the landfill to the uppermost aquifer during the landfill's active life, closure, and post-closure periods. The latter exemption is available only to owners and operators of landfills in approved states.

For existing MSW landfills and lateral expansions of such units, compliance with the monitoring requirements will be phased in over a five-year period (by October 9, 1996), although approved states may use an alternative (though no more lengthy) implementation schedule. However, within the five-year period, the EPA has established priorities based upon the distance between the existing MSW landfill unit (or lateral expansion) and a "drinking water intake" (which can be located above or below ground). If the landfill unit is less than one mile from the intake, monitoring must be in place within three years (by October 9, 1994); if the landfill-intake distance is between one and two miles, monitoring must be in place within four years (by October 9, 1995); finally, if the distance is greater than two miles, monitoring must be in place within five years (by October 9, 1996). New units must be in compliance with the monitoring requirements before waste can be placed in the unit.

Each groundwater monitoring system must consist of a sufficient number of appropriately located wells to be able to yield groundwater samples from the uppermost aquifer that represent the quality of background groundwater and the quality of groundwater passing a specified relevant point of compliance. Each monitoring system must be certified by a qualified groundwater scientist or approved by an approved state.

The rule states detailed sampling procedures and requires that samples be taken at least every six months. Sampling is aimed at measuring the levels of 47 volatile organic compounds and 15 metals (listed in Appendix I to the rule). The Appendix I monitoring is known as "detection monitoring." Examples of Appendix I substances include arsenic, lead, and benzene. Approved states have been given the authority to delete any of the Appendix I parameters (where it can be shown that certain substances are not "reasonably expected" to be in or derived from the waste in the unit), to establish alternative parameters, or to vary the frequency of sampling where appropriate.

If any of these compounds are measured at a statistically significant level over background concentrations, the owner or operator must move to a second step known as "assessment monitoring." In this monitoring phase, sampling must be performed for a lengthy list of Appendix II substances. All of the substances listed in Appendix I are included as part of the Appendix II listing.

If subsequent assessment monitoring shows that the levels of detected Appendix II substances are at a statistically significant amount above the relevant Ground Water Protection Standard (GWPS), the owner or operator must evaluate alternative corrective action measures. The assessment must be completed within a "reasonable period" of time, following which the selected remedy must be implemented.

In selecting a remedy, the regulations mandate that the ultimate choice be protective of human health and the environment, and that the selection be based on consideration of several detailed factors, including long- and short-term effectiveness; the extent to which the remedy will control the source, thereby reducing further releases; difficulty of implementation; technical and economic capability of the owner or operator; cost to implement the remedy; and degree to which the remedy reflects community concerns. As part of the selected remedy, the owner or operator must specify an initiation and completion schedule. In addition, as part of the process of evaluating potential remedies, the owner or operator must hold a public meeting. A record of the selected remedy must be placed in the facility's operating record.

The director of an approved state can waive the remediation requirement where the contaminated groundwater is not a source of drinking water, remediation is neither feasible nor expected to be helpful, or remediation would have other undesirable impacts.

In addition to corrective action, which may take years to plan and carry out, if there is a threat to human health or the environment, the state may require the landfill owner or operator to take other interim measures, such as providing a temporary alternate water supply.

Once implemented, corrective action must continue until the owner or operator achieves compliance with the GWPS for a period of three consecutive years (or an alternative determined by an approved state).

FINANCIAL ASSURANCE

The EPA's regulations will require that owners or operators of both new and existing MSW landfills demonstrate financial assurance for three types of future costs: closure, post-closure, and corrective action for known releases. The EPA fears that, absent these requirements, the government will ultimately be responsible for funding these activities. State and federal government owners or operators are exempt from these requirements, but local governments (including general purpose, *e.g.*, cities and special purpose, *e.g.*, public authorities units) are not. The requirements are presently scheduled to become effective April 9, 1995, for all landfills.

The amount of financial assurance required is based on written estimates of the costs of hiring a third party to: (1) close the largest area of the MSW landfill in the most expensive manner; (2) conduct all activities over the entire post-closure activities period; and (3) if corrective action is needed, perform the corrective action in accordance with the regulations.

The regulations also specify financial mechanisms that may be used to demonstrate financial responsibility. The general standard is that the financial mechanism chosen must ensure that the requisite funds be available when needed, and in a timely manner. The rule permits the use of one or more of the following: (a) trust fund with a pay-in period; (b) payment or performance surety bond; (c) irrevocable standby letter of credit; (d) insurance; (e) any other state-approved mechanism; and (f) a determination by the state that it will assume financial responsibility. The EPA has proposed additional mechanisms for use by local governments, but these proposals were not final as this book went to press.

CONCLUSION

Economics is an inescapable consideration in implementing regulatory compliance. Ideally, compliance costs and possible contingencies are included in the budgeting process. However, it is often difficult to estimate the cost of regulatory compliance, especially without knowing current waste management costs. For example, municipal waste collection and disposal costs may be lumped together as part of a general fund appropriation; municipally owned disposal facilities may subsidize costs for other municipal divisions; replacement cost or depreciation of vehicles and equipment may be excluded from waste management expenses; and private operators may be unwilling to disclose their cost figures.

In addition, waste management facilities often create economic impacts on the municipal infrastructure that are difficult to quantify. For example, diversion of household hazardous wastes may require municipalities to provide for hazardous waste disposal and waste-to-energy plants may require significant water for cooling and fire protection.

Economic tradeoffs exist as well. For example, curbside collection programs divert recyclables and unacceptable materials from the landfill, thus extending landfill capacity — but the direct cost to collect the material may exceed the revenues from sale of the recyclable materials. However, while a curbside program's initial labor, equipment, and startup costs may seem high, such programs may bring down total system costs over the long term. In addition, the avoided costs of landfill operation — particularly given the new federal requirements — may make such short-term costs even more acceptable.

The key to determining the financial impact of regulatory compliance is knowing what today's costs are. Without a solid base of current cost information, planning future expenditures will be difficult. Municipal officials must amass data on all the costs of solid waste management, direct and indirect, obvious and obscure, to determine the financial needs of compliance programs.

Decisions must be assessed in economic as well as environmental terms. In other words, prevention efforts that seem expensive today may forestall even costlier cleanup costs tomorrow.

CHAPTER **4**

Emergency Planning and Community Right-to-Know

Mark S. Hegedus and Lisa G. Dowden

This chapter discusses local government compliance with laws concerning emergency planning for releases of hazardous substances and the public's right-to-know information about the use of such substances at, and the release of them from, facilities in their communities. The primary governing law is the Emergency Planning and Community Right-to-Know Act (EPCRA), 42 U.S.C. § 11001 *et seq.* The regulations issued under EPCRA can be found at 40 C.F.R. § 350 *et seq.*, § 355 *et seq.*, § 370 *et seq.*, and § 372 *et seq.* The purpose of EPCRA is to require anyone who manufactures, processes, stores, or uses hazardous chemicals to report this information to state and local officials who are responsible for developing emergency response plans for use in the event that an emergency arises. Much of the reported information will also be made available to the public.

EPCRA imposes three distinctly different kinds of requirements. One is *emergency planning.* For any covered facility (*e.g.*, wastewater treatment plant, utility generating plant, vehicle maintenance garage), you must participate in efforts to plan a coordinated response to a serious emergency (*e.g.*, spill, explosion, or fire involving toxic chemicals) in your community. Such efforts are coordinated by state and local emergency response committees. The second is *general public reporting and disclosure requirements.* If you are covered by these requirements, you must make general disclosures about the potentially hazardous chemicals that your facilities use. The third is *emergency reporting requirements.* Once again, if you are covered, you must report certain emergency spills and other releases "into the environment."

Bear in mind that the EPCRA imposes requirements on local governments both as regulated entities and as regulators. Local governments and fire departments are expected to participate in the local emergency planning efforts required by the law. In addition to complying with the regulations, your city, county, or town may have to budget resources for participation in planning for your community.

1-56670-098-1/95/$0.00+$.50
© 1995 by CRC Press, Inc.

In order to achieve compliance with the EPCRA, your local government will probably have to designate a coordinator to ensure that city facilities make all required submissions. Many municipalities give this responsibility to the fire department, which is automatically part of the EPCRA process in any case. You will also need to think carefully about how your employees should comply with the emergency reporting requirements. In general, it is better that contact with regulators be made by employees who are trained to recognize when reporting is necessary, and who have experience dealing with regulators. On the other hand, all employees should be able to recognize when a release has occurred which may require notification, so that they can contact the appropriate personnel.

This chapter will briefly explain the operation of state and local emergency response committees, which comprise the bureaucratic structure that implements the statute. It will then consider the EPCRA reporting requirements, certain miscellaneous provisions, EPCRA's enforcement and civil action provisions, and recordkeeping.

It is particularly important to remember that this chapter discusses only the requirements imposed by federal law. Many states have adopted community right-to-know legislation, and federal law expressly does not preempt state and local requirements. This failure to preempt means that, even if your local government's facilities are exempt from certain federal reporting obligations (and some are), they could very well be subject to the same or more stringent obligations under state and local law. State law might also impose different or more stringent reporting obligations in instances where you are obligated to report under federal law. In most cases, you must fulfill both the federal and state obligations. It is vital that your local government be aware of applicable state and local laws.

In addition to the differences between state and federal laws, the state and local emergency response committees established by the federal law (discussed more fully below) are permitted to impose requirements in addition to those imposed by EPCRA. For example, local committees could decide to regulate chemicals other than those on the EPA list, and state commissions have the power to designate facilities for compliance that would otherwise not be covered by the EPCRA. Therefore, your state and local response committees, established under the EPCRA, can ask you for more information than is discussed here and have the right to receive it.

STATE AND LOCAL EMERGENCY RESPONSE COMMITTEES

The first important obligation under the EPCRA is knowing to whom you must report. Reporting under the EPCRA is made to emergency response committees, which are responsible for community emergency planning, gathering information about hazardous chemicals present in their communities, and forming plans for evacuation and other emergency responses. The EPCRA set up a timetable for states to establish the framework for state and local emergency planning, and in most localities the required committees have been established. The EPCRA required each state governor to appoint a state emergency response commission (SERC). If you do not know how to contact your SERC, you should call your governor's office. The SERC was responsible for establishing local emergency planning districts, and appointing local emergency planning committees (LEPCs). These committees should consist of local emergency response personnel such as fire department personnel and representatives from local industries and citizens groups. If your community does not have an LEPC, or if you don't know how to contact your LEPC, you should contact the SERC for your state. In the absence of an LEPC, you should still make all notifications required under the EPCRA to the SERC. The LEPCs should have produced community emergency response plans.

EPCRA GENERAL REQUIREMENTS

The EPCRA requires you to report the presence of designated quantities of certain extremely hazardous substances at covered facilities so that the local committees can use this information in preparing emergency response plans. The EPCRA also requires emergency reporting of chemical releases. The EPA has published a list of "extremely hazardous substances," and for each chemical the EPA has established both a "threshold planning quantity" (TPQ) and a "reportable quantity" (RQ). The listed chemicals and their TPQs and RQs are found at 40 C.F.R. § 355, Appendices A and B. The TPQ and the RQ are usually different, and the TPQ is generally a higher number than the RQ. The TPQ's significance is that, if you have more than the TPQ of any listed chemical present at your facility, you must report this fact to the SERC and the LEPC. The RQ's significance is that, if your facility releases any of the chemical into the environment in an amount in excess of its RQ, you must make an emergency notification to the same officials.

EMERGENCY PLANNING

The first step in determining reporting obligations is to determine whether any of the extremely hazardous substances on the EPA's list are present at your facility. The EPA's definition of "facility" under EPCRA requires you to consider all buildings, equipment, machinery, and vehicles stored on contiguous (or adjoining) sites as one facility. Remote, noncontiguous locations are treated as separate facilities. Therefore, if several of your departments, *e.g.*, vehicle maintenance and parks and recreation, share a service yard or storage facility, it will be considered a single facility for EPCRA reporting purposes, and all of the chemical present *at the facility* must be counted.

Once you have determined that a particular listed chemical is present at your facility, you must determine how much. If the amount of an extremely hazardous substance present at your facility exceeds its TPQ, you are obliged to report. In order to determine whether a listed chemical at your facility exceeds its listed TPQ, you must count all of the chemical present. The location or locations of the chemical, the number of containers, and the method of storage do not matter. (For instance, sulfuric acid in batteries is counted.) The fact that the chemical may be present as an ingredient in a mixture does not matter. If the chemical constitutes more than 1 percent by weight of a mixture or solution, you must count it. To calculate the composition of a mixture, you multiply the percentage of the chemical present in the mixture or solution by the mass, in pounds, of the entire mixture. Mixtures and solutions are combinations that can be separated into their component parts. Alloys and amalgams are not mixtures, and their components need not be counted, unless the alloy or amalgam is itself a listed substance.

In the case of purchased chemical products, you may not know the amount of an extremely hazardous substance present in a mixture. Sometimes this information can be obtained from the manufacturer's Material Safety Data Sheet (MSDS) or from the label. Under the EPCRA, you are obliged to make the calculations if you know, or reasonably know, what is in a purchased mixture. You are not obliged to make inquiries from the manufacturer. However, even though you are not required to make inquiries, in many cases federal or state Occupational Safety and Health Act (OSHA) regulations may require you to have the MSDS available for your workers. If you have failed to satisfy this requirement, enforcement officials may decide that you should have known what was in a substance. It is important to bear in mind that, while local governments are generally exempt from federal OSHA requirements, they are likely to be subject to these requirements in states with OSHA programs.

If you determine that one or more of the hazardous substances listed by the EPA is present at your facility in an amount in excess of the TPQ, you must notify the SERC and the LEPC that your facility is a covered facility. While the regulations do not specifically state that you must identify the types and amounts of regulated substances present, it is clear that the SERCs and LEPCs have the right to obtain this information from you. This notification should have been made some time ago and must be made within 60 days of the time your facility first becomes a covered facility. If your facility begins to use a new listed substance in excess of its TPQ, or if a new substance is listed that you already use in excess of its TPQ, you must renotify the SERC within 60 days. You are further required to inform your LEPC of any changes at your facility that are relevant to emergency planning, and to promptly provide any information requested by the LEPC that is necessary for the development and implementation of emergency plans.

Two things should be obvious from the above discussion. First, you will be able to decrease your regulatory responsibilities by cutting down or eliminating use of listed chemicals at your facility. Substitute other products wherever possible. Second, you will need an ongoing compliance program at your facility to evaluate and check new chemicals against the lists and to keep you aware of new chemical listings. Once you have a compliance program in place, the reporting process can become routine.

EMERGENCY REPORTING

Emergency reporting under the EPCRA is fairly straightforward and consists of two components. Under the first, facilities must report releases of substances designated on the extremely hazardous substances list when the amount of chemical released exceeds the listed reportable quantity (RQ). Under the second, even if the release would not otherwise be reportable according to the EPCRA list, facilities are also required to report releases for which a report to the National Response Center is required under the Comprehensive Environmental Response, Compensation and Liability Act of 1980 ("CERCLA" or "Superfund"). See Chapter 5 for more information. You are responsible for complying with both components.

When to Report

The EPCRA's emergency reporting requirements apply when there is a "release" of a listed chemical. The regulations define a "release" of a listed chemical as "spilling, leaking, pumping, pouring, emitting, emptying, discharging, injecting, escaping, leaching, dumping or disposing" of the chemical into the environment. Release also covers disposing of drums, cans, or other receptacles containing the chemical.

When you are determining whether a release has exceeded the substance's designated RQ, you are not required to aggregate multiple releases of the same chemical released from different facilities or to aggregate different chemicals from the same facility. In addition, there are some circumstances when EPCRA emergency reporting is not required. These include when

- The release is completely confined to the site where the facility is located and only persons solely within the site are exposed to the release, as long as the environment outside the site (including land, air, and water) is not exposed to the release. *If it gets into the air, the release is probably reportable.*
- The release is a federally permitted release such as a discharge specifically permitted pursuant to the Clean Water Act or the Clean Air Act.
- The release is a "continuous" release subject to annual reporting requirements under Superfund. Statistically significant deviations from a Superfund continuous release must be reported, under both Superfund and the EPCRA.
- The release is use of a registered pesticide in accordance with the instructions on the label.

The emergency reporting requirements began in 1987. Accordingly, if your facilities experience any releases of designated chemicals, you must report them immediately to your SERC and LEPC.

Where to Report

In the event of a reportable release from any facility, the owner or operator must immediately make the report, by telephone, radio, or in person, to each of the following:

- The Community Emergency Coordinator, if one has been appointed, for each community likely to be affected by the spill.
- The LEPC, if there is no Community Emergency Coordinator, for each community likely to be affected by the spill.
- The SERC, for each state likely to be affected by the spill.
- For spills from "transportation facilities" (*i.e.*, trucks, trains, or storage facilities used during transportation, etc.), the above requirements are satisfied by dialing 911, the operator, or local emergency number (whichever is applicable in the community) and making the report.

Do not forget that many releases will also require a call to the National Response Center (1-800-424-8802 and 202-267-2675 in the D.C. metro area) under Superfund. Reports to state and local officials do not satisfy this requirement, and a call to the Coast Guard National Response Center does not satisfy EPCRA reporting requirements. In many cases, you will be contacting emergency response personnel, such as fire departments, police, or ambulances at the same time. See Chapter 5 for more information on what and how to report.

PROVISION OF INFORMATION TO MEDICAL PROFESSIONALS

You may also need to provide information to medical professionals, and a special section of the EPCRA deals with this issue. Health professionals, including doctors and nurses, may apply directly to your facility in order to obtain information to treat a patient they believe has been exposed to a hazardous chemical. Local governments may also hire health professionals to conduct health studies of exposed populations or to develop preventive health measures for the local community. These professionals also may apply directly to covered facilities for information, bypassing the LEPC. In general, you will not be able to (or wish to) deny information to medical professionals.

INVENTORY REPORTING REQUIREMENTS

There are additional EPCRA reporting requirements which *only* apply to facilities covered by federal OSHA requirements. The EPA has determined that local governments, which are not generally subject to federal OSHA requirements, are exempt from these additional EPCRA provisions. However, not all states agree with the EPA's determination, and these states intend to enforce the requirements against local governments. In addition, many states have enacted their own EPCRA requirements which often expressly apply to local governments. You must still investigate state and local community right-to-know requirements before you can be sure of the full extent to which your local government's facilities are regulated.

Because some states will require you to comply with these OSHA-triggered requirements, and because the EPA encourages you to comply with them voluntarily, these additional requirements are explained below. You will also need to be familiar with them to provide medical personnel with some of the information they request.

The EPCRA inventory reporting requirements require facilities to turn over certain types of information to their SERCs, LEPCs, and local fire departments. Facilities must turn over copies of their MSDSs or lists of the chemicals for which they have MSDSs, and each facility must fill out an inventory form for each chemical, containing certain detailed information about the chemical. These forms must be filed on an annual basis.

The OSHA Hazard Communication Standard requires manufacturers and importers of chemicals to identify hazards associated with the chemicals they import or produce. Once the hazards are identified, the chemicals must be properly labeled and shipped with an MSDS which identifies the hazards. All employers, whether they are in the chemical manufacturing business or merely purchase the chemicals for their own use, must make these MSDSs available to their employees. Certain training and awareness programs are also required. Note that, while the applicability of EPCRA requirements is somewhat confused, the OSHA Hazard Communications Standard was enacted in such a way that it covers everyone, including local governments, through federal or state programs.

OSHA is not a "list-driven" statute. In other words, the government has not provided all-inclusive lists of chemicals (like the EPCRA list) to assist manufacturers and importers in their hazard evaluations, although some lists exist for certain chemicals. OSHA requires evaluations of all "hazardous chemicals." Under OSHA, a hazardous chemical is defined as any element, chemical compound, or mixture of elements and compounds that is a physical or health hazard. "Hazards" can be physical hazards (such as flammable or reactive chemicals) or health hazards (such as substances known to cause cancer). Mixtures can be evaluated as mixtures, or by separate components. Local governments, which are not generally involved in the chemical manufacturing or importing business, are unlikely to have to perform hazard evaluations. Instead of performing their own hazard evaluations, local governments may rely on any MSDS provided by a manufacturer or importer.

You are responsible for making certain that your facilities obtain an MSDS for each hazardous chemical you have on the premises to which your workers might be exposed. *OSHA requires that manufacturers and importers label chemicals to indicate hazards.* This requirement means that an employer can tell whether or not an MSDS is required by examining the label of the chemical. If the label indicates a hazard, you know that an MSDS is required and you must obtain one from the manufacturer. This statement assumes that the manufacturer is following the labeling requirements correctly. Regardless of the label, if you have reason to believe a chemical presents a hazard, you should request an MSDS. If you have chemicals on hand that you purchased long ago, prior to the OSHA labeling requirements, you should evaluate whether you need them around. If you are going to keep them, you should request an MSDS.

While we have not described your responsibilities to your employees under the Hazard Communication Standard, the standard has been discussed because EPCRA requirements are triggered by the OSHA requirements. If you are unaware of your general OSHA responsibilities, you should take steps to learn what they are.

MATERIAL SAFETY DATA SHEETS

Under the EPCRA, facilities that are required by the OSHA Hazard Communication Standard to prepare or have available an MSDS for a hazardous chemical must provide a copy of that MSDS to the LEPC, the SERC, and the local fire department with jurisdiction over the facility where the chemical is present. Alternatively, a list of such chemicals may be provided in place of copies of each MSDS.

The definition of "facility" is the same one given above. Remember that *facility* means *buildings and operations located on contiguous pieces of land.* If you use or store chemicals at remote facilities, you must make separate notifications for *each* location. There is one exception to this rule for the purposes of the requirements explained here. Transportation facilities, which include vehicles in transit and facilities where materials are temporarily stored while en route to another destination, are not covered for these purposes. A vehicle used as a storage facility on your property is covered by these regulations. In other words, your trucks used for hauling chemicals outside the facility are not regulated by this section of the EPCRA, but you cannot store chemicals in a truck parked in your vehicle yard and call that a transportation facility.

It bears repeating that the definition of "hazardous chemical" is not related to the list of Extremely Hazardous Substances that determines the application of the EPCRA provisions described previously. For the purposes of the MSDS requirement and the chemical inventory form requirements described here, the list of Extremely Hazardous Substances has no application.

Under the broad OSHA definition, almost any chemical for which OSHA requires an MSDS would be a hazardous chemical. Accordingly, any MSDSs your facilities have (or are required by OSHA to have) should probably be turned over to the SERC, LEPC, and fire departments at the appropriate time.

As stated above, the EPCRA provides two options for MSDS compliance. Your facility may submit all its MSDSs or it may submit a list of all chemicals requiring an MSDS. The requirement of submission of an MSDS for each chemical is probably the simpler of the two options. The alternative, submission of a list of chemicals present at a facility, as explained below, requires consideration of more factors, and you are responsible for separating the listed chemicals into hazard categories. For MSDS submission, a facility need only gather the MSDSs for each chemical, and submit copies to the SERC, the LEPC, and the fire department with jurisdiction over each facility.

The only potential difficulty involves the treatment of mixtures. The EPCRA allows the facility to submit either an MSDS for the mixture as a whole or an MSDS for each of the hazardous chemicals which comprises the mixture. If the facility chooses the second method, and a hazardous chemical present in one mixture is also present in others, the facility may submit one MSDS for that chemical. The regulations do state that a facility should treat mixtures consistently, and not provide an MSDS for mixtures in some cases and for ingredients in others. Since most of the hazardous chemicals your local government has on hand will be commercial chemical products, often mixtures, you should decide which approach your facilities will use.

A facility must submit a new MSDS to the LEPC and SERC within three months of the discovery of significant new information concerning the hazardous chemical. A facility also has three months to submit an MSDS after a new chemical becomes present at the facility.

REQUIREMENTS FOR SUBMISSION OF CHEMICAL LIST

As stated above, you have the option of submitting a chemical listing of the hazardous chemicals present at your facilities instead of submitting an MSDS for each chemical. Any list submitted by a facility must contain each hazardous chemical present at the facility for which an MSDS is required under OSHA. The chemicals on this list must be grouped into hazard categories. The hazard categories are "immediate health hazard," "delayed health hazard," "fire hazard," "sudden release of pressure," and "reactive." You are responsible for assigning chemicals to the proper category. The MSDS may provide this information for each chemical. In order to prepare the list, you will probably need to gather all your MSDSs and segregate them according to hazard categories.

The chemical list must also provide the chemical or common name of each hazardous chemical, as supplied from the MSDS, in addition to any hazardous component of a chemical derived from the MSDS. The treatment of mixtures for the chemical list is the same as for submission of MSDSs. Facilities may list mixtures either as mixtures, or by their individual components, but they should be consistent in the chosen method.

If a facility chooses to submit a list instead of an MSDS for each chemical, the LEPC may still request the MSDS of any chemical on the list, and the facility will be obligated to provide it. Similarly, members of the public are entitled to request any MSDS from the LEPC, which will provide it, or obtain it from the facility if the LEPC does not have the MSDS. As you can see, providing the MSDSs is generally the easier route.

Chemical Inventory Forms

Facilities are required annually to submit a chemical inventory form for each hazardous chemical for which OSHA requires the facility to have an MSDS. These forms must be provided to the SERC, the LEPC, and the fire department with jurisdiction over the facility in question, and serve the purpose of making extensive information available to the public. There are two types of inventory forms, called Tier I and Tier II. Tier I calls for aggregate information about chemicals according to the hazard classes discussed above in the list reporting section. Tier II calls for more specific information about each hazardous chemical. The facility owner or operator makes the initial decision as to which information to provide unless the state or the LEPC chooses to require one form or the other. Many states require or strongly encourage use of the more-detailed Tier II forms. Annually on March 1, facilities are required to submit forms reflecting all hazardous chemicals that were present at the facility during the previous calendar year and that were present in any amount. Forms are also required for extremely hazardous substances from the EPCRA list present in quantities exceeding 500 pounds or 55 gallons, or the TPQ, whichever is less.

Tier I Information

Sample forms requesting Tier I and Tier II information are available from EPA or your state. The Tier I form requires you to separate the hazardous chemicals present at your facility into the hazard categories discussed earlier. This information should be obtainable from the MSDS of each chemical.

Once you have categorized the chemicals, you must provide an estimate of the maximum amount of all chemicals in each category present at the facility during any time in the previous calendar year. These are aggregate numbers. You are not reporting the amount of any specific chemical present, but the total amount of chemicals present in each category. You must also provide an estimate (in ranges, as shown on the form) of the average daily amount of hazardous chemicals present in your facility.

Tier II Information

Tier II forms request the following:

- The chemical or common name of each hazardous chemical, from the MSDS.
- An estimate (in ranges) of the maximum amount of the hazardous chemical present during the previous calendar year.
- An estimate (in ranges) of the average daily amount of the hazardous chemical present during the previous calendar year.
- A brief description of the manner of storage of the hazardous chemical.

- The location of the hazardous chemical at the facility.
- An indication of whether the owner elects to withhold information of a specific hazardous chemical from disclosure as a trade secret.

Mixtures can be reported as mixtures or by individual components as described above, but again consistency is desired. Your facility should use the same method used for MSDS or list reporting.

INFORMATION AVAILABILITY

State and local officials and the public may obtain access to Tier II information by requesting it from the LEPC. The LEPC can obtain the information from the facility if it cannot satisfy the request from information already reported. The fire department is entitled not only to obtain Tier II information, but also to conduct an on-site inspection of the facility. You may not withhold specific location information from the fire department.

MISCELLANEOUS PROVISIONS

Several EPCRA provisions are referred to only briefly, either because they are unlikely to apply to local governments or because no action on the part of a facility is involved. For instance, Section 313 of the EPCRA, which requires covered facilities to submit toxic chemical release forms, is an important part of the EPCRA, but it applies only to facilities engaged in manufacturing, and is therefore not discussed here. The EPCRA also makes provision for the protection of trade secrets, when information about a chemical required to be reported could be made available to the public. Since most of the hazardous chemicals present at local government facilities are purchased commercial chemical products, it is unlikely that you would need to make use of the trade secret provisions.

RECORDKEEPING

The EPCRA does not impose any specific recordkeeping requirements. However, accurate and complete records are the only way for you to prove that you have complied with environmental requirements. Remember the cardinal rule: if you don't write it down, it might as well never have happened if a regulatory agency (*or* a citizens' group) ever checks your compliance. Therefore, you should maintain copies of all notifications, annual reports, and other correspondence addressed to (or received from) your LEPC and SERC. Detailed memos to the files should document all verbal communications.

CONCLUSION

The EPCRA requirements are designed to protect your communities in the event of a release of a hazardous substance. Perhaps the most difficult part of the EPCRA requirements is establishing the reporting procedures. Once this is completed, however, EPCRA compliance should be routine.

CHAPTER **5**

Emergency Notifications

Mark S. Hegedus and Rena I. Steinzor

Several environmental laws require individuals or entities to report to government agencies if they experience spills, leaks, or escapes of hazardous substances from their facilities into the environment. These laws apply with full force to local government facilities; this chapter will discuss your notification obligations in the event of an emergency. Local governments should be aware that there are stiff criminal and civil penalties for failure to report a release in a timely fashion, and failure to make a required report is one of the offenses for which the federal government is most likely to prosecute.

Obviously, local governments should have procedures in place for responding to emergency spills or leaks. You may be wondering where such emergencies are most likely to arise in your municipality. For most cities and towns, the greatest risk is chlorine gas, which is used at wastewater and drinking water treatment plants and sometimes at their associated facilities. It may also be used in pools. Not only is chlorine gas deadly, but it is likely to be present at water facilities in large amounts. If your local government operates a utility, oil and PCB spills could also trigger these requirements. Although somewhat less likely, accidents with pesticides, hazardous waste, solvents, or paint are possible. The parks department especially should be aware that a pesticide spill could qualify as a release.

The environmental notification requirements most likely to apply to local governments include:

- Superfund (for releases of listed hazardous substances) 42 U.S.C. § 9601, 40 C.F.R. § 302.
- Clean Water Act (for spills of oil or hazardous substances into navigable waters and noncompliance with NPDES permits) 33 U.S.C. § 1251, 40 C.F.R. § 117.
- Toxic Substances Control Act (TSCA) (for releases of PCBs) 15 U.S.C. § 2601, 40 C.F.R. § 761.

- Resource Conservation and Recovery Act (RCRA) (for releases of hazardous wastes) 42 U.S.C. § 6901, 40 C.F.R. § 260.
- Emergency Planning and Community Right-to-Know Act (EPCRA) (for releases of extremely hazardous substances) 40 C.F.R. § 300.

Notification requirements under most of these laws are set up along similar lines. EPA regulations generally include:

- Lists or categories of chemicals and other dangerous substances covered by the notification requirement;
- Reportable quantities (RQs) for each of those substances (*i.e.*, how much must be released in order to trigger the notification requirement);
- Guidance as to when, how, and to whom notifications are to be made.

Overall, the key to compliance with all federal notification requirements is to know where and when you might experience a spill or other release, figure out what hazardous substances might spill in those circumstances, and then determine their RQs. Once you have made those determinations, you can train personnel who deal with spills to make notifications in accordance with statutory and regulatory requirements.

SUPERFUND NOTIFICATION REQUIREMENTS

Although most people think of Superfund as the comprehensive national hazardous waste cleanup law, it also covers emergencies such as spills, fires, and explosions. The Superfund program funds a National Response Center which tracks emergency releases. It also provides limited funding for actual responses to emergencies.

The general Superfund notification rule is as follows:

Where there has been a "release" of a "hazardous substance" "into the environment," in an amount equal to or greater than the substance's "reportable quantity," immediate notification must be provided to:

The Coast Guard National Response Center (1-800-424-8802). This number is a 24-hour hotline. (In the D.C. metro area the number is 202-267-2675.)

The State Emergency Response Commission of any state that is likely to be affected by the release. If no state commission exists, you are required to make your report to the Governor's office.

The Local Emergency Planning Committee. If no local committee exists, you must notify your local police and fire officials (which you may be doing anyway, depending on the nature of the emergency).

Notification can be made by telephone. As soon as is practicable, telephonic notice must be followed by a written report (or reports, if necessary) to the applicable state and local entities, updating the information contained in the telephone report. No written follow-up to the National Response Center is necessary.

Below we will review (1) the types of events that are considered "releases" under Superfund and the situations in which those releases are "into the environment"; (2) substances that are considered "hazardous"; (3) how to determine a substance's "reportable quantity" and how to measure when a spill has exceeded it; (4) when and how to notify the proper authorities; and (5) what records to keep about the spill.

While the focus of the following discussion is on immediate notification in the event of an emergency situation, you should also keep in mind that, whenever you discover a release that would have been reportable under Superfund at the time that it initially started, you are under an ongoing obligation to report it. For example, if you uncover several drums of hazardous substances buried in your local landfill, and the amount of these substances exceeds their RQs, you are under an obligation to report, even though the circumstances of the release are no longer an ongoing emergency. As you read the discussion of notification requirements below, you should keep in mind that, if you discover a release in other than emergency circumstances, you are still obligated to report it. If you are in doubt about your reporting obligations, you should consult an expert.

"RELEASES" COVERED UNDER SUPERFUND

Under Superfund, virtually any spill, explosion, leak, or purposeful dumping or pouring of a listed hazardous substance on land, into air, or into water qualifies as a "release" covered by the notification requirements. Proper notification must be made if the spill or other release equals or exceeds the substance's RQ. While there are some exceptions to the Superfund notification rule, they are extremely limited. *When in doubt as to whether any of the exceptions apply to your spill, it is best either to consult immediately with an expert, or to give notice in accordance with the regulations.*

The EPA requires notification only when a hazardous substance is released "into the environment." For purposes of determining when a release is "into the environment," the EPA has drawn an imaginary line at the boundary of the facility in which the discharge has occurred. Hazardous substances are released into the environment if they are discharged outside the boundaries of the facility. Substances may also be released into the environment, even if they are initially discharged onto plant or installation grounds, if they later make their way outside of the facility through the ground, water, or air. Examples of such releases include spills from tanks or valves onto concrete pads or into lined ditches open to the outside air. If the substances vaporize into the air or reach groundwater, they become releases into the environment.

On the other hand, where a substance remains within the boundaries of a facility you need not give notification under Superfund. Hazardous substances may be spilled at a plant or installation but not enter the environment. An example of such a release is the accidental spill of PCB-contaminated oil or spent solvents onto the concrete floor of an enclosed manufacturing plant. This type of release does not require Superfund notification. These releases may require notification under TSCA or RCRA, however.

The following releases, which might occur in the course of normal municipal activities, do not require notification under Superfund:

- Emissions of hazardous substances in engine exhaust from a motor vehicle, rolling stock, aircraft, vessel, or pipeline pumping station.
- Fertilizers released during normal application.
- Pesticides released during normal application, even when they are applied in concentrations greater than those specified on the label. Spills that occur during application are required to be reported, however.

There are two additional categories of releases that are exempt from the Superfund notification requirements: (1) "permitted" releases and (2) releases that are "continuous and stable in rate and quantity."

First, Superfund notification is not required for releases that are expressly allowed by a permit issued under any of several federal laws. In order to qualify for this exemption, the releases must occur in accordance with permit conditions. Releases that are *not* covered by permit conditions *are* Superfund releases and require notification if an amount equal to or greater than the substance's reportable quantity is released. An example of a federally permitted release would be a discharge by your wastewater treatment plant into surface waters in accordance with a Clean Water Act permit. Be careful, though, to make sure that the specific chemical in question is named in the permit. General permit categories such as "volatile organic compounds" will not exempt large releases of specific chemicals within that class. Moreover, accidental releases that are not associated with permitted operations are covered by Superfund notification requirements.

Categories of federally permitted releases that are relevant to typical local government operations and that are exempt from Superfund notification requirements include:

- Releases from point sources with National Pollutant Discharge Elimination System permits.
- Releases under Clean Water Act Section 402 permits.
- Underground injections authorized pursuant to the Safe Drinking Water Act.
- Emissions subject to Clean Air Act controls.
- Under certain specifications, the introduction of pollutants into publicly owned treatment works.

The qualifications for the exemption categories listed above are complex and must be closely reviewed before a decision on exemption is made. If you believe that you may qualify for exemption, you should consult with an expert prior to deciding not to notify under Superfund.

Although federally permitted releases are generally exempt from Superfund notifications, you must be aware of one important permit rule. Many permits, especially Clean Water Act or Clean Air Act permits, have separate requirements to notify appropriate officials if and when your discharges exceed federal requirements. These separate permit notification requirements are very important and should not be overlooked.

The second category of releases exempt from Superfund notification requirements are those that are "continuous and stable in rate and quantity." This category is not generally applicable to municipal operations.

SUBSTANCES COVERED UNDER SUPERFUND

The EPA has compiled a list of hazardous substances. Do not confuse the list with the lists of hazardous wastes regulated under the RCRA; the Superfund list includes all the RCRA wastes, but adds many more substances. The Superfund hazardous substance list is published at 40 C.F.R. § 302.4.

REPORTABLE QUANTITIES

How much of a hazardous substance must be released before you are obligated to make a notification? You will have to calculate how much of a hazardous or extremely hazardous substance has been released, and whether or not the substance's RQ has been exceeded. The RQ for covered substances is stated in terms of pounds. For example, a list will say that the RQ for Chemical X is 1,000 pounds, meaning that any spill above 1,000 pounds must be reported. The RQ usually depends on the relative degree of hazard posed by a spill or other release of the substance. In general, the most hazardous substances have the lowest RQ amounts, and therefore the most demanding notification requirements.

It can sometimes be very complicated to calculate whether you have experienced a release of an amount of a substance equal to or greater than its RQ. For one thing, the RQs are calculated on the basis of the *dry weight* of such substances within another liquid. If you spill 1,000 gallons of liquid containing 10 percent of a hazardous substance and 90 percent other material, you have only spilled 100 gallons of the hazardous substance.

The EPA has also adopted rules for dealing with two potentially troublesome release calculation situations. These are situations in which (1) there is a release that contains several hazardous substances or (2) there are multiple releases of the same substance over a 24-hour period. If you have a release that contains more than one Superfund hazardous or extremely hazardous substance, *you need to report the release under Superfund only if one or more of the hazardous (or extremely hazardous) substances is discharged in a quantity equal to or greater than its RQ.* Discharges of different hazardous substances should not be added together. In other words, if a spill contains half the RQ of one substance, and half the RQ of another substance, there is no notification requirement under Superfund. In applying this rule you must make an effort to calculate and itemize the RQs of the substances that were spilled. If you have any questions about how to determine the components of a mixture, you should contact EPA or your state agency, or an expert in the operation of these requirements. If you have multiple releases of a hazardous substance over a 24-hour period, you must measure the release over the 24-hour period. An initial release of a substance may not equal or exceed its RQ, but when added to additional releases over the following 24 hours the release may equal or exceed the RQ. When the amount of a substance released within a 24-hour period equals or exceeds its RQ, notification must be made immediately.

NOTIFICATION MECHANICS

When the amount of a Superfund hazardous substance release equals or exceeds its RQ, the person in charge — once he knows of the release — must *immediately* notify the Coast Guard National Response Center and the state and local emergency planning committees. Notifications must contain the following information:

- Chemical name or identity of the substance involved.
- An indication of whether the substance is on the EPA extremely hazardous substances list.
- An estimate of the quantity of the substance that was released into the environment.
- The time, duration, and location of the release.
- The medium or media into which the release occurred (*e.g.*, water, soil, air).
- Any known or anticipated acute or chronic health risks associated with the emergency and, where appropriate, advice regarding medical attention necessary for exposed individuals.
- Proper precautions to be taken as a result of the release, including evacuation.
- The name and telephone numbers of persons to be contacted for further information.

As soon as practicable after the initial verbal report, you are required to give state and local officials (as applicable) a written follow-up emergency notice that contains all the information contained in your telephone report, updated and corrected as necessary. Additional follow-up notices may be necessary as more information becomes available after the first report has been made. In addition, the follow-up notice should describe the actions you have taken to respond to the spill or other release, any known or anticipated acute or chronic health risks associated with the release, and, where appropriate, advice regarding medical attention necessary for exposed individuals.

Finally, an important note about recordkeeping. You should keep in your permanent records copies of all written notifications you have made. It is also a good idea to write memoranda to your files concerning telephone notifications, indicating the date and time of your call, the person with whom you spoke, and the content of the conversation.

OVERLAP WITH OTHER STATUTES

Some hazardous substances are also regulated under other federal environmental laws and regulations. These other laws contain their own reporting requirements. Superfund notification of the release of a hazardous substance also fulfills the reporting requirements under the Clean Water Act, the RCRA, and the Hazardous Materials Transportation Act (administered by the Department of Transportation). Once notification has been given under Superfund, additional notifications under these laws are not required. Note that, although Superfund releases also trigger EPCRA reporting requirements, these requirements are not satisfied by a Superfund report.

CLEAN WATER ACT NOTIFICATION REQUIREMENTS

The Clean Water Act (CWA), codified at 33 U.S.C. § 1251 *et seq.*, contains its own notification requirements, which — like Superfund — come into play when an amount of a hazardous substance equal to or greater than the substance's RQ is discharged into navigable waters. The important practical point to be made concerning the CWA is that with one notable exception, the CWA substances are the same as the Superfund hazardous substances. The RQs are also the same. In other words, reporting under Superfund is required for every type of release of a hazardous substance that is subject to reporting under the CWA. The EPA has stated that notification in accordance with Superfund requirements satisfies your obligations under the CWA to notify in the event of a discharge of a hazardous substance into navigable waters.

The notable exception concerns oil. There is a specific CWA regulation requiring notification in the event of a discharge of oil into navigable waters. Oil is not a Superfund hazardous substance. Under CWA regulations, oil is defined as

> Oil of any kind or in any form, including but not limited to, petroleum, fuel oil, sludge, oil refuse, and oil mixed with wastes other than dredged spoil.

The CWA notification program covers discharges of oil into navigable waters or adjoining shorelines in quantities that "may be harmful to public health or welfare." "Harmful" oil discharges include those that (1) violate applicable water quality standards; (2) create a film or sheen upon or discoloration of the surface of the water or adjoining shorelines; or (3) deposit sludge or an emulsion beneath the surface of the water or upon adjoining shorelines. "Navigable waters" is broadly defined, and includes almost any body of water. If you spill oil in a harmful quantity, you must immediately telephone the 24-hour Hotline at the Coast Guard National Response Center (1-800-424-8802). (In the D.C. metro area the number is 202-267-2675.)

TOXIC SUBSTANCES CONTROL ACT

The Toxic Substances Control Act (TSCA), codified at 15 U.S.C. § 2601 *et seq.*, has its own set of notification requirements. If your local government owns and operates an electric utility, the most important requirement concerns the circumstances under which you are required to give notice of a spill of polychlorinated biphenyls (PCBs). In general, spills of as little as one pound of PCBs can trigger federal reporting requirements, and even lesser amounts carry notification obligations if spilled into sensitive areas such as surface water, drinking water, sewers or treatment facilities, grazing lands, or vegetable gardens. If PCBs are an issue for your local government, a spill response policy should be part of an overall PCB management plan. Most utilities have such a plan, and in any case a description of individual notification obligations in specific situations is beyond the scope of this book. Readers should consult an expert to obtain advice tailored to their individual situations.

RESOURCE CONSERVATION AND RECOVERY ACT

The EPA has issued a comprehensive system of notification requirements under the Resource Conservation and Recovery Act (RCRA), codified at 42 U.S.C. § 6901 *et seq.*, which apply to those persons who generate, import, transport, treat, store, or dispose of hazardous wastes. All hazardous wastes under the RCRA are also hazardous substances for purposes of Superfund. Therefore, where there is a release of a hazardous waste under the RCRA that is equal to or in excess of the designated Superfund RQ, you must give notification in accordance with Superfund. Where a reportable quantity of a waste has been spilled, notification under Superfund satisfies any notification obligation you may have under the RCRA.

Some RCRA notification obligations exist even if less than an RQ has been spilled. Large- and small-quantity generators (see Chapter 2) storing hazardous wastes for disposal must notify the Coast Guard National Response Center in the event that a release of hazardous waste could threaten human health outside the facility or if they have knowledge that a release has reached surface water.

When such notification is given, the waste generator must provide the following information:

- Name, address, and EPA identification number.
- The date, time, and type of incident.
- The quantity and type of hazardous waste involved.
- The extent of injuries, if any.
- The estimated quantity and disposition of recovered materials, if any.

EMERGENCY PLANNING AND COMMUNITY RIGHT-TO-KNOW ACT

Emergency reporting under the Emergency Planning and Community Right-to-Know Act (EPCRA), codified at 42 U.S.C. § 11001 *et seq.*, is fairly straightforward and consists of two components. Under the first, facilities must report releases of substances designated on the Extremely Hazardous Substances List, 40 C.F.R. § 355, Appendices A and B, when the amount of chemical released equals or exceeds the listed RQ. Under the second, even if the release would not otherwise be reportable according to the EPCRA list, facilities are also required to report releases for which a report to the National Response Center is required under the Comprehensive Environmental Response, Compensation and Liability Act of 1980 (CERCLA or Superfund). You are responsible for complying with both components.

WHEN TO REPORT

The regulations define a "release" of a listed chemical as "spilling, leaking, pumping, pouring, emitting, emptying, discharging, injecting, escaping, leaching, dumping or disposing" of the chemical into the environment. Release also covers disposal of drums, cans, or other receptacles containing the chemical. The EPCRA requires the reporting of such a release in the following instances:

- When the released chemical is on the EPCRA list, and the amount released equals or exceeds the designated RQ. This type of release must be reported regardless of whether it is also reportable under Superfund.
- When the chemical release is required to be reported under Superfund, regardless of whether the substance is on the EPCRA list or whether the spill equals or exceeds the EPCRA RQ.

When you are determining whether a release has equalled or exceeded the substance's designated RQ, you are not required to aggregate multiple releases of the same chemical released from different facilities, or to aggregate different chemicals from the same facility. In addition, EPCRA reporting is not required when:

- The release is completely confined to the site where the facility is located and only persons solely within the site are exposed to the release, as long as the environment outside the site (including land, air, and water) is not exposed to the release. *If it gets into the air, the release is probably reportable.*
- The release is a federally permitted release such as a discharge specifically permitted pursuant to the Clean Water Act or the Clean Air Act.
- The release is a "continuous" release subject to annual reporting requirements under Superfund. Statistically significant deviations from a Superfund continuous release must be reported, under both Superfund and EPCRA.
- The release is use of a registered pesticide in accordance with the instructions on the label.

WHERE TO REPORT

In the event of a reportable release from any facility, the owner or operator must immediately make the report, by telephone, radio, or in person, to each of the following:

- The Community Emergency Coordinator, if one has been appointed, for each community likely to be affected by the spill.
- The Local Emergency Planning Committee (LEPC), if there is no Community Emergency Coordinator, for each community likely to be affected by the spill.
- The State Emergency Response Commission (SERC), for each state likely to be affected by the spill.
- For spills from "transportation facilities" (*i.e.*, trucks, trains, or storage facilities used during transportation, etc.) the above requirements are satisfied by dialing 911, the operator, or local emergency number (whichever is applicable in the community) and making the report.

You should know how to contact your Community Emergency Coordinator or LEPC and your SERC. If not, contact your governor's office.

Do not forget that many releases will also require a call to the National Response Center under Superfund. Reports to state and local officials do not satisfy this requirement, and a call to the National Response Center does not satisfy EPCRA reporting requirements. In many cases, you will also be contacting emergency response personnel, such as fire departments, police, or ambulances at the same time.

Keep the phone numbers of your SERC, LEPC, and Community Emergency Coordinator by any telephones from which a release might be reported. While this step is not expressly required by the regulations, it will save time in an emergency. Another practical step would be to keep a written record containing the name of each person you speak to and a summary of what was said. This record will provide added verification that you made the required calls, and will be helpful when you prepare the required written follow-up report.

WHAT TO REPORT

The EPCRA specifies the information that must be included in the verbal emergency reports. However, if you do not know all of the information required by EPCRA at the time of the spill, you should not delay reporting for this reason. The gaps can be filled in later. The required information is:

- The chemical name or identity of all substances involved.
- An indication of whether the substance is on the EPCRA list.
- An estimate of the quantity released into the environment.
- The time and duration of the release.
- The medium or media into which the release occurred (*i.e.*, air, water, land).
- Any acute or chronic health risks that you know or suspect might follow from the emergency, and any information or advice you have regarding medical attention needed for exposed individuals.
- Proper precautions to be taken. For instance, should the area be evacuated? Should people not drink water?
- The name and address of persons to be contacted for further information.
- While it is not expressly set out in the statute or regulations, it is clear that you should provide all information relevant to emergency response, including the location of the release, and anything else response personnel deem necessary.

As soon as it is practical after the emergency situation has been contained, you must provide the Community Emergency Coordinator or LEPC, and the SERC, with a written follow-up report. The follow-up report must contain and update the information you gave in your verbal notification, in addition to setting out additional information about actions you took to contain the release, any acute or chronic health effects which you know or suspect may result from exposure, and any information you have about necessary medical attention. Hazardous waste and Superfund reports may be necessary as well.

CONCLUSION

In the event of a release of a hazardous substance in your community, it is vital that you contact the appropriate local, state, and federal officials to ensure a proper and timely response. Putting a compliance program in place or making sure that your existing compliance programs are operating satisfactorily will help to ensure that your community will be protected in an emergency. In addition, there is no substitute for effective employee training in responding to emergencies most likely to arise at your facilities.

CHAPTER 6

Oil and Fuel Management

James F. Short, John M. McNurney, and David R. Meyer

In the wake of the Exxon Valdez oil spill into Prince William Sound, AK, in 1989 and the Ashland oil spill into the Monongohela River at Floreffe, PA, in 1988, pollution caused by oils and fuels has received much attention from the EPA and the public in recent years. However, the EPA has estimated that such incidents are responsible for only a small fraction of the total amount of oil that is released into the environment. The majority is released through small spills, leaks, and intentional discharges that occur as part of everyday activities in industry, government, and the home. The EPA and Congress have responded by regulating the storage, handling, and disposal of used oil. Local governments do not have to worry too much with respect to spilling crude oil into the sea from a fleet of supertankers, but they do have to worry about gasoline tanks and 55-gallon drums of used oil.

The storage and management of petroleum is primarily regulated under three major environmental laws: the Clean Water Act, the Resource Conservation and Recovery Act (RCRA), and the Oil Pollution Act. The regulations most likely to apply to oil used by local governments are the used oil rules (40 C.F.R. § 279) and the rules for Spill Prevention, Control, and Countermeasure Plans (40 C.F.R. § 112). Other laws and regulations may also come into play. For example, dielectric fluids containing PCBs are regulated as simply as oils with respect to the oil pollution prevention regulations, but they are also regulated by PCB regulations under the Toxic Substances Control Act (TSCA). Similarly, used oil that is not handled properly can become a solid waste or even a hazardous waste subject to RCRA. Many states have their own regulations that reflect the federal programs and are sometimes even more strict. It is important to be aware of these requirements because local governments are responsible for complying with all of them simultaneously. While many federal agencies, including the Department of Transportation (DOT), the U.S. Coast Guard, the Occupational Safety and Health Administration (OSHA), and the Federal Emergency Management Agency (FEMA), have some responsibilities under these programs, most of the requirements are administered by the EPA and, in some cases, state environmental agencies.

When you check your local government facilities for oil that may be subject to the regulations, you are looking for tanks of gasoline, diesel fuel, or any other oil used for fuel, oil filters (spin-on or cartridge), lube oils, hydraulic oil, and dielectric fluids. The oil may be new or used. Likely departments include vehicle maintenance, the municipal airport, electric utilities, fuel farms (for police, fire, and other city vehicles), and departments where large equipment is maintained (sanitation or parks). Vehicle maintenance and electric departments will probably have the greatest need for oil and fuel management programs.

USED OIL MANAGEMENT

Standards for the reuse and management of used oil took effect in March 1993 in states not then authorized by the federal government to administer that aspect of the hazardous waste program. States with authorization for their own programs must amend them to incorporate the new rules and you should check your individual state program for changes. According to EPA, used oil is "any oil that has been refined from crude oil, or any synthetic oil, that has been used and as a result of such use is contaminated by physical or chemical impurities." Used oils can include motor oil, synthetic motor oil, transmission fluid, hydraulic oil, mineral oil dielectric fluid, synthetic dielectric fluid, cutting oils, and others. Vehicle and equipment maintenance are the most common activities that generate used oil. Your local government may also collect waste oils as part of a "household hazardous waste" collection program. Local governments must develop and maintain a prudent, knowledgeable approach to dealing with the waste oils generated by their operations and stored on their property to avoid significant liability for improper oil handling.

The used oil management standards attempt to set out a program that protects the environment while still encouraging the recovery and recycling of used oil. The used oil standards are intended to encourage recycling by providing an avenue for disposing of used oil that doesn't require the use of expensive hazardous waste disposal companies.

When you generate (produce) used oil, you must store it in tanks or containers. All above-ground tanks and containers must be in good condition, with no signs of severe rusting, structural defects, or deterioration, and free from leakage. Each container must be clearly marked "used oil." Underground tanks are subject to their own set of state and federal regulations. If municipalities store used oil in above- or below-ground tanks, the fill pipes must be clearly marked "used oil." Remember, it is important, as explained further in this section, to avoid mixing any hazardous wastes with used oils, as this would trigger rigorous (and expensive) hazardous waste management and disposal restrictions.

The used oil regulations assume that used oil will be recycled, that is, it will be processed, re-refined, or burned for energy recovery. If the oil is otherwise disposed of, it will be subject to either the solid waste or the hazardous waste RCRA regulations depending on whether it qualifies as hazardous waste. See Chapter 2 for more information on this possibility.

Even if you do intend to recycle or burn your used oil, you may be prevented from doing so if your used oil is contaminated with other hazardous chemicals. Used oil mixed with hazardous wastes becomes a hazardous waste, so it is prudent to carefully segregate waste oils from other material, including cleaning solvents and vehicle antifreeze, to avoid possible contamination. On the other hand, used oil that is *not* mixed with hazardous wastes is not a hazardous waste, even if it fails one of the four hazardous characteristic tests (see Chapter 2) as long as it is recycled or burned for energy recovery.

Burning for energy recovery is lightly regulated. The EPA has adopted regulations designed to encourage the burning of used oil for energy recovery purposes and the recycling of used oil; several states have passed largely identical laws. These rules create a definite incentive for used oil generators to burn their oil in this manner. Burning oil for energy recovery is a good option, particularly where the oil meets the definition of "on-spec" used oil. On-spec oil must meet certain limits for the metals arsenic, cadmium, and chromium; total halogens; and flash point in order to be burned without restriction under RCRA management standards. You can only claim that your oil is on-spec if you have the test results for each container of oil to prove it. Keep the test results for each container of oil in case questions arise in the future (you are required to keep them for three years). However, even oil that does not meet the standards (off-spec oil) can be burned or marketed for burning under certain regulatory controls, as long as it has not been mixed with hazardous waste.

Mixtures of hazardous waste and used oil are regulated in several ways, depending on the hazardous waste generator status and the nature of the waste itself. If the used oil is mixed with a RCRA-listed hazardous waste, the oil is subject to regulation as a hazardous waste. If the used oil is mixed with a characteristic hazardous waste and does not exhibit any hazardous characteristic, it is subject to the used oil regulations. Other mixtures of characteristic wastes are subject to hazardous waste regulations. If your facility is a conditionally exempt generator, it can mix its hazardous waste and used oil and the resulting mixture is regulated as used oil.

If your local government decides to recycle its used oil, you should know how the proposed recycler will process and market it. Because the term "recycling" can cover a multitude of activities, you must be sure that the contracted recycler is engaging in a bona fide recycling activity that continues to ensure that you are protected from excessive liabilities and risks.

For example, the law restricts the use of used oil as a dust suppressant. Federal laws prohibit anyone from spreading used oil contaminated with hazardous wastes on road or land surfaces for dust suppression.

If your local government aggregates and stores used oil from all of your facilities at a central location, that facility becomes a *used oil aggregation point,* which is subject to certain requirements discussed above. If you accept used oil from "do-it-yourselfers" (DIYs) maintaining their personal vehicles, you will not be subject to any additional regulations for that reason. However, if you accept oil from other generators, such as commercial or industrial facilities, your facility will be a *used oil collection center* and subject to licensing by the state.

The EPA has developed standards for used oil transporters and transfer facilities, but there are steps municipalities can take to avoid having to qualify as transporters when they move used oil between their own facilities. If the city hauls used oil in shipments of 55 gallons or less from a generator facility to either a used oil collection center or an aggregation point, it is exempt from EPA regulations on used oil transporters. However, it is your responsibility to ensure that, after that point, the oil is moved only by certified transporters who have obtained EPA identification numbers. It is important to note here that, if a city hauls oil from an aggregation point to a used oil collection center, it is not exempted from these regulations even if the shipment is 55 gallons or less. The exemption only applies to the generator of the oil (the person who first produced it) and it is site, or facility, specific. For example, cities may collect used oil at several locations around the city and haul it to a central aggregation point owned and operated by the city without being regulated as a used oil transporter by the EPA as long as individual shipments are 55 gallons or less. If the DIY oil is then hauled from the aggregation point to a used oil collection center, the person hauling it must comply with the used oil transporter regulations.

Used oil filters (spin-on or cartridge type) from light- or heavy-duty vehicles are exempt from the hazardous waste regulations as long as they are not coated with terne (an alloy of tin and lead) and as long as they are gravity hot-drained. Gravity hot-draining means that the filters are held up and allowed to drain for a period of several hours (12 hours recommended) at a temperature near the engine operating temperature and above room temperature. The drained filters can be recycled, or crushed and disposed of with your solid waste.

OIL SPILL PLANNING

In an effort to ensure that facilities using fuels and oils are adequately prepared to prevent accidental discharges to the environment, the government requires the preparation of plans to prevent and respond to oil spills. The purpose of these plans is to protect health, safety, public welfare, and the environment. A good plan can help avoid damage suits, legal fees, penalties, and cleanup expenses.

There are two types of plans generally applicable to petroleum management. One is the Spill Prevention, Control and Countermeasure (SPCC) Plan, required under the Clean Water Act. Its primary purpose is to reduce the likelihood of oil spills. Further, an SPCC Plan serves as a guideline to control a spill if one occurs and to mitigate damaging effects on the environment. The second type is an Oil Spill Response Plan, required by the Oil Pollution Act. An Oil Spill Response Plan describes how to clean up a spill after it occurs.

SPCC PLANS

An SPCC Plan should address both the prevention of a harmful discharge and measures to control and contain material if a discharge occurs. Each plan should provide for:

- Appropriate containment and/or diversionary structures or equipment to prevent discharged oil from reaching navigable waters.
- Procedures to minimize potential for a discharge to occur.
- Adequate training of employees to reduce the possibility of releases or discharges.
- Periodic inspection and review of operating procedures for facilities and equipment to handle discharges.

Portions of an SPCC Plan may be common for facilities with similar equipment, but location and terrain variables require unique plan provisions and features for each location.

It is illegal to discharge oil into "regulated waters" without a permit — and an accidental spill is a discharge without a permit. Regulated waters means virtually every body of water — rivers, harbors, lakes, streams, ponds, creeks, wetlands, and even dry river washes. The regulations prohibit the discharge of "harmful quantities" of oil. A harmful quantity of oil can be a very small volume, and is defined as any amount of oil that would cause any of the following conditions:

- Creation of a film or sheen on the water.
- Endangerment to health or the environment.
- Violation of water quality standards.
- Deposits of sludge onto the shore or beneath the water surface.

While the government obviously cannot require you to get a permit for an accidental discharge you do not anticipate, it does require you to take steps to prevent such occurrences.

Your local government must have an SPCC plan at all facilities that use or store oil at locations where spilled or discharged oil could reasonably be expected to reach navigable waters in harmful quantities and where any of the following are true: (1) the facility has a total above-ground oil storage capacity greater than 1,320 gallons; (2) the facility has an oil storage capacity in a single container greater than 660 gallons; or (3) underground storage tank capacity is greater than 42,000 gallons. The EPA treats oil-containing electrical equipment such as transformers and circuit breakers as bulk storage tanks for the purposes of these regulations.

The owner or operator of every facility must determine whether the facility could "reasonably be expected" to discharge oil into regulated waters or upon adjoining shorelines. Making this decision is difficult and requires sound professional judgment. If the facility is far removed from regulated waters, the probability of discharge into regulated waters may be remote. Among the factors to consider are:

- Spill history.
- Location (proximity to regulated waters).
- Potential size of discharge.
- Soil and terrain conditions.
- Frequency and amount of rainfall.

In addition to over-ground transport, oil may be able to reach regulated waters by means of storm drains. Oil sent through a sewer line can also cause repercussions at the treatment plant.

It is not true that secondary containment is required only for tanks or equipment that have a storage capacity greater than 660 gallons. That threshold is used only in the determination of the applicability of the regulations. Some containers greater than 660 gallons may not warrant a separate secondary containment system while other containers much smaller than 660 gallons might. It is up to the engineer developing the plan to determine what, if any, containment is needed at a given facility to provide reasonable protection against a spill reaching navigable waters.

SPCC Plan Requirements

The EPA regulations offer guidance for developing SPCC Plans. Those requirements are summarized here, but personnel responsible for preparing SPCC Plans should refer to the actual regulatory text when drafting the plans. The following is a brief summary of those requirements:

- A discussion of spill events in the 12 months prior to the date of the plan and a description of how further spills will be avoided.
- A prediction of the direction, rate of flow, and total volume of oil that could be discharged where experience indicates a "reasonable potential" for equipment failure.
- A description of secondary containment systems in place and how they will work, including the volumes such systems can contain, leaving sufficient freeboard for rain.
- A description of facility drainage systems and how oil will be kept out of sewers, storm drains, and water courses.
- A schedule and forms for inspections including primary equipment, secondary containment systems, retained stormwater, and drainage systems.

- Where appropriate, a description of oil transfer operations and procedures to follow that will ensure a spill does not occur including pipe/hose and joint inspections.
- A description of facility security including valve locks, pipe caps, fences, gates with locks, and lighting.
- A discussion of personnel training in spill prevention including notification hierarchy, proven response methods, equipment maintenance, and knowledge of pertinent state and federal regulations.

If secondary containment for a facility is not practicable, the owner or operator must clearly demonstrate the impracticability and develop an oil spill contingency plan following the provisions found at 40 C.F.R. § 109. The owner must also provide a written commitment of manpower, equipment, and materials required to expeditiously control and remove any harmful quantity of oil discharged.

The oil spill contingency plan should describe: (1) the authority, responsibilities, and duties of all persons in planning or directing the oil removal operations; (2) the establishment of notification procedures including current names, addresses, and phone numbers of responsible persons and agencies, provisions for access to reliable communications systems, and a prearranged procedure for requesting assistance in the event the situation exceeds the response capability of those present; (3) provisions to assure manpower equipment, materials, and supplies are available; and (4) provisions regarding the specific actions to be taken in the event of a discharge.

Anticipated Regulatory Changes

The EPA has proposed new regulations that will affect the existing SPCC Plans. Some of the expected changes include a notification requirement for facility owners, changes in when plans must be prepared, and exemption of underground tanks from the plans.

OIL SPILL RESPONSE PLANS

The Oil Pollution Act (OPA) requires facilities to prepare plans to respond to a worst-case discharge of oil, and sets forth specific requirements for the development of such plans. The EPA has issued rules and the U.S. Coast Guard has proposed rules that will implement the law. The rules will require the owner/operator of any on-shore facility that could reasonably be expected to cause substantial harm to the environment as a result of a spill of oil from the facility into or on navigable waters, adjoining shorelines, or the exclusive economic zone to prepare a response plan. This requirement is separate from any requirement to prepare an SPCC Plan. An SPCC Plan describes how to prevent or contain a spill. A response plan describes how to clean up the spill after it occurs.

If you have a facility that transfers, stores, or handles substantial amounts of oil (over one million gallons unless the oil is transported over water, in which case 42,000 gallons is the triggering amount) and is located next to a navigable waterway, the requirement to prepare a response plan may apply. The administrative responsibility for reviewing oil spill response plans is split between the U.S. Coast Guard and the EPA. The Coast Guard deals with marine transport-related facilities (excluding storage tanks) while the EPA is responsible for on-shore oil storage facilities (tanks).

If your city, county, or town has a fuel unloading pier or transfer terminal, it may be necessary to prepare a response plan for a spill resulting from the transfer operation and submit it to the U.S. Coast Guard. This requirement is limited to a spill of oil associated with the transfer operation and does not require inclusion of a spill resulting from a leak or rupture of on-shore storage tanks. However, if you have on-shore oil storage (with or without marine transfer facilities), you may need to prepare a response plan and submit it to the EPA.

The major thrust of the response plan guidelines is to assure that there is a thoughtful written plan for responding to an oil spill. The plan should include provision for cleaning up the spill in the immediate vicinity and should identify the means to protect important economic and environmental areas that could also be affected. Another major emphasis is to assure that the necessary equipment, personnel, and other resources have been identified and will be available in the case of an emergency.

The OPA requires that certain critical items and issues be addressed in response plans including:

- Consistency with the National Contingency Plan and Area Contingency Plans.
- Identification of a qualified individual having full authority to implement removal actions, and initiate immediate communication between that person and appropriate federal authorities and responders.
- Identification of available resources to remove, to the maximum extent practicable, a worst-case discharge.
- Description of training, testing, unannounced drills, and response actions of persons at the facility.
- Periodic updates.
- Resubmittal for approval of each significant change.

The EPA has developed a model plan to help owners and operators of affected facilities prepare their plans. This model, which is similar to the Coast Guard model, includes the following elements:

- Emergency response action plan (what to do when a discharge occurs).
- Facility name, type, location, and the names of owners and operators.
- Emergency notification, equipment, personnel, and evacuation information.

- Identification of potential spill hazards and previous spills.
- Identification of small-, medium-, and worst-case discharge scenarios and response actions.
- Description of discharge detection procedures and equipment.
- Detailed implementation plan for containment and disposal.
- Facility response resource self-inspection, training, and meeting logs.
- Diagrams of facility and surrounding layout, topography, and evacuation paths.
- Security measures such as fences, lighting, alarms, guards, emergency cut-off valves, locks, and others.

Much of this information is the same as that contained in a good SPCC Plan. While the EPA believes these plans have different purposes, it recognizes some sections may be identical. Therefore, if you have an existing SPCC Plan, you may be able to simply reproduce appropriate and suitable sections for inclusion in the response plan.

Even if your facility does not store enough oil to trigger the requirement for a spill response plan, you must still execute a self-certification for each facility. The certification says that you have examined the rules and determined that the facility is not covered. Keep the certification with your SPCC plan. Officials may ask to see it during inspections.

NOTIFICATIONS

Several major federal environmental laws require facility operators to notify federal, state, or local agencies when they become aware of a spill, leak, or other release of a variety of substances (including oils and fuels) from a facility into the environment. These notices help to mobilize emergency personnel and ensure that the spill or release is cleaned up promptly and properly. Stiff criminal and civil penalties are imposed for failure to notify or to respond properly to a spill. Notification does not eliminate liability for cleanup costs or for natural resource damages associated with the release of a substance. For more information on emergency notification requirements, turn to Chapter 5.

CONCLUSION

Plans for the management and storage of oil are essential if local governments are to manage their used oil in compliance with the environmental laws.

CHAPTER 7

Underground Storage Tanks

Wendy S. Lader and Rena I. Steinzor

This chapter concerns underground storage tanks or "USTs" and the regulatory program that governs them. To be considered a UST, a tank, together with its associated piping, must have at least 10 percent of its volume below the ground. The UST regulations only apply to tanks containing petroleum products and certain chemical substances. Tanks containing hazardous wastes are subject to even more stringent regulations which are not discussed here. Because local governments rarely, if ever, store chemicals in USTs, this chapter will deal exclusively with the regulations applicable to USTs storing new or used petroleum products.

Where should you look for USTs in your local government operations? Fuel farms, of course, are the most obvious places. If your municipality operates locations for fueling government vehicles, it is almost guaranteed that there will be underground tanks there. If you operate a municipal airport, there is probably also a fuel farm for aircraft. You should also consider any areas where vehicle (including aircraft) maintenance occurs. Vehicle maintenance generates substantial quantities of used oil which must be accumulated for proper disposal or recycling. It is not uncommon to accumulate such oil in underground tanks. Finally, you should consider facilities with emergency generators. Hospitals, water and wastewater treatment plants, and police and fire stations often have them. Airports are another common site. The fuel supplies for these generators may be stored in USTs. While USTs associated with emergency generators are exempt from some requirements, they are subject to many of the regulations and should be considered in any UST management program.

Before examining the federal regulations, you should also be aware that an increasing number of states have initiated regulatory programs covering petroleum and hazardous substance UST systems. The EPA regulations provide for the implementation of new regulations carried out at the state level as long as these regulations are at least as stringent as the federal regulations. If your state has an approved program, you will need to comply with the state's regulations.

1-56670-098-1/95/$0.00+$.50
© 1995 by CRC Press, Inc.

The federal UST regulations are part of the RCRA hazardous waste program and are located at 40 C.F.R. Part 280. The federal program covers four important areas:

- *Notification* involves notifying your state government about all of your USTs. Some states collect annual registration fees.
- *Technical standards* involve meeting strict criteria regarding the composition of your tank, and its leak detection and other mechanisms. Older tanks that do not meet the criteria must be retrofitted according to a schedule.
- *Emergency response requirements* involve the procedures you must follow to respond to leaks or spills.
- *Financial assurance* requires you to have financial mechanisms in place to guarantee that your local government has funds available to cover cleanup costs and third-party liability resulting from its USTs.

This chapter will discuss the requirements in each of these areas. First, however, we will discuss some general issues.

There are a number of categories of tanks that are exempted from the EPA UST regulations by law. Tanks exempted by law and likely to be located at city facilities include

- Tanks storing heating oil for consumptive use on the premises where stored.
- Tanks holding 110 gallons or less.
- Equipment and machinery that contain regulated substances for *operational* purposes, including *electrical equipment* such as vaulted underground transformers.
- Emergency spill or overfill tanks used to hold regulated substances only for a short period of time, provided that such tanks are expeditiously emptied after use. However, sumps used to store petroleum or hazardous substances during periodic cleaning or maintenance of equipment (*e.g.*, turbine oil sumps used during maintenance of power generation turbines) *are covered* by the rules.
- Septic tanks.
- Storm water or wastewater collection systems.
- Flow-through process tanks.
- Storage tanks situated on or above the floor of underground areas (such as basements, shafts, or tunnels).
- Tanks that store fuel solely for use by emergency power generators do not have to comply with release detection requirements but otherwise have to follow *all other* requirements in the new UST rules.

A word of caution in reading the rest of this section: the technical rules often vary according to whether the tank is an "existing" or a "new" tank. An existing tank is one for which, as of the effective date of the regulation, an owner or operator had obtained all required federal, state, and local permits and had *either* begun physical installation of the tank *or* had signed contracts for such installation which could not have been canceled or modified without substantial loss.

Existing petroleum UST systems must comply with the new regulations by December 1998 (10 years after the rules became effective). A new tank is one installed after the effective date of the regulation, which must comply with the regulation upon installation. This chapter will discuss the different sets of regulations applying to existing versus new tanks where applicable.

Even before the technical rules were issued in 1988, an "Interim Prohibition" was established. This prohibition, issued on May 8, 1985, applied to all tanks installed between May 8, 1985, and December 22, 1988.

The Interim Prohibition made it illegal to install any new UST system unless the three following requirements were met: the system had to prevent releases due to corrosion or structural failure; protect against corrosion; and, finally, be compatible with the substance to be stored.

You should therefore make sure any tanks installed during the 1985 to 1988 time period comply. The EPA recognizes several different types of corrosion protection devices that will satisfy the Interim Prohibition. For bare steel tanks, many owners and operators employ "cathodic protection" systems which involve deflecting the electric currents between the tank and the ground that typically cause corrosion. Other corrosion protection methods include coating the tank with fiberglass-reinforced plastic to prevent rust.

NOTIFICATION

Turning to the four major regulatory requirements, the first important obligation to be aware of is the notification requirement. All owners were required to notify state officials by May 8, 1986, concerning any tank that has been used at any time since November 8, 1984. Owners of tanks taken out of use between January 1, 1974, and November 8, 1984, but still in the ground, also had to notify state officials. Owners of tanks subsequently brought into use have 30 days from the time they start using the tank to notify state agencies. Although most tank technical standards apply to both owners and operators, the notification requirements are limited to owners, those holding title to the tank, to simplify the inventory process.

The EPA has put out a standard form for registering notifications which is used by most, but not all, states. You should check with your state's environmental protection agency to get copies of the appropriate form used in your location.

TECHNICAL STANDARDS

CERTIFICATION OF PROPER INSTALLATION

You must also comply with a series of design and performance standards. If you install a new UST, you must follow industry codes and standards for proper installation and certify that your tank was installed properly by filing a *notification form* with your state that you have put a new UST into service. There is no analogous requirement for existing tanks.

Proper installation standards and codes cover a variety of factors, including excavation, siting, burial depth, tank system assembly, backfilling of the tank system, and surface grading. Many mistakes can be made. For example, work crews can mishandle the tank and damage it, lay piping runs improperly, tighten joints incompletely, or cover the tank inadequately especially if it is in a heavily trafficked area. To avoid these problems, you should make sure that your contractor or work crew carefully follows the codes and standards.

PREVENTION OF SPILLS AND OVERFLOWS

You are also required to take certain steps to prevent spills and overflows. Releases of petroleum into the environment from spills and overfills are at least twice as numerous as actual leakage from tanks or their piping. Such accidents happen most often when the delivery truck comes to replenish the supply of gasoline in the tank.

The technical regulations require that

1. You make sure that the UST has enough room in it to hold a new delivery *before* the transfer is made.
2. The operator of the UST and the delivery truck operator *watch constantly* during the transfer to prevent overfilling and spilling.
3. You use equipment to prevent and contain spills and overfills, such as spill catchment devices and dry disconnect couplings. Such equipment either automatically shuts off the flow of fuel or sounds an alarm when the tank is nearing capacity.

All *new* USTs have been required to follow regulatory requirements to prevent spills and overfills since December 22, 1988. All *existing* tanks must follow these requirements by December 1998, but it is a good idea to get into compliance as soon as you can because you will always be liable for the cleanup of spills or overfills no matter when the rule goes into effect. The *only exception* to these requirements is for tanks that are filled by *separate* transfers of *no more than* 25 gallons each.

CORROSION PROTECTION

As of 1988, the EPA determined that some 80 percent of existing UST systems were constructed of unprotected — or "bare" — steel that has no special capacity to resist corrosion. These tanks are, therefore, far more likely to leak. As a result, the technical regulations require that tanks be protected from corrosion. Again, new tanks must comply with this requirement when installed, and existing tanks must be retrofitted and upgraded by 1998. You would be well advised to upgrade as soon as possible since it is far less expensive than cleaning up a spill.

There are several ways to accomplish compliance with this crucial requirement. Steel tanks *and* piping can be coated with a corrosion-resistant material and "cathodically" protected. Alternatively, tanks *and* piping can be made *totally* of a noncorrodible material such as fiberglass-reinforced plastic (FRP). Lastly, to enable ongoing technological developments, the EPA rule allows the regulatory authority (either your state or EPA itself) to approve new methods that are as effective as the ones mentioned above.

LEAK DETECTION

The regulations also require that you outfit USTs with leak detection systems that provide for monitoring of leaks at least every 30 days. The permissible forms of leak detection provided in the rule vary depending on whether the tank is a new or existing UST.

For *new* tanks, there are at least six different options available for monthly monitoring:

- Tank tightness testing every five years combined with monthly inventory control (dispatching and reconciling). After *10* years, you must use one of the other approved methods of leak detection.
- Monitoring for vapors in the soil.
- Monitoring for liquids in groundwater. This method cannot be used if the water table is more than 20 feet beneath the surface of the ground.
- Automatic in-tank "gauge" monitoring. This method uses *automated* processes to monitor product level and to help control inventory.
- Interstitial monitoring within secondary containment. This method applies to USTs that are double walled, fitted with internal liners, or equipped with partial interception barriers located below the UST.
- Other approved methods.

As for *existing* tanks, the EPA rule phased in the requirement for leak detection systems over a five-year period. All existing USTs should by now be equipped with leak detection.

- You can use any of the monthly monitoring methods explained above in our discussion of new tanks.
- *If* your existing UST has corrosion protection or internal tank lining, as well as devices that prevent spills and overfills — in other words, if it is an upgraded tank — you can *combine* monthly inventory control with a complete tank tightness test every *five* years. *However*, this choice can only be used for *10 years* after the tank is upgraded.
- If your tank is *not upgraded*, you can still do monthly inventory control but you must combine it with *annual* tank tightness testing. Even this alternative is allowed *only until* December 1998. After that, your UST must use a *new* tank leak detection method.

Piping must also be protected against leaks. The degree and type of leak detection method depends on whether the piping is "pressurized" piping or "suction" piping.

If your piping is of the *pressurized* variety, you must have devices that either automatically shut off or restrict the flow through the pipe when it begins to leak or that sound an alarm in the event of a leak *and* you must either conduct an annual tightness test or use a monthly monitoring method.

If your piping is of the *suction* variety, leak detection requirements depend on the precise kind of piping you have. If the piping is especially safe, no leak detection is required. "Safe" piping is installed below grade and on a slope and has only one check valve per suction line below the suction pump. If these criteria are not satisfied you must monitor the piping monthly or perform a tightness test once every *three* years.

All piping in *existing* tanks should have been upgraded with appropriate leak detection devices.

Remember also that you can only prove compliance with these detailed and copious requirements if you keep equally careful and copious records. You should keep records showing that you have monitored your tank's performance and that you regularly maintain it and its leak detection system.

RECORDKEEPING

The recordkeeping requirements in the EPA regulations are very stringent, so the best rule of thumb is "when in doubt, do not throw it away." You must keep records showing that you installed the appropriate type of new tank or leak detection system. You should also keep records showing that you have monitored your tank's performance and that you regularly maintain it and its leak detection system. You should retain records showing that the last two inspections of your corrosion protection system were carried out by properly trained professionals. You must also have paper to demonstrate that you repaired a leaking tank in the required manner. You should retain copies of all notifications you furnish to a state or federal agency in the event of a leak. You must also retain full records showing that you have taken appropriate corrective action in response to a leak.

The absence of such records not only is a separate violation in and of itself, it could leave you defenseless in the event of an enforcement action claiming that you neglected these important substantive requirements.

Records required to be kept by tank owners and operators must either be available on site or accessible for inspection on 24-hours notice. The rule does not set any time limit on how long you need to keep these records, except that it says that you only need to keep closure records for three years. We recommend that you keep all records indefinitely.

CORRECTIVE ACTION REQUIREMENTS

The ultimate goal of the UST rule is to prevent leaks by requiring owners to upgrade their tanks. Although the EPA hopes that leaks will be a relatively rare occurrence, the agency has received alarming data indicating that a significant percentage of the 1.6 million tank systems in the U.S. are in fact leaking. In 1992, the EPA found that 184,000 tanks were leaking and estimated that number will increase by 50,000 every year.

Since leaks can cause serious, irreversible damage, especially to the groundwater supply, the cleanup of ongoing pollution is a major preoccupation of the federal UST rule. The regulations provide requirements for reporting and corrective action as soon as you suspect that a UST has developed a leak.

What should you do if you suspect a leak? If evidence of spilled petroleum appears (*e.g.*, a distinctive smell in the area, or a strange taste in drinking water), you must take three steps as soon as possible. These three steps apply to both new and existing tanks.

- Report your discovery of environmental damage *immediately* to the appropriate state agency.
- Conduct tightness tests of the entire UST system.
- Investigate the UST site for additional evidence on the extent and nature of environmental damage.

You must also take these three steps if monitoring results from your leak detection system indicate a leak may have occurred, unless your monitoring device is found to be defective and is immediately repaired or replaced. If you are using an inventory control method of leak detection, you must report unless a second full month of data does not confirm the initial result.

Once you have confirmed the existence of a leak, and its nature and scope, the regulations require you to undertake corrective action. Corrective action requirements are generally divided into two stages. Stage I involves immediate action to stop the leak, notify the relevant agencies, and to clean up the spill. Periodic reporting to your state agency is likely to be necessary. Bear in mind that you may also have other notification obligations under Superfund or the Clean Water Act. See Chapter 5 for more information. Stage II cleanups can be required for more serious leaks. If you are in a Stage II situation, you will have to develop a cleanup plan that must be approved by the state agency.

Finally, what do you do with the tank once you have discovered that it is leaking? You may repair it if the person who does the work carefully follows standard industry codes and standards that establish proper methods for such procedures. Within 30 days after the repair, you must prove that the repair has actually worked by doing one of the following three things:

- Have the tank inspected internally *or* subjected to tightness testing following standard industry codes.
- Use one of the specified *monthly* leak detection methods required by the regulations for new tanks, except that you may *not* use the method combining inventory control and tank tightness testing.
- Seek special permission from your state regulatory authorities for an alternative method.

Six months after repair, all USTs with cathodic protection must be tested to show they are working properly. As for leaking *metal* pipes, you *cannot* repair them — they must be replaced, unless loose fittings are the source of the problem in which case you should tighten them. If your piping is made of FRP, you *can* repair it but only in accordance with the manufacturer's instructions or national codes of industry practice. Within 30 days of the repair, you must test the FRP piping in the same way you would test a tank repair.

FINANCIAL RESPONSIBILITY REQUIREMENTS

Finally, we come to the financial responsibility requirements. These regulations require all owners or operators of petroleum USTs to demonstrate financial responsibility for the costs of corrective action, such as cleaning up leaked petroleum and correcting environmental damage, as well as third-party liability in the event of a release, such as compensating people for personal injury or property damage. You should note that the rule applies to all petroleum USTs included in the final technical rule and follows the same exemptions and deferrals. If you have taken a UST out of operation before the compliance dates in this rule, you do not have to obtain financial assurance.

The regulations establish a number of financial assurance mechanisms to meet the requirements of the rule, discussed below under the "1988 Rule" section. Especially noteworthy are the four additional compliance mechanisms that the EPA made available to local governments. It is important to familiarize yourself with these procedures, discussed in detail below in the "1993 Rule" section, since they should make it far easier for local governments to comply with the financial responsibility requirements. Local governments had until February 18, 1994, to comply with these requirements.

1988 RULE

The EPA issued the rule establishing the financial responsibility requirements in 1988. That rule determines the amount of financial responsibility all owners or operators of petroleum USTs must maintain as well as the financial mechanisms available to satisfy that requirement.

Under this rule, all owners or operators must obtain financial assurance of at least $500,000 "per occurrence" as well as maintain an "aggregate" of $1 million for one to 100 tanks, and $2 million for 101 or more tanks. The aggregate amounts are intended to provide assurance for all leaks that might occur in one year. Per occurrence coverage pertains to each tank and is limited to $500,000 only if your tank is *not* used in petroleum production, refining, or marketing *and* has a monthly throughput of 10,000 gallons or less. If your tank does not meet this description, the level of per occurrence coverage required is $1 million.

Please keep in mind that the amount of financial responsibility that you must show does not limit your total liability for damages caused by a leak from your tank system. Compliance with financial responsibility requirements means that you should be well prepared to pay for cleanup costs or other damages in the event of a leak, because the average leak costs significantly less than $1 million, or $500,000 for that matter. However, you can still be sued for amounts well in excess of these figures and compliance with the financial responsibility rule will not exempt you from liability.

In addition to establishing the amount of financial responsibility, the rule identifies several financial assurance mechanisms that could be used to meet the requirements of the rule. A "phase-in" compliance schedule is set out which gives owners or operators different compliance deadlines depending on which "ownership category" they fall into. Local governments fall into Category IV and, as established in the 1993 rule, had until February 18, 1994, to comply.

Although local governments can take advantage of all the financial assurance mechanisms, they may find the four additional compliance mechanisms established in the 1993 rule more suitable. All of the mechanisms are described briefly below. You should note that you may use any one or a combination of the financial assurance mechanisms identified in the rule to obtain a total of $1 million per occurrence and appropriate aggregates coverage, provided both corrective action and third-party coverage are fully satisfied. The financial test of self-insurance cannot be combined with a guarantee, however, where the financial statements of the owner or operator and the guarantor are consolidated.

Financial Test of Self-Insurance

There are two financial tests devised by the EPA to assess self-insurance capacity, both geared to corporate structures. The firm must demonstrate a net worth of at least $10 million for both tests. In Alternative I, the firm must have a tangible net worth equal to ten times the aggregate coverage required, demonstrated by financial statements filed with the Securities and Exchange Commission or with Dun and Bradstreet. In Alternative II, the firm must have a tangible net worth of at least six times the required coverage and a bond rating higher than BBB from Standard and Poor's or Baa from Moody's.

Guarantee

A guarantee is a promise by one party (guarantor) to pay specified debts or meet specified obligations for another party (principal) in the event the principal fails to do so. Under the final rule a guarantee may be provided by related firms or by unrelated firms that have a substantial business relationship with the owner or operator. The regulation requires that guarantors demonstrate their capacity to provide financial assurance by meeting the criteria in the Alternative I or Alternative II financial test. The rule also requires a "standby trust fund" in the event that funds must be expended for UST corrective action or third-party liability claims.

Pollution Liability Insurance and Risk Retention Group Coverage

Owners and operators selecting the insurance option may demonstrate financial responsibility by obtaining private insurance either as a separate policy or as an endorsement to an existing policy. Since insurance coverage is often unavailable, the rule also allows for coverage by a risk retention group (RRG). The RRG can provide environmental impairment liability coverage for its members, those who contribute the group's capitalization.

Surety Bond

The regulation permits use of a surety bond to demonstrate financial responsibility as long as the company that issues the bond is among those listed as acceptable sureties on federal bonds in the latest Circular 570 of the U.S. Department of the Treasury. Those using this mechanism must also establish a "standby trust fund."

Letter of Credit

Again, if an owner or operator uses a letter of credit that conforms to specific requirements, there must also be a standby trust fund in place.

Trust Fund

A fully funded trust fund may be used to demonstrate capacity or, if partially funded, it may be used in combination with another mechanism. The amount of the trust fund is determined by the owner or operator. The EPA has included exclusionary language for defining the terms of this instrument in the final rule.

State Mechanisms

Some states have not yet obtained authorization for their UST regulatory program, but many have financial responsibility requirements in place. Because state programs must meet a "no less stringent" standard before approval is granted, state-required mechanisms can be substituted to satisfy federal requirements. In addition, some states have developed state funds to provide financial assurance. These funds vary from state to state and may provide only partial coverage.

1993 RULE

Because the EPA considers local governments to be more financially stable than private companies, the Agency established alternative financial mechanisms that should enable local governmental entities to comply more easily (58 Fed. Reg. 9026). These additional mechanisms include a bond rating test, a worksheet test, a governmental guarantee, and maintenance of a fund balance.

These mechanisms apply to local governments which are defined as both general purpose and special purpose governments. General purpose local governments include municipalities, counties, townships, towns, villages, parishes, and New England towns. Special purpose local governments are those entities that perform a single function or limited range of functions. This class includes public authorities or special districts such as school districts, water and sewer authorities, transit authorities, or power authorities. As noted above, you had until February 18, 1994, to comply with the financial responsibility requirements.

Bond Rating Test

Local government entities satisfy the financial responsibility requirements if they have $1 million or more of total outstanding issues of general obligation bonds that are currently rated at least "investment grade" by Moody's or Standard & Poor's. Municipalities and special districts that cannot issue general obligation bonds can satisfy this test if they have $1 million or more of outstanding revenue bonds that have earned investment-grade rating.

If you have used the bond rating test but can no longer meet these requirements, the rule requires that you find alternative coverage within 150 days of the change in status.

Local Government Financial (Worksheet) Test

The local government financial, or worksheet test is available for those local governments that cannot use the bond rating test because they have less than $1 million in outstanding investment bonds. However, the worksheet test is not available to local government entities that have outstanding debt rated lower than investment grade.

The worksheet test is set out in the final rule and requires that a local government calculate nine financial ratios using available financial data. A government that passes the threshold value satisfies the financial responsibility requirement. Since special districts may not have access to the financial information needed, it is unlikely that they can avail themselves of this test.

Governmental Guarantee

The governmental guarantee mechanism provides local governments with an option similar to the corporate guarantee mechanism established in the October 1988 rule. Under this option, a governmental entity may be the guarantor as long as it can pass the bond rating, the worksheet test, or the fully funded fund balance test.

Unlike the corporate guarantee mechanism, the governmental guarantee option provides the choice of establishing a guarantee *with or without a standby trust*. If a governmental guarantee is established without a standby trust, the guarantor is required to pay for corrective actions on an as-needed basis as directed by the implementing agency.

The February 1993 rule also requires that the local governments entering into an agreement demonstrate a "substantial governmental relationship" with the governmental guarantor. Such a relationship requires a commonality of interests, which could include common constituencies shared by a state and a local government or a demonstrated mutual impact by neighboring counties in the event of a UST release, for example. The EPA has established, however, that a guarantee from a risk pool does not satisfy the substantial relationship test.

Maintenance of a Fund Balance

Under this option, a local government may satisfy the financial responsibility requirement by creating a dedicated fund pledged for use in the event of UST releases or general catastrophic events. The fund must meet the government's aggregate financial responsibility requirements.

There are three types of funds that can be used in satisfying this option. The *fully funded dedicated fund* can be administered by the local government itself, but must be established as an irrevocable fiduciary or trust account in the amount of the aggregate financial responsibility requirements. The *catastrophic events contingency fund* permits local governments to combine funds to cover both UST costs and other emergency costs. It must contain at least $5 million. Finally, the *incrementally funded trust fund* permits a local government to fund a dedicated fund in annual increments equal to at least one seventh of the aggregate liability each year. Until the fund is fully funded, the government must demonstrate the authority to issue a specified amount of general obligation bonds that would be sufficient to respond to a UST release.

Recordkeeping and Reporting Requirements

As always, you must maintain all records indefinitely. A copy of the financial assurance mechanism(s) must be kept on site or at the place of business.

In four instances, you also need to report or file a copy of your financial assurance documentation with the implementing agency (EPA or state):

- When installing a new tank system.
- After a known or suspected release.
- Upon receiving notice that a method of coverage will be canceled or will not be sufficient, and you are unable to obtain alternate coverage.
- When the EPA or a state agency requests it.

CONCLUSION

Obviously, compliance with the UST regulations can best be achieved by giving one person or department the responsibility for establishing your local government's UST compliance program. Implementing such a program is a vital component of reducing your city's potential for incurring environmental liability.

CHAPTER **8**

Pesticides

Russell F. Smith III and John M. McNurney

Most local governments use pesticides to control unwanted plants or animals in and around municipal facilities. While municipal pesticide use is most likely to occur at parks, public golf courses, and athletic fields, you may also find that crews responsible for maintaining street or utility right-of-way use pesticides for that purpose. It is extremely important that local government employees store, use, and dispose of pesticides properly, both to protect their own health and that of the public and to prevent pesticide contamination which could leave the city responsible for cleanup costs.

Under the law, the term "pesticides" refers to herbicides, insecticides, rodenticides, fungicides, disinfectants, plant growth regulators, and any other chemicals used for pest or plant control.

The Federal Insecticide, Fungicide, and Rodenticide Act (FIFRA) regulates the storage, use, and disposal of chemical pesticides. The law is found at 7 U.S.C. § 136 *et seq.* The regulations are codified at 40 C.F.R. § 152 *et seq.* Only pesticides that have been registered with the EPA pursuant to the FIFRA may legally be sold or used in the U.S. While the FIFRA is the primary source of federal regulation of pesticides, the Resource Conservation and Recovery Act (RCRA) is also applicable in circumstances where a pesticide constitutes a hazardous waste. This chapter focuses on the FIFRA, RCRA, and the regulations that have been promulgated under those statutes. State and local government laws and regulations are not covered here.

The FIFRA is one of the simplest environmental statutes because its requirements for entities using and applying pesticides (as opposed to manufacturing them) can be boiled down to two simple rules:

- Always follow the directions on the pesticide label precisely.
- If an activity is *not* described on the pesticide label, don't do it.

Basically, the FIFRA requires pesticide manufacturers to include detailed instructions on every pesticide label. These labels are often lengthy, and some are even small booklets. However, these labels cover every aspect of proper use, storage, and disposal for that pesticide. Using the pesticide in any other manner is unlawful. Accordingly, training for local government employees should always stress the importance of complying fully with the requirements on the label.

Two other common sense rules are also necessary to a good pesticide program:

- Always use the least toxic product available to get the job done.
- Maintain an inventory of the pesticides you currently have in storage.

The first rule simply encourages risk reduction by minimizing the toxicity of products your local government keeps on hand. The inventory is necessary because sometimes the EPA cancels the registration or "bans" a pesticide currently in use. If you have a banned pesticide in storage, you must tell the EPA and you may no longer use the pesticide, even in accordance with the label. The inventory lets you quickly determine whether you have a banned pesticide. All of these concepts are further discussed below.

SELECTING A PEST CONTROL METHOD

By carefully choosing your pest control methods, you can reduce potential harm to persons and the environment, and reduce the cost of pest control. Weeds, rodents, insects, and other pests can be managed in a number of ways. The methods of control chosen have important implications for the types of protective schemes that must be established by a local government. While one effective method of control is to employ pesticides, pesticide usage forces a local government to bear the costs and liabilities of handling, storing, and disposing of hazardous substances. Improperly engaging in any of these activities can cause injury to people, animals, plants, and the environment. In addition, it can result in a local government being found financially responsible for the injuries caused or for cleanup costs.

A local government can reduce its exposure to these potential costs and liabilities by engaging in *pesticide source reduction*. This can be accomplished by using pesticides only when other methods of pest control are not effective. Alternative pest control methods include trapping, weeding, heating, freezing, and using natural predators.

If the use of alternative pest control measures is impractical, you can still practice source reduction by minimizing the amount of pesticide used. This is accomplished, in part, by using the smallest possible amount of pesticide to achieve your purpose. You should also always select the least toxic pesticide that will do the job. Decreasing the volume or the toxicity of the pesticide used decreases the potential for harm to humans and the environment. It may also decrease your costs associated with the proper use, storage, and disposal of pesticides. Finally, it may help to reduce the local government's potential liability in the event of an accidental spill or unintended exposure.

Another way to reduce the potential cost and liabilities is to use only those pesticides that are not persistent in the environment and that do not bioaccumulate. Pesticides are said to be persistent in the environment if they retain their chemical composition for a long time after they are introduced into the environment. Pesticides considered persistent in the environment are said to bioaccumulate when they are retained in living tissue, and thus become more concentrated as they are passed up the food chain. For example, if a population of insects each receives one unit of a pesticide that bioaccumulates, a fish that eats ten of the insects will store ten units of the pesticide in its flesh. A person eating ten such fish would receive 100 units of the pesticide, and could suffer serious health effects. To find out if the pesticides you use or are considering using persist in the environment ask the manufacturer, or call the National Pesticides Telecommunications Network at 1-800-858-7378.

LABEL INSTRUCTIONS

Pesticide labels convey a great deal of information. Whenever you apply a pesticide, you must read the information on the label carefully, and comply with all of the instructions. The EPA requires that certain information be printed on the label of all pesticide containers in order to ensure their safe use. It is a violation of federal law to use a pesticide in a manner other than that described on the label. If you do you may be subject to civil and criminal penalties. More importantly, you could needlessly put your health or the health of others in danger.

Pesticide labels indicate how toxic the pesticide is by using the words "DANGER," "WARNING," or "CAUTION." Those labeled CAUTION are the least toxic, and those labeled DANGER are the most toxic. (Some highly toxic pesticides may also be labeled "POISON.") In addition, the label will also tell you whether you need to contact an appropriate state agency to determine if your intended pesticide application will affect an endangered species, a protected body of water, or some other element of the environment.

The pesticide label will also enable you to determine whether the pesticide has been classified by the EPA as a *restricted-use pesticide* or as *nonrestricted-use pesticide*. All pesticides receive one or the other classification. The EPA classifies a pesticide as restricted use if it determines that the pesticide can be highly toxic if it comes in contact with skin or is inhaled. It is always preferable to use nonrestricted-use pesticides.

Handling pesticides can be hazardous. Persons applying a pesticide must always read and follow the safety and first-aid precautions listed on the pesticide label, including use of all appropriate protective equipment. In addition, they should

- Inspect all pesticide containers for leaks before handling them.
- Refrain from drinking, eating, or using tobacco products in areas where pesticides are present.
- Wear rubber gloves while handling pesticide containers.
- Wash with soap and water after using pesticides, and launder clothes before wearing them again.
- Avoid inhalation of pesticides. Never spray outdoors on a windy day.
- Mix pesticides carefully to avoid splashing. If someone spills pesticides on skin or clothing, wash immediately with soap and water and change clothes.
- Always wear all protective clothing specified on the pesticide container label, including respirators.

Information on the proper application and disposal of the pesticide will be on the pesticide container label. It may also be included in additional information that may accompany the pesticide product. The pesticide label will tell you how much of the pesticide should be applied. *Never apply more than the amount of pesticide specified on the label.* Ten times as much does *not* mean ten times as good. Overdoses of pesticides can harm you and the environment and can subject you to liability for environmental cleanup and for civil and criminal penalties. In addition, application of a pesticide in a dosage in excess of that provided on the label may constitute illegal disposal of a hazardous waste, an offense that could subject the applicator to civil or criminal penalties under the RCRA.

APPLICATOR CERTIFICATION
AND RESTRICTED-USE PESTICIDES

Under the FIFRA and its implementing regulations, pesticides labeled "RESTRICTED USE" may only be purchased and applied by, or under the direct supervision of, a certified applicator. The certified applicator is responsible for ensuring that any pesticide handled under his or her direct supervision is handled properly. If noncertified applicators operating under the certified applicator's direct supervision violate the law or otherwise cause harm through the improper use of pesticides, the certified applicator may be held liable. If a restricted-use pesticide is misused by a noncertified applicator, the EPA can initiate an enforcement action against both the noncertified applicator and the certified applicator who supervised the use. For example, many pesticides are sold in a concentrated form, and must be diluted with a specified amount of water. If the concentrated product is not diluted sufficiently, environmental harm may result. The certified applicator is responsible for assuring that the pesticide is diluted with the appropriate amount of water. If it is not, then the certified applicator may be the subject of an enforcement action.

Many local governments choose to have one or more of their employees trained and licensed as certified applicators. Other local governments seek to avoid setting up their own pesticide programs by hiring private contractors when necessary, instead of using their own employees. Bear in mind that certified applicators who are not in the direct employ of a municipality may nonetheless be considered agents of the municipality. If a certified applicator violates any provision of the FIFRA or its implementing regulations while applying pesticides on behalf of a local government, the local government may be liable for civil and/or criminal penalties. Do not make the mistake of thinking that you can hire out or contract away your liability for improper pesticide storage, use, or disposal. Local governments that have pesticides applied by outside applicators or commercial firms should ensure that any restricted-use pesticides are applied by or under the supervision of a certified applicator. A representative of the local government should also review the label of any pesticide to be applied, ask the applicator to explain how each pesticide will be applied, and ensure that the label instructions are being followed. When contracting with an outside firm, your city will want to verify that firm's licenses and certifications and may wish to seek indemnification protection for any environmental problems that may result from the activities of the private applicators. Do not allow any private firm to require your local government to assume responsibility for liability stemming from the private firm's pesticide waste disposal.

If you choose to have local government employees certified for pesticide application, the employee must complete an EPA-approved state certification program. Such programs are sometimes available at community colleges. Certification generally requires attendance at a training program that provides instruction on the proper handling of toxic chemicals and successful completion of a written examination and/or performance test. In order to become certified, an applicator must show competency in the use and handling of pesticides, including the ability to understand labels, safety requirements and procedures, environmental consequences of use and misuse, and application techniques. Some states have additional certification requirements. The EPA certifies applicators in states where no state certification program exists. The certification training program will vary with the type of pesticides to be applied and the environment in which they will be applied. Your employees will need to renew their certifications periodically.

STORAGE OF PESTICIDES

Proper storage of moderately or highly toxic pesticides is extremely important. Improper storage can create many unnecessary risks of harm to health and the environment. For example, if incompatible materials are stored together and accidentally mixed, violent reactions and the release of toxic fumes may occur. In the case of other pesticides, exposure to temperature extremes alters the chemical properties of the pesticides, possibly rendering them ineffective or even more dangerous to health and the environment. Exposure to the elements can also cause pesticides to leak, and accidents can occur if unauthorized personnel have access to stored pesticides. Improper storage may also lead to civil or criminal penalties.

In order to avoid harm to human health or the environment, pesticides should be stored in strict compliance with the directions on the label and in any other material provided by the manufacturer of the pesticide. In addition, EPA suggests the following:

- Pesticides should be protected from the elements and temperature extremes in a secure, dry, well-ventilated separate room, building, or covered area where fire protection is provided.
- Only authorized persons should be able to enter the storage area. The storage area should be surrounded by a fence, and doors and gates should be kept locked to prevent unauthorized entry.
- Signs reading "DANGER," "POISON," and "PESTICIDE STORAGE" should be prominently placed outside the storage area. A list of the types of pesticides stored within should also be posted.
- Drainage from the site should be contained, tested periodically, and, if contaminated, disposed of as an excess pesticide.
- Equipment used for handling pesticides should be labeled "CONTAMINATED WITH PESTICIDES." Equipment that is contaminated with pesticides should not be removed from the site unless thoroughly decontaminated.
- Provisions should be made for decontamination of personnel (*e.g.*, showers), and all contaminated water should be disposed of as an excess pesticide.
- Pesticide containers should be stored off the ground, with the label plainly visible. A complete inventory of all pesticide containers should be maintained.
- Each pesticide product and waste should be separately stored. Pesticide wastes should also be segregated according to their method of disposal (see below), to ensure proper disposal.
- Containers should be checked regularly for corrosion and leaks. If any pesticide spill is discovered, it should be cleaned up immediately, and all residues disposed of properly.
- All containers should have accurate labels. Labels should be replaced if they fall off, become illegible, or if they do not accurately describe the contents of the containers.
- Procedures should be posted for handling any emergencies involving stored pesticides, including spills (see below) and accidental poisonings.

RECORDKEEPING

Recordkeeping requirements for pesticide use vary from state to state, and you must be sure to comply with applicable state or local guidelines. The EPA has established minimum recordkeeping requirements for all EPA-approved state certification plans. The federal regulations specify that state plans must, at a minimum, require that certified applicators who apply restricted-use pesticides keep and maintain for a period of at least two years records containing information on kinds, amounts, uses, dates, and places of application of restricted-use pesticides. State plans must also require that such records be available for inspection by appropriate state officials. You should ensure that accurate pesticide application records are kept in a central location by city personnel and outside applicators in order to comply with this requirement.

NOTIFICATION OBLIGATIONS

Numerous pesticides are classified under federal regulations as hazardous substances, and states may have their own classifications that cover additional substances. If there is a spill of a pesticide classified as hazardous in an amount in excess of that substance's "reportable quantity," you may have notification obligations under Superfund and the Community Right-to-Know law. There may be notification obligations under other laws as well. Failure to adhere to notification requirements in a timely fashion can lead to stiff criminal and civil penalties. Therefore, you should compile and maintain information that will permit the city to comply with its notification obligations in a place easily accessible to those who use or supervise the use of pesticides. This information should include

- The reportable quantities for the pesticides you use.
- The number for the Coast Guard National Response Center (1-800-424-8802).
- The number for any state and local planning commissions and/or community emergency coordinator that must be notified. The number of your employee who is responsible for coordinating pesticide use.

For more information on your obligations when there is a spill of a pesticide, see Chapters 4 and 5.

You may also be required to notify the EPA if you have a certain pesticide in your possession. The EPA has the power temporarily or permanently to ban the use of a pesticide by canceling or suspending the pesticide's registration. Commercial applicators who possess such a banned pesticide, including municipal employees registered as commercial applicators, have notification responsibilities under the FIFRA. If the EPA cancels or suspends registration of a pesticide that is in your possession, you must notify the EPA, along with state and local officials, that you have some of the pesticide, how much you have, and where it is stored. It is therefore wise not to keep pesticides you no longer use on hand, because their regulatory status may change. Have your employees properly dispose of all pesticides no longer being used. If you are unsure whether a pesticide's registration has been canceled or suspended, you may call the National Pesticides Telecommunications Network at 1-800-858-7378.

DISPOSAL

The same characteristics that make pesticides useful products when properly applied — toxicity to pests — also make their proper disposal essential, because they are often toxic to the environment. Pesticide wastes are often considered hazardous when disposed, and some wastes are even considered acutely hazardous, which subjects them to highly stringent regulation. Even pesticide wastes that are not regulated on the state or federal level as hazardous or acutely hazardous may have toxic characteristics and must be handled with caution. You will need to develop and implement a program to ensure that all pesticide wastes are being handled correctly. Such a program should include the proper elimination of excess or unused pesticides; procedures to ensure proper handling and disposal of wastes generated from the use of pesticides; proper cleaning and disposal of pesticide containers; and proper disposal of any residue from pesticide spills.

Wastes from pesticides in use include any unused pesticide concentrate remaining in a tank or container that you do not intend to use in a later application; any excess spray mixture you do not intend to reuse; rinse waters from the rinsing of containers, holding tanks, or mixing tanks, unless you intend to apply the rinsate; and any residues from tank filters.

For all these types of waste, you should follow the instructions on the pesticide label for disposal. The label should indicate the federal classification of the pesticide waste and provide the EPA recommendations concerning appropriate disposal methods. You should also contact the appropriate state agency to determine if your state adds any disposal requirements. If the pesticide waste is a hazardous waste, you will have to meet all state and federal disposal requirements. The federal disposal requirements are discussed at length in Chapter 2. You should read and become familiar with that material. In addition, your state may adopt disposal regulations that are even more stringent than the federal scheme. You must also become familiar with applicable state regulations.

Because the applicable regulations are less stringent if you generate a lower volume of waste, it is to your advantage to minimize the amount of waste generated. You should apply excess pesticides or pesticide rinsate from one job to another suitable application, being careful not to alter the proper concentrations. Moreover, because full regulation applies even to very small quantities of acutely hazardous pesticide wastes, it remains a sound strategy to consider using substitute products that do not result in the creation of acutely hazardous wastes.

The pesticide label is also your best guide to the appropriate disposal of empty containers. It should indicate how to dispose of the container. If pesticide containers are not being recycled or reused, they are considered wastes. If the pesticide involved is not a state or federal hazardous waste when disposed, the container is not likely to be a hazardous waste either. It should be cleaned and disposed of according to the label instructions. If, however, the pesticide involved is regulated by the federal or state government as a hazardous or acutely hazardous waste when it is disposed, then the container will also be regulated as a hazardous or acutely hazardous waste when it is disposed, unless it is "empty." Not surprisingly, there are detailed federal regulations defining which containers are empty for disposal purposes, and the definition hinges upon the toxicity of the pesticide in the container. Refer to Chapter 2 for information on when a container with hazardous waste residues is considered empty.

After the container is empty, you may be able to ship it back to the manufacturer for reuse with the same class of pesticides. Contact the manufacturer to find out if this is possible. Other pesticide containers can be sent to sanitary landfills in accordance with local and state regulations, although it is a good idea to puncture them to prevent reuse.

PESTICIDE SPILLS

The final step in ensuring proper disposal of pesticide wastes is to make sure that debris from the cleanup of pesticide spills is handled appropriately. Such debris, including soil, water, solvents used for cleanup, and any other contaminated debris, should be handled as hazardous waste if the pesticide involved is hazardous when disposed of, and as acutely hazardous waste if the pesticide involved is acutely hazardous when disposed of. Obviously, the best way to deal with such spills is to prevent them from occurring, and good housekeeping practices can reduce the chances of a spill. These practices include performing pesticide mixing activities in paved areas over containers where liquids may be collected and reused; rinsing any spray equipment over the containers in which rinse water will be stored or in an area where liquids may be collected; and storing any partially full, empty unrinsed, or empty rinsed containers in paved areas where liquids or residues will not reach the soil or surface water.

CONCLUSION

Local governments operating pesticide programs must monitor pesticide applications, whether they use their own employees or outside contractors. Minimizing the use of pesticides, and particularly of more toxic pesticides, is the best way to minimize the potential for problems.

CHAPTER 9

Asbestos

Scott H. Strauss

Many of the environmental regulatory programs discussed in this guide can be implemented by local government employees who have studied the relevant regulations. However, for most local governments, compliance with the regulatory requirements applicable to asbestos is *not* a do-it-yourself proposition. In many cases, the regulations require the use of certified asbestos abatement professionals and, even where the use of such professionals is not legally required, it is extremely risky not to use them. In some sensitive individuals, exposure to as little as a single fiber of asbestos can be enough to trigger serious and fatal illness. The risks to your employees and members of the public are simply too great to take unnecessary chances.

Just because you will hire a contractor, however, does not mean that you need not know anything about the rules, because you will still be responsible for making sure the contractor follows them. In addition, you should be able to recognize situations where the potential for exposure to asbestos fibers may arise at municipal facilities.

Asbestos is a substance used for insulation, soundproofing, fireproofing, pipe and boiler wrap, and more than 3,000 other commercial purposes. It is widely found in public and commercial buildings, particularly those built prior to the mid-1970s. The presence of asbestos-containing materials (ACMs) in a building has potential health consequences for you and your employees. When asbestos fibers are released into the air, they can be inhaled by building occupants. Medical research has found that diseases can result from inhaling airborne asbestos fibers, including asbestosis, lung cancer, and mesothelioma. While the EPA has found that there is no "safe" level of exposure to airborne asbestos fibers, it has also stated that not every exposure to asbestos is inherently dangerous.

Exposure to asbestos fibers is likely to occur where ACMs have become "friable," *i.e.*, when they flake or crumble when subjected to normal hand pressure. Materials become friable as they age, or when they are damaged by heat or water. The fibrous or fluffy spray-applied asbestos materials found in many buildings for fireproofing, insulating, sound proofing, or decorative purposes often are friable. Pipe and boilerwrap materials are also often friable and are found in numerous buildings. Some materials, such as vinyl asbestos floor tile, are considered non-friable and generally do not emit airborne fibers unless subjected to sanding or sawing. Other materials, such as asbestos cement sheet and pipe, can emit asbestos fibers if the materials are broken or crushed during demolition of buildings that contain them. Asbestos cement pipe is relatively common in water distribution systems in the southwest, and may turn up in other water systems as well.

In this chapter we will discuss the three EPA regulations that concern the inspection, assessment, abatement, and disposal of ACMs. The regulations are the

National Emissions Standard for Hazardous Air Pollutants (NESHAPs) for asbestos (40 C.F.R. § 61.140). NESHAPs prescribes procedures to be followed to minimize the release of asbestos fibers into the air during demolition and renovation operations where ACMs are present.

Asbestos-In-Schools Rules (40 C.F.R. § 763.80). These regulations, issued pursuant to the Toxic Substances Control Act (TSCA), govern all phases of the inspection, assessment, cleanup, and disposal of hazardous ACMs in schools. While these regulations are binding only with respect to schools, they contain a roadmap for addressing asbestos problems in other contexts as well.

Worker Protection Rule (40 C.F.R. § 763.120). This regulation requires that the worker health and safety precautions prescribed in the OSHA regulation on asbestos apply to public employees engaged in asbestos abatement projects.

In addition, we will mention the EPA's most recent "guidance" document on the management of ACM in buildings. While there is no legal requirement that the EPA's guidance be followed, the document does represent the Agency's latest, state-of-the-art thinking on the asbestos issue. Along with complying with regulatory requirements, implementing EPA's guidance document recommendations is the best means of protecting building occupants from exposure to airborne asbestos fibers.

Concerns about dealing with ACMs, which the EPA defines as materials that contain more than one percent asbestos, may come up in a variety of operational situations undertaken by municipal governments. The most common problems are potential exposure to friable asbestos or concerns related to ACM that will be disturbed during demolition or renovations of older buildings. You should also consider asbestos when you buy or sell an older building. In each of these contexts, the following types of questions are raised:

Was asbestos used for soundproofing, architectural treatment, or pipe insulation in a building to be purchased or sold?

How should you treat ACMs during the course of demolition and renovation activities?

How should you address the need to maintain safe working conditions in buildings with ACMs?

How should you decide how to clean up ACMs in your building, apart from demolition and renovation operations?

How should you deal with the disposal of asbestos-containing wastes?

In brief, the alternatives available to you in the event you discover the presence of friable ACMs in a municipally owned structure are to

Remove the material from the facility. This operation will require compliance with a variety of worker and occupant protection practices designed to minimize the potential for both asbestos fiber release and asbestos fiber inhalation by removal project workers and members of the public.

Encapsulate the material, which means treating ACMs with a substance that surrounds or embeds asbestos fibers in an adhesive to prevent the release of fibers.

Enclose the material, which involves constructing an airtight, impermeable, permanent barrier around the ACM to prevent the release of fibers.

Repair the damaged ACM by using any of a variety of methods (including painting and taping), such that material is returned either to an undamaged condition or to an intact state, so as to prevent further asbestos fiber release. In addition, if you decide not to remove the ACMs, the EPA recommends the implementation of a pro-active, in-place *management program* for ACMs.

The EPA has enumerated five facts to be aware of upon discovering the presence of ACMs in your building:

- Asbestos is hazardous, but the risk of asbestos-related disease depends upon exposure to airborne asbestos fibers.
- Available data show that the average asbestos air level in buildings is low. This is an indication that the risk of developing asbestos-related disease facing building occupants who are unlikely to be involved in the disturbance of ACMs is low. Of course, building workers, if not properly trained and protected, may disturb ACMs, thereby increasing the risk to themselves and others.
- Removal is often not a building owner's best course of action to reduce asbestos exposure. Without proper application of all safeguards, removal of asbestos can increase rather than decrease the risk of asbestos-related disease.
- The EPA *requires* asbestos removal in order to prevent significant public exposure to airborne asbestos fibers during activities such as building demolition or renovation.
- The EPA *recommends* a pro-active, in-place management program whenever ACMs are discovered.

In determining the presence and condition of ACMs, and deciding what action to take, it is crucial that you engage competent, accredited (licensed) asbestos abatement contractors to help you. Determining how to address the dangers posed by ACMs is an extremely complicated matter. Improperly performed abatement actions may make matters far worse rather than better. Using expert help will make it more likely that your local government will select the proper course of action, and that the action will be carried out correctly.

If you do decide to handle asbestos "in-house," you must ensure that your staff is properly trained. In November 1991, the EPA published a national directory of "accredited" training courses and approved training providers for asbestos-related activities. Under federal law, asbestos inspection and abatement activities conducted in school buildings must be performed by accredited personnel. To the extent you decide to conduct asbestos inspection or abatement activities in-house, this national directory will give you ready access to courses (or individuals) that can be used in training your staff in all facets of asbestos activities, including inspection, preparation of asbestos "management plans," and conduct of abatement activities. The directory, which is updated quarterly, can be ordered from NDAAC Clearinghouse, c/o ATLIS Federal Services, 6011 Executive Blvd., Rockville, MD 20852.

NESHAPs: RENOVATION AND DEMOLITION

The focus of the NESHAPs regulation is prevention of the emission of asbestos fibers into the air during building demolition and renovation activities. NESHAPs applies not when you make a specific decision to investigate and abate asbestos hazards in your facilities, but rather when you are planning to demolish or renovate a building containing asbestos and where your operations will disturb ACMs.

The EPA has delegated authority to enforce NESHAPs regulations to most states. EPA enforces the regulations (through its regional offices) in those states where there has been no delegation, and it retains the authority to enforce the regulations even where there has been a delegation.

The applicability of the NESHAPs regulations depends upon the nature of the operation you are planning to perform and the amount of (1) friable ACMs that will be removed, stripped, or disturbed as a result of your operation and (2) non-friable ACMs that will become friable as a result of the demolition or renovation activities. The NESHAPs regulation refers to these two categories of materials collectively as "regulated asbestos-containing material" or RACM. As a general matter, you will be required to comply with the NESHAPs regulations if (1) you are performing a demolition or renovation operation and (2) as a result you will need to remove or strip at least certain threshold quantities of RACM. The basic NESHAPs requirements may be summarized as follows:

Before you renovate or demolish a building

Notify the EPA that you intend to do renovation or demolition work.

Remove RACM located in the work site before beginning any wrecking or dismantling activity that would break up the asbestos material.

During your renovation or demolition operation

Limit asbestos emissions from the site by keeping the ACM wet from the moment it is disturbed until it is disposed. The NESHAPs regulation requires that there be no visible emissions (*i.e.*, emissions of asbestos fibers that you can see without visual aids) during all handling of removed asbestos.

Ensure that the workers conducting the demolition or renovation work are protected in accordance with the EPA's "worker protection" rule, where applicable.

After you complete your renovation or demolition operation

Ensure that there are no visible emissions of asbestos fibers during the collection, packaging, transportation, or depositing of asbestos waste at the disposal site.

Ensure that asbestos waste is deposited as soon as is practical in a landfill that is covered daily with at least six inches of clean fill. There must be no visible emissions of asbestos fibers from the asbestos waste disposal site.

Maintain a properly completed "waste shipment record" on file for at least two (2) years.

Failure to comply with the applicable NESHAPs requirements can result in the imposition of civil or even criminal penalties.

To decide whether the NESHAPs regulatory scheme applies, you must answer two questions: (1) are you conducting a "demolition" or "renovation" operation? and (2) if so, does the facility where the operation will be conducted contain RACM equal to or in excess of the NESHAPs threshold levels?

NESHAPs defines demolition work as that including the wrecking or taking out of any load-supporting part of a facility, such as a wall or a beam, together with any related handling operations, or the intentional burning of any facility. The regulations cover demolition work performed either at the election of the facility operator or by order of a governmental agency.

A NESHAPs renovation operation, on the other hand, is any job that involves the alteration in some way of one or more non-load-supporting facility components (*e.g.*, pipes, ducts, boilers, tanks, reactors, turbines, furnaces, or other parts of a building), including the stripping or removal of RACM from any facility component. The EPA divides renovation operations into three types: planned, emergency, and nonscheduled.

Once you have determined that your operation qualifies as NESHAPs demolition or renovation work, you must determine the amount of RACM in the facility you want to demolish, or the amount to be removed or stripped from the facility you want to renovate.

The November 1990 revision to the NESHAPs regulation explicitly requires a "thorough inspection" for the presence of asbestos prior to the conduct of demolition or renovation activities. The EPA does not require that the individual conducting the inspection be accredited or certified, though common sense dictates that only a qualified inspector should be used. The EPA states that an ACM building inspection should be conducted by a "trained, experienced and qualified inspector, who is able to perform the sampling of suspect ACM for laboratory analysis."

For purposes of determining the quantity of friable asbestos material that will be affected by your operation, the EPA includes asbestos-containing materials which either are in a friable condition at the outset of the demolition or renovation operation or will become friable as a result of the demolition or renovation work. In other words, regardless of the condition of the material *prior to* doing the work, if as a result of the demolition or renovation the material will be disturbed to the point of becoming friable, you should include it in your calculation of the amount of RACM in your facility.

To aid in making this determination, the EPA describes two types or "categories" of non-friable materials, and explains how these materials should be treated when conducting demolition or renovation activities.

Category I non-friable asbestos-containing materials (ACM) includes resilient floor covering, roofing products, gaskets, and packings. These materials are not subject to the NESHAPs regulation (and do not have to be stripped, removed, and disposed of in accordance with the regulation) unless (1) they are in poor condition *and* are friable or (2) as a result of the demolition or renovation process, they will be subject to "sanding, grinding, cutting or abrading." If either of these circumstances applies, the materials are to be treated as friable ACM and dealt with in accordance with NESHAPs. For example, if asbestos-containing floor tiles are removed through a process that results in the tile being broken into small fragments, the NESHAPs regulation requirements must be met with regard to that material.

Category II non-friable ACM includes any material not in Category I which, when dry, cannot be crumbled, pulverized, or reduced to powder by hand pressure. These materials must be examined on a case-by-case basis to see if, as a result of the renovation or demolition activity, they will be subject to NESHAPs. If the material is ACM, and the demolition or renovation process will crumble, pulverize, or reduce the material to powder, then the NESHAPs requirements must be followed.

As explained earlier, the recent NESHAPs revision also describes a third, composite category known as regulated asbestos-containing materials or RACM. RACM consists of (1) friable ACM; (2) Category I non-friable ACM that has become friable; (3) Category I non-friable ACM that has been or will be subjected to grinding, sanding, cutting, or abrading; or (4) Category II non-friable ACM that has a "high probability" of becoming crumbled, pulverized, or reduced to powder as a result of the forces at work in the course of the demolition or renovation activity.

Once you have calculated the amount of RACM to be disturbed during the project, you can determine whether you meet the threshold level triggering the rules. The threshold asbestos level is 80 linear meters (260 linear feet) on pipes, 15 square meters (160 square feet) on other facility components, or at least 1 cubic meter (35 cubic feet) off facility components where the length or area could not be measured previously. In determining whether or not the regulation applies, you must compare the threshold levels to the predicted total amount of ACMs to be removed or stripped within one year.

ASBESTOS IN SCHOOLS

The EPA issued 1987 regulations that cover the cleanup of hazardous ACM in school buildings. By now, all local governments operating schools should have conducted asbestos inspections (using certified inspectors) and should have developed asbestos management plans (and undertaken abatement where necessary). Although there is no federal cleanup requirement for buildings other than schools, there are three important reasons why the EPA's guidance on school cleanup should be carefully considered in deciding whether to voluntarily initiate cleanup of potentially hazardous ACMs in your facilities.

First, it is clearly in the best interest of all building operators to minimize the potential for occupant inhalation of asbestos fibers.

Second, to the extent you can prove that you have taken action on asbestos that is in accordance with the EPA's standards on the cleanup of asbestos, you will stand a better chance of defending your actions and avoiding liability if a suit should be filed claiming harm caused by asbestos hazards in your buildings.

Third, EPA regulations on asbestos cleanup in schools establish a systematic approach for the inspection, assessment, and abatement of hazardous ACMs and provide at least a general roadmap for dealing with asbestos contamination in all buildings.

The major requirements are summarized below.

INSPECTION AND REINSPECTION REQUIREMENTS

The first stage in formulating an adequate cleanup plan is to inspect a building thoroughly, identify *all* ACMs, and then separate such materials into categories depending on whether they are friable or not. Although friable ACMs require the most immediate and thorough attention, materials that are currently non-friable must be watched over time to make sure that, if they become friable, appropriate action is taken. Under the school rule, inspections must be carried out by persons who have been trained and certified under applicable state programs. The EPA's July 1990 guidance document similarly recommends that a trained, qualified inspector be used. It is best if you engage a certified inspector to inspect your facilities. If the certified inspector finds material that he suspects contains friable asbestos, the usual procedure is to send "bulk" samples of the material to a certified laboratory where it is tested to confirm the inspector's diagnosis. The school regulations include protocols for labs to follow in testing such samples. The certified inspector should be able to direct you to the appropriate lab for analysis. Alternatively, you can omit lab testing and instead simply assume that the inspector's diagnosis that the material contains asbestos is correct.

The last phase of the inspection process is an assessment by the inspector. The inspector identifies not only which ACMs are friable as opposed to non-friable, but assesses the degree of damage friable materials have undergone. The nature and scope of cleanup required depends on whether friable asbestos is considered to be undamaged, damaged or "significantly" damaged, or whether such materials have the "potential" to become damaged or significantly damaged. The assessment required under the regulation amounts to a judgment by the expert inspector regarding the category into which the various kinds of ACMs should be placed. Once the ACM is categorized, appropriate cleanup plans can be developed.

It is important to note that the EPA rule requires the expert inspector to make a subjective determination regarding how bad the damage is, based on his or her visual inspection of the material, not on the basis of the results of air monitoring of the facility. You should be skeptical of any contractor who recommends air monitoring as a viable approach to determining the need for cleanup. This technique is expensive, it doesn't work well, and it is not approved by the government unless supplemented by the visual inspections described above.

The regulation also requires reinspection at least once every three years to ensure that previously identified non-friable asbestos has not become hazardous (*i.e.*, friable) and that any cleanup short of removing the material from the facility, *e.g.*, enclosure of friable materials, is in fact still preventing the release of asbestos fibers. The EPA's July 1990 guidance document notes that the three-year reinspection interval may also be appropriate in non-school settings.

DEVELOPMENT OF A MANAGEMENT PLAN

Once an inspection has been completed and an assessment performed, the next stage in the process is to develop a "management plan." The plan should be a detailed blueprint for how cleanup of hazardous ACMs will be conducted. Under the EPA rule, school management plans must be prepared and implemented by certified abatement contractors.

Management plans should contain the following items of information:

Plans for the cleanup of all friable ACMs, and a schedule for carrying out such actions.

Detailed descriptions of any ACMs that will remain once cleanup has been completed, and a plan for conducting long-term surveillance and "operations and maintenance" activities (designed to prevent new damage to such materials).

Plans for periodic reinspection of ACMs.

Statements showing that the inspections were carried out, that abatement action plans were developed by persons accredited by the state, and that lab analyses were conducted by accredited laboratories.

An evaluation of the resources that will be necessary to carry out the plan.

The plan should, of course, be kept in your records and, upon request, made available to employees or members of the public. The development and timely implementation of the plan is evidence that you are making a serious, substantial effort to address any danger posed by ACMs in your facilities.

CLEANUP STANDARDS

The regulation divides friable ACMs into four distinct categories, depending on the severity of damage that has occurred or could occur in the future: (1) damaged, (2) significantly damaged, (3) potentially damaged, and (4) potentially significantly damaged. The degree of cleanup required depends on the degree of damage.

Cleanup approaches also depend on what kind of ACMs are at issue:

Thermal system insulation ACMs are those that have been applied to pipes, fittings, boilers, breeching, tanks, ducts, or other interior structural components to prevent heat loss or gain or water condensation.

Surfacing ACMs are those that have been sprayed on, troweled on, or otherwise applied to surfaces such as acoustical plaster on ceilings and fireproofing materials on structural members.

Miscellaneous ACMs are interior building materials such as floor and ceiling tiles that are not otherwise included in the surfacing and thermal categories.

Once damage requiring abatement action has been identified through a visual inspection by an accredited expert, there are four cleanup options available: (1) *remove* the ACM, (2) *enclose* the material so that, even if it crumbles or flakes, releases of fibers do not occur, (3) *encapsulate* the material so that releases of fibers do not occur, or (4) *repair* (*e.g.*, tape or paint) the material so that releases of fibers do not occur.

The EPA recommends that a building owner, with the assistance of a qualified expert, make a decision about whether to perform an abatement action on the basis of an assessment of the ACM's characteristics, quantity, location in the building, and building use.

Following cleanup of friable materials, the regulation requires that the area in which the cleanup project was performed be visually inspected, and that the air be tested to determine whether it is safe for building occupants to reoccupy the area. For this particular stage of the process, the EPA has decided to adopt an air monitoring approach because the areas to be tested will be relatively limited and there is no issue of permitting releases that could have been prevented.

EPA regulation currently recognizes two ways in which to conduct air monitoring analysis: (1) phase contrast microscopy, or PCM or (2) transmission electron microscopy, or TEM. Although PCM is cheaper than TEM, it is well known that PCM is far less accurate than TEM in identifying the presence of asbestos fibers in the air. EPA's regulation required the phase out of the use of PCM in verifying school abatement project completion by October 1990. The EPA guidance document recommends the use of TEM to determine if an abatement action has been properly completed.

OPERATIONS AND MAINTENANCE

As soon as it is discovered that a building contains ACMs, whether friable or non-friable, the regulations require the initiation of an operations and maintenance plan. Such plans serve two fundamental purposes. First, the plans will help building owners determine whether non-friable ACMs have deteriorated to the point where cleanup is required. Second, the plans will help ensure that remedies short of removal continue to work and, if they prove inadequate, that further cleanup actions are taken.

Operations and maintenance plans include worker training on the hazards posed by asbestos releases and how to avoid them; periodic surveillance of areas containing ACMs to evaluate the condition of such materials; and routine cleaning to remove any traces of fiber releases. The worker training requirements include

> Two hours of asbestos awareness training for all maintenance and custodial workers in a building that may contain ACMs.
>
> Fourteen hours of additional training for all staff who conduct activities that may result in the disturbance of ACMs.

This additional training should include information on the use of respirators as well as the contents of the EPA school asbestos regulation.

Because some of the worst asbestos problems have been discovered in maintenance areas such as boiler rooms, which tend to have significant amounts of thermal and surfacing insulation, the EPA regulation requires that all ACMs left in such maintenance areas — whether friable or non-friable — be labeled with a visible, easily readable warning that says

CAUTION: ASBESTOS
HAZARDOUS
DO NOT DISTURB WITHOUT PROPER TRAINING
AND EQUIPMENT

You should make certain to train adequately all maintenance personnel in dealing with ACMs.

In order to ensure that building occupants are not exposed to asbestos fibers during cleaning activities that may disturb friable ACMs, you should (1) restrict entry into the area; (2) shut off (or temporarily modify) the air handling system in the building; (3) if possible, wet down the areas where cleaning activities will be conducted; and (4) place asbestos debris in sealed, leak-tight containers.

RECOMMENDATIONS ON ASBESTOS OPERATIONS
AND MAINTENANCE PROGRAMS

The EPA recommends the implementation of a pro-active, in-place management program as soon as ACM is discovered. The EPA states that a successful plan will include the following elements:

Notification: A program to tell workers, tenants, and building occupants where ACM is located, and how and why to avoid disturbing the ACM. All persons affected should be properly informed.

Surveillance: Regular ACM surveillance to note, assess, and document any changes in the ACM's condition.

Controls: A work control/permit system to control activities that might disturb ACM.

Work practices: Basic operations and maintenance (O&M) work practices to protect employees from potential exposure and to plan for a potential release of asbestos fibers.

Recordkeeping: Proper documentation of O&M activities should be maintained.

Worker training: The EPA recommends an appropriate level of maintenance worker training, depending on whether the employee will do simple maintenance, repair, or abatement.

EPA'S WORKER PROTECTION RULE

The EPA has issued a rule that applies the substance of the OSHA asbestos worker protection standard to employees of public entities such as local governments who are not covered by federal OSHA. The EPA rule applies solely to public employees conducting asbestos cleanup projects, as well as demolition and renovation operations that are the subject of the NESHAPs regulation. Municipalities that conduct demolition or renovation work (whether or not covered by NESHAPs) that puts employees in contact with ACM must ensure that the work is conducted in accordance with the procedures contained in the EPA worker protection rule. If the NESHAPs standards are also applicable, the demolition or renovation job must be conducted in accordance with the NESHAPs requirements as well.

The worker protection rule establishes certain practices that you must follow to minimize the extent to which persons performing cleanup work or demolition and renovation are exposed to airborne asbestos fibers. The requirements of this regulation are summarized below.

SMALL-SCALE, SHORT-DURATION PROJECTS

The worker protection rule exempts projects that are defined as "small scale" and "short duration" from many of its requirements. Examples of such projects include:

Removal of asbestos-containing insulation on pipes, on beams, and above ceilings.
Replacement of an asbestos-containing gasket on a valve.
Installation or removal of a small section of drywall.
Installation of electrical conduits through or proximate to ACMs.

An appendix to the worker protection rule contains a set of practices to be followed in conducting these projects in place of the practices stated in the rule itself. Most importantly, if you choose to follow the appendix practices, you will *not* be required to notify the EPA, to monitor the air before beginning work, or to establish a negative pressure enclosure (including the use of hygiene and decontamination facilities).

The practices specified in the rule appendix which *must* be followed in performing small-scale, short-duration projects include (1) removal of all movable objects from the work area prior to beginning the abatement operation; (2) wetting ACMs throughout performance of the abatement operation; and (3) use of "glove bags" during removal operations.

Glove bags are approximately 40-inch wide by 64-inch long bags fitted with arms through which the work can be performed. These bags create a temporary, small work area enclosure to permit the performance of a removal operation while leaving workers isolated from the ACM. Glove bags must completely cover the pipe or other work structure where the asbestos work is being done, and the employee using the glove bag must wear at least a half mask dual-cartridge HEPA-equipped respirator. Respirators should also be worn by those employees who will be in close contact with the glove bag.

The asbestos removed into the glove bag must be thoroughly wetted and then removed using whatever tool (razor knife, mesh scissor, etc.) is appropriate for the type of material being removed. The surface from which the asbestos has been removed must be thoroughly cleaned and any asbestos-containing insulation edges exposed as a result of the operation must be encapsulated. Once the job is finished, a vacuum hose from an HEPA-filtered vacuum must be inserted into the glove bag to remove any remaining asbestos fibers.

In some instances, a glove bag may not be large enough to enclose the work area. You can still comply with the appendix by constructing a "mini-enclosure" around the work area. Such enclosures should be constructed of 6-mil-thick polyethylene plastic sheeting, and be small enough to restrict entry to the work area to one worker. The appendix contains detailed instructions on the creation of the mini-enclosure.

The appendix also requires the initiation of an asbestos maintenance program in all facilities with ACM. Elements of the program include (1) development of an inventory of ACM in the facility; (2) periodic examination of such materials; and (3) written procedures for handling the materials during small-scale, short-duration projects, during disposal, and during emergencies. You must also provide training to members of the building staff who may be required to handle ACM, including information on the hazards posed by ACM and the use of respirators. The training should also describe to the staff "prohibited" activities, such as (1) drilling holes into ACM; (2) sanding asbestos-containing floor tiles; and (3) using an ordinary vacuum to clean up asbestos-containing debris.

LARGER PROJECTS

The EPA worker protection rule establishes more stringent requirements for larger jobs that do not fall into the small-scale, short duration exemption above. Since most local governments would be well advised to use outside contractors for large abatement actions, this book does not describe the requirements in detail. The rule provides for advance notification to the EPA regional coordinator, air monitoring, establishment of a negative pressure enclosure in the work area, engineering controls, special work practices, respirator protection for employees, special clothing and hygiene facilities, training, and recordkeeping. You will also have to arrange for regular medical examinations for your employees.

A WORD ON ASBESTOS CEMENT PIPE

As noted earlier in this chapter, it is not uncommon for water distribution systems (particularly in the southwest) to contain asbestos cement pipe. Although the chance of transmission of fibers from cement pipe is low, some states do require local governments to report the existence of such pipe in their systems. Most importantly, however, your employees must be trained to handle the pipe properly (no cutting, sanding, etc.) when making repairs, to take proper precautions and to ensure correct disposal.

CONCLUSION

Friable asbestos is one of the most dangerous substances that local government employees may encounter, and municipalities should attempt to identify and plan for asbestos management before problems arise. Use certified inspectors and abatement professionals to make certain the job is done correctly.

PART II

Permits

CHAPTER 10
Wastewater and Stormwater Discharges

Mark A. Keyworth and John M. McNurney

Local governments play many roles with respect to wastewater and stormwater permitting under the Clean Water Act. A city may be a regulated entity required to hold permits for point source discharges from city facilities such as wastewater or drinking water treatment plants or from municipal stormwater systems. A city may also regulate discharges by industrial users to its *publicly owned treatment works (POTW)* or stormwater systems. In addition, a city may need stormwater runoff permits for city operations that meet the definition of an "industrial facility." Careful planning and monitoring is required to ensure that your local government fulfills its responsibility as both regulator and regulated entity.

The Clean Water Act (CWA) regulates discharges of pollutants into the waters of the U.S. The CWA is found at 33 U.S.C. § 1251 *et seq.* Implementing regulations are codified at 40 C.F.R. § 117 *et seq.* The CWA establishes the National Pollutant Discharge Elimination System (NPDES), under which the EPA issues permits for point source discharges of pollutants into surface waters. In many states, the EPA has delegated permit writing authority to a state agency. The EPA can advise you whether it has delegated that authority in your state.

Anyone discharging pollutants directly into "waters of the United States" (almost any body of water, including lakes, rivers, streams, wetlands, ponds, lagoons, or even dry river washes) from a "point source" (*e.g.*, a pipe, culvert, or ditch) is a "direct discharger." Direct dischargers must have an NPDES permit that specifically allows them to discharge the particular pollutants in their waste stream. The permit lists the pollutants the facility may discharge and limits the monthly, weekly, or daily discharge of each. NPDES permits may also include standards and requirements for sludge use and disposal unless the sludge is regulated under separate solid waste permit provisions.

Facilities that discharge pollutants into a POTW, *i.e.*, a public sewer, are "indirect dischargers." Indirect dischargers do not need federal NPDES permits, but state programs often require them. The CWA does require indirect dischargers to comply with pretreatment standards so that untreated wastes will not pass through or interfere with the operation of the POTW.

The EPA and the states can penalize violations of permit requirements through fines and imprisonment. They can also directly enforce standards against indirect dischargers or force the operator of the POTW involved to sue the indirect discharger. Discharging oil wastes, hazardous wastes, or any other waste into sewers without proper pretreatment violates the law. Any planned discharge into sewers or open waterways should be reviewed with the EPA or the appropriate state authority. Accidental discharges of oil or hazardous substances must be reported to regulatory agencies under the CWA.

FACILITIES THAT MAY REQUIRE DISCHARGE PERMITS

- Airports
- Departments of public works
- Incinerators
- Industrial/manufacturing facilities
- Landfills

- Municipal buildings
- Power plants
- Recycling facilities
- Refuse transfer stations
- Water and sewage treatment plants

APPLYING FOR AN NPDES PERMIT

Any facility planning a new discharge must submit a permit application, which may include a requirement to develop a best management practices (BMP) plan, to the appropriate state authority or EPA at least 180 days before discharge begins. An individual permit may not be needed if the proposed discharge is covered by a general permit. General NPDES permits are issued for specific discharges, such as those that are common throughout a defined political (state) or geographic (drainage design) area.

Most local governments retain consultants to assist them through the permitting process, but bear in mind that permit applications and other reports must be signed by a municipal employee with the authority and responsibility to certify under the penalty of law that the document is accurate and complete.

NPDES permits commonly limit not only the final discharge, but also its component waste streams. Monitoring requirements may also address internal flows and the composition of the final effluent. Therefore, the plant discharge can be in compliance when the internal waste stream is not. These requirements are intended to prevent dilution of low-volume/high-strength waste streams with high-volume/low-strength waste before discharge.

Permit-issuing agencies rely heavily on EPA effluent guidelines in determining permit limitations. Effluents authorized under an NPDES permit must also be certified by the state water resources agency (even if the NPDES is issued under federal law by the EPA). The certification verifies that the

Table 1   Application of Various Effluent Guideline Categories

Effluent Guideline Category	Source Type		Discharge Point		Pollutant Types	
	Existing	New	Navigable Waters	POTW	Conventional	Toxic or Non-conventional
BPT	X		X		X	X
BAT	X		X			X
BCT	X		X		X	
PSES	X			X	X	X
NSPS		X	X		X	X
PSNS		X		X	X	X

effluent's impact on the receiving water is consistent with the state water quality standards.

GUIDELINES FOR DIRECT DISCHARGERS

The CWA requires the EPA to establish effluent guidelines for various industries. The EPA determines the level to which technology can reduce the discharge of a particular pollutant and sets the effluent limitations at that level. The appropriate level of technology is determined in part by the quality of the receiving water. The effluent discharge must not affect public or commercial water usage or the associated fish and wildlife populations. The remaining considerations vary, depending on whether a new source or permit renewal is involved; whether the pollutant is designated as conventional, nonconventional, or toxic; and whether the discharge is direct or indirect.

The categories of technologies that may be required include:

- Best Practicable Control Technology Currently Available (BPT), which has been required for all dischargers since March 1989.
- Best Available Technology Economically Achievable (BAT), which has been required for all dischargers of toxic pollutants since March 1989.
- Best Conventional Pollutant Control Technology (BCT), which has been required for all dischargers of conventional pollutants since March 1989.
- Pretreatment Standards for Existing Sources (PSES), which have been required since July 1984.
- New Source Performance Standards (NSPS), which must be achieved by all new sources.
- Pretreatment Standards for New Sources (PSNS), which must be achieved by all new sources discharging to a POTW.

Table 1 summarizes how these technologies are applied. Any of the technologies could apply to renewal permits for existing facilities, because variances are available and technological standards have not been established for some specific effluents (*e.g.*, there is no BAT or BCT technology designated for some specific industrial discharges).

PRETREATMENT STANDARDS

The pretreatment regulations were enacted to reduce degradation of the nation's waters by ensuring a consistent quality of the water discharged from POTWs that accept industrial wastes. Pretreatment is intended to prevent industrial dischargers from introducing certain types of pollutants that can pass unaffected through the treatment process of a POTW or interfere with the normal operation of the treatment facility, including recycling or reclaiming wastewaters and sludges.

The responsibility for complying with pretreatment standards rests on both the industrial discharger and the POTW. The POTW can develop and enforce special limits supplemental to the federal prohibitions if proper notification is given to the industrial discharger. The regulating authority — the state or the EPA — can enforce pretreatment standards by serving notice to either the industrial discharger or the POTW. Unless the NPDES authority assumes local responsibility, any combination of POTWs operated by the same entity with a total design flow exceeding five million gallons per day (MGD) must develop a pretreatment plan. The regulating authority may also require a POTW with a flow of less than 5 MGD to create a pretreatment plan if the volume or nature of the industrial effluent will have a significant impact on effluent quality, sludge disposal procedures, or normal plant operations.

To maintain safe, consistent operation of the POTW, the federal government prohibits certain discharges:

- Pollutants that can create a fire or explosive hazard in the POTW.
- Pollutants that can cause corrosion/structural damage or have a pH less than 5 (without special dispensation).
- Pollutants with a concentration or flow rate that can disrupt POTW operations.
- Effluents heated above 104°F that can affect biological treatment activity.
- Solid or viscous wastes that can cause obstruction in the POTW.

The POTW can limit the concentrations of pollutant discharges that will affect its individual treatment processes. The pretreatment plan must first be submitted to the regulatory authority for approval; then the POTW must notify all existing dischargers of the imposed limits and compliance schedule. New sources are required to meet pretreatment standards before starting operations.

The federal government has created national pretreatment standards categories that specify the quantity, concentration, and characteristics of pollutants that may be discharged into the POTW by new and existing sources. Specific standards for industrial source categories will be established in addition to the general prohibitions discussed above.

When a new category is certified, existing sites have three years to meet the effluent limits unless otherwise provided. New sources must have a determination of categorical status and all pollution control devices must be operational before beginning discharge. New sources have a maximum of 90 days after beginning discharge operations to come into categorical compliance.

STORMWATER RUNOFF NPDES PERMIT

The Clean Water Act has traditionally addressed industrial pollution emanating from point source discharges. However, a growing concern for many state agencies is the degradation of water quality from other nonconventional sources, specifically stormwater runoff. The EPA defines stormwater runoff as:

- Surface runoff.
- Wash waters from street cleaning or maintenance.
- Infiltration (except for water contaminated with seepage from sanitary sewers or other discharges).
- Drainage from storms or snow melt.

Urban stormwater runoff is considered a major source of lead, cadmium, arsenic, pesticides, and organics found in water. The quality of that water is further affected by industrial and construction site runoff containing sediments, petroleum products, chemicals, and fertilizers. In 1990, the NPDES permit application regulations for stormwater discharges were published (40 C.F.R. Parts 122, 123, and 124). The EPA intends to utilize a four-tier strategy for regulating industrial stormwater discharges, beginning with baseline permitting, followed by watershed, industry- and facility-specific permitting.

PERMIT CLASSIFICATIONS AND REQUIREMENTS

The regulations focus on three categories of discharges:

- Medium-sized cities with populations greater than 100,000.
- Large cities with populations greater than 250,000.
- Discharges associated with industrial and construction activities.

The stormwater regulations affect approximately 170 cities nationwide and will probably be extended to smaller communities in the future as the regulatory trend toward local responsibility for stormwater runoff continues. Permits for the affected urban areas will resemble complex management plans requiring:

- Storm system mapping.
- Source and outfall identification.
- Prohibition of illegal sewer hookups.
- Implementation of jurisdiction-wide programs.

The type of management controls will vary by regulated area. Less developed areas will require more structural controls — retention basins, first flush diversion systems, and infiltration systems. Controls for more developed areas will include erosion control, watershed management, street cleaning operations, and public education programs.

INDUSTRIAL STORMWATER

The EPA defines industrial stormwater as stormwater associated with industrial activity, which can include many facilities typically owned and operated by municipalities. Regulated facilities likely to be operated by local governments include

- Landfills, land application sites, and open dumps that have received any industrial wastes.
- Steam electric power-generating facilities, including on-site and off-site transformer storage areas.
- Transportation facilities in SIC classifications 40 through 45 and 5171 (airports, public transport depots, municipal maintenance garages), which have vehicle maintenance shops, material-handling facilities, equipment-cleaning operations, or airport de-icing operations, but only that portion of the facility involved in vehicular maintenance, loading, unloading, and storage and equipment cleaning operations.
- POTW lands used for land application treatment technologies, sludge disposal, waste handling and processing areas, and chemical handling and storage areas.
- Construction activities involving the disturbance of more than five acres of land (less if the construction is part of a larger development).
- Facilities involved in significant recycling of materials, including metal scrapyards and battery reclaimers.
- Facilities subject to effluent limitation guidelines, new source performance standards, or toxic pollutant effluent standards.

Permits regulating stormwater from industrial facilities will require sampling procedures, erosion control measures, and appropriate technologies unless the facilities discharge into a municipal separate storm sewer system. Municipal separate storm sewer systems are considered point sources subject to previously enacted NPDES regulation; they are *not* considered POTWs because they do not convey the water discharge to a POTW. Permits for stormwater runoff will be separate from any existing NPDES permits your facility may have. Your permit may include comprehensive stormwater monitoring requirements for constituents of stored material or chemicals that could be carried off-site in runoff.

IMPACT

Older cities typically have combined sewer overflow systems that convey stormwater and municipal sewage through a single piping system to a POTW.

Since the contents are not directly discharged to waters of the U.S., the systems are not subject to NPDES regulation. However, during storms, the systems can overflow, triggering discharges of untreated waters directly into surface waters. Such systems will be subject to future regulation. Although the regulations are not final as this guide goes to press, compliance is expected to be very expensive, possibly over $100,000 for a medium-sized municipality.

APPLYING FOR THE STORMWATER RUNOFF NPDES PERMIT

Enactment of the new stormwater permitting system is proving to be a complex administrative and technical burden for both the permittees and regulators. The regulations are still being debated and are subject to change, especially with regard to permit application deadlines.

The requirements for obtaining the proposed stormwater permits for municipal separate storm sewer systems are quite different from those typically used under the NPDES program. Typical NPDES permits are relatively simple, specifying sampling and monitoring programs to be followed, pollutant volume and concentration limits to be met, and reporting requirements. The proposed municipal separate sewer system stormwater permits resemble drainage basin management programs, requiring long-range planning, analysis of source information, and a requirement that stormwater discharge be reduced to the "maximum extent practicable." The permits will be based on site-specific, best-professional-judgment evaluations of appropriate pollution control measures.

Facilities associated with industrial activity will be required to follow the regulations and apply for an NPDES permit for stormwater discharge to any lake, stream, river, estuary, or other water of the U.S., *unless* they discharge to a municipal separate storm sewer system *and* meet the following additional requirements:

- The municipality has been notified of the discharge and has been provided a certification that the discharge has been evaluated for the presence of non-stormwater discharges.
- The discharge is composed entirely of stormwater and does not contain a hazardous substance in excess of federal reporting requirements under the CWA and the Superfund law.
- The discharge is in compliance with any management program established for the municipal separate storm sewer system.

In some circumstances, the EPA or the state could determine that a separate permit must be obtained for an industrial discharge to a municipal separate storm sewer system. Where industrial facilities discharge into a private stormwater sewer, either the discharger or the system must obtain a permit. Unlike the municipal separate storm sewer systems, a private (or federal) system can refuse to incorporate access for an industrial discharger in its permit.

The proposed regulation contains a two-part application process for all municipal systems. The applications require significant investigations into current conditions and plans for monitoring and managing stormwater. Most cities will wish to hire consultants to assist them through this process.

APPLICATIONS

Under the new regulations, individual or group applications may be submitted for subcategories of industry groups or for sufficiently similar groups. The group application will cover only the individual facilities listed within it, not the industry as a whole. The EPA will then use the group application to develop a model permit that each individual permittee would receive.

General permits issued by your state or the EPA establish standard conditions for an entire industry. Once a general permit for a state is issued, individual facilities seeking coverage under the general permit can file a notice of intent (NOI) within 180 days. General permits are not available in all states. All discharges covered by a general permit must be composed entirely of stormwater and the owner/operator of the facility must develop a stormwater pollution prevention plan within 180 days of the date that the general permit is issued. The prevention plan is similar to a best management plan (BMP).

Each permit is likely to require at least annual monitoring and reporting for the following parameters: oil and grease, pH, BOD, COD, TSS, total phosphorus, total Kjeldahl nitrogen, nitrate plus nitrite nitrogen, and any pollutant limited in any applicable effluent guideline. Sampling procedures for these parameters include one grab sample for detention ponds and both a grab and a composite sample for all other discharges.

In general, permits for most facilities should have been submitted by this time.

OPERATING UNDER AN NPDES PERMIT

NPDES permits contain certain general conditions that apply to all facilities, as well as site-specific conditions unique to each permitted facility. General conditions may or may not be spelled out in each permit, but they are part of the NPDES regulations and are incorporated in each permit by reference. Compliance with the general conditions associated with all NPDES permits are duties of the permittee. These duties include:

- Complying with new CWA effluent standards or prohibitions established for toxic pollutants as they are promulgated.
- Reapplying 180 days before an existing permit expires.
- Operating and maintaining treatment systems properly.
- Providing information requested by the permitting authority.
- Allowing inspections at reasonable times.
- Monitoring operation and keeping monitoring records for three years.

- Reporting the following to the NPDES regulatory agency:
  Planned facility modifications.
  Anticipated noncompliance.
  Monitoring efforts.
  Compliance schedules.
  Actual noncompliance.

Any noncompliance that could endanger health or the environment must be reported verbally within 24 hours and in writing within five days to the state or federal regulatory agency. Any bypass or unintentional temporary malfunction (upset) that causes the discharge to exceed any effluent limit in the permit or any problem causing the facility to exceed a maximum daily discharge limit must be reported according to federal guidelines.

NPDES permits sometimes have to be modified. The modification process is usually triggered by operational changes or construction at the existing site. All facility changes should be evaluated to ensure compliance with the current permit conditions.

The specific conditions of a permit are established by the responsible regulatory agency. States authorized to issue NPDES permits may enact more stringent requirements than the federal ones, and some states without NPDES authority issue their own discharge permits in addition to the federal NPDES permit.

REAPPLYING FOR AN NPDES PERMIT

A local government with an existing NPDES permit must apply for a new one prior to expiration of the existing permit. The time period will be specified by the regulatory agency. If the permit is not issued on time because of delay by the permitting agency, the existing permit will continue in force under an administrative action. Reapplication is different from a first application because the discharges have been regulated and monitored for some period. Therefore, data are available describing how the discharge has performed in comparison to regulatory requirements.

Do not assume that the discharge will be repermitted with the same discharge limitations as the previous permit. Effluent guidelines at the federal level changed during the early 1980s. Subsequently, the requirements in many states were altered to reflect the federal changes. States may also have changed their own specific requirements. Since NPDES permits are typically issued for five years, significant changes may occur during the life of an existing permit.

Changes in effluent guidelines deserve your attention. The federal NPDES guideline changes include important procedural items and new effluent guidelines. Specific industry subdivisions are now combined to establish minimal, universal effluent guidelines that generally apply without exception. Furthermore, permitting authorities are now encouraged to set both concentration and mass limits in permits where only mass limits were previously used. This change restricts operating variability in many cases, since it prevents varying the concentration of a pollutant.

PENALTIES

Failure to comply with NPDES regulations can result in substantial fines, imprisonment, or both. Noncompliance with permit conditions such as effluent limitations, monitoring requirements, or reporting schedules can be penalized by civil penalties of up to $25,000 for each day of noncompliance. Criminal penalties can be imposed in some cases, including fines of $2,500 to $25,000 per day of violation, imprisonment up to one year, or both.

An action that you take knowing that it may cause death or serious injury is subject to fines up to $250,000, up to 15 years in prison, or both. Subsequent offenses of this nature are subject to fines of up to $500,000, 30 years in prison, or both. An organization violating this "imminent danger" provision is subject to a fine of up to $1 million for a first offense and up to $2 million for subsequent offenses.

It is worth noting that some municipal employees have been sent to prison for violations of the CWA and most of those were convicted of falsifying information on monitoring reports required by their permits. It is therefore very important to ensure that employees with monitoring responsibility understand the importance of performing those duties with care.

CONCLUSION

The wide-ranging regulations of the CWA make permitting for wastewater and stormwater discharges an area of particular interest to local governments. The complexities of meeting permit requirements are increasing, as the challenges of maintaining water quality in areas with growing populations and thriving industry multiply.

CHAPTER 11

Municipal Sludge Management:
The other Side of Clean Water

Robert J. Schafish

Our wastewater disposal practices have come a long way since the days when sewage was discharged directly into a nearby river. While the amount of pollutants generated has actually increased, today most are removed before reaching lakes and rivers. Although accumulation of various toxins and metals in the tissues of aquatic animals remains a severe problem (especially in the Great Lakes), we have virtually eliminated the discharge of untreated sanitary wastewater into our inland waters. The result has been dramatically improved water quality throughout the nation.

The tremendous reduction in wastewater pollutants is largely the result of the Clean Water Act (CWA) and the National Pollution Discharge Elimination System (NPDES), which resulted in the construction of thousands of publicly owned treatment works (POTWs) over the past two decades. (See the sections on Wastewater Permits, the Safe Drinking Water Act, and Air Permits for more information about compliance with these requirements.)

POTWs, however, are not a waste management panacea. In the process of removing pollutants from wastewater discharges, POTWs generate vast quantities of sludge that must be treated and disposed of in an environmentally sound manner.

Today's dilemma: successfully addressing our water pollution problem has created a difficult solid waste disposal problem. The same environmental concern that spurred the CWA and NPDES now restricts traditional sludge disposal practices and causes storage and transportation problems. Accordingly, local governments must face the problem of disposing of sludge from their wastewater treatment plants.

WHAT IS SLUDGE?

Sludge is the by-product of water pollution control. As defined in federal regulations, it means solid, semi-solid, or liquid residue generated during the treatment of domestic sewage in a treatment plant. Ironically, it is the result of an environmental tradeoff: we have removed waterborne pollutants and converted them to a residual requiring separate environmental management.

Sludges are generated principally in sewage and wastewater treatment and potable (drinkable) water treatment plants. While many other pollution abatement processes also generate concentrated sludges (especially treating industrial wastewater), this chapter will focus on sludges generated by municipal POTWs that treat sewage. POTW sludge contains suspended solids removed by initial settling (primary sludge) and other solids that are the product of conversion of soluble pollutants to solids that can settle (secondary sludge). The proportion of primary and secondary solid constituents in POTW sludge is unique to the characteristics of the raw sewage, the treatment technology, and the degree of purification required by local and federal (NPDES) regulation.

The chemical characteristics of POTW sludges also depend on the characteristics of the raw sewage, since many of the waterborne pollutants accumulate in the sludge residual. In fact, most of the regulations that limit the acceptable means of sludge management concern pollutants converted and/or accumulated from the raw sewage. The term "biosolids" refers to domestic wastewater residual solids which have been processed for future beneficial use. The term is gradually replacing the term "sewage sludge."

HOW MUCH SLUDGE DO WE GENERATE?

According to the EPA's nationwide survey, there are approximately 12,570 POTWs of which about 25 percent are considered "major" POTWs — those serving populations greater than 10,000 or having flows greater than one million gallons per day (MGD).

Total annual POTW sludge generation in the U.S. is almost 6 million tons (dry weight). That represents 30 billion gallons of liquid sludge every year — enough to fill almost 500 Superdomes. All of that — current and future — must be disposed of with minimal harm to the environment.

The volume of sludge generated by individual POTWs varies widely, depending on the character of the raw sewage and the degree to which it is purified. The daily inflow of raw sewage to a particular POTW is obviously the largest factor, but generated volumes also depend on how sludge processing occurs ahead of the disposal system. The POTW sludge product is typically either a slurry (water/insoluble solids mixture) with 97 to 99 percent moisture, a viscous semisolid with 90 to 94 percent moisture, or a cake with 60 to 80 percent moisture. In general, as the sophistication of the POTW increases, the sludge moisture content is reduced. Although the dewatering process often requires extensive additional facilities, many treatment works of all sizes are now justifying the additional cost of generating a sludge product with a low moisture content.

Bone dry, POTW sludge contains approximately 70 percent volatile matter and 30 percent inert matter. Often the volatile fraction can be further reduced by additional processing within the POTW. Such sludge stabilization may reduce the volatile matter by as much as 50 percent, thereby lowering overall generated volumes and often reducing moisture in the resulting slurry, semi-solid, or cake.

In general, sludge solids produced by a modern POTW range from 0.15 to 0.27 pounds per capita per day (bone-dry basis). Sludge stabilization processes may reduce that volume by approximately 25 to 35 percent.

HOW IS SLUDGE MANAGED TODAY?

Sludge management techniques generally can be separated into two broad categories: sludge treatment (stabilization) and dewatering. Treatment reduces the volatile fractions of the sludge solids. Treatment options include anaerobic digestion, filtration, heat treatment, wet oxidation, chemical treatment, and composting. The practices used depend on local regulations and disposal methods. Dewatering simply uses gravity or a mechanical process to remove excess water from sludge.

In 1988, the EPA performed a survey of sludge disposal practices. The survey showed that 34 percent of the sludge is disposed of in landfills along with municipal solid waste. Only 3 percent goes to sludge monofills — landfills licensed to accept sludge only. With municipal landfill disposal becoming more costly and scarce, disposal of sludge in municipal solid waste landfills is likely to become more difficult and expensive.

Nationwide incineration is used by about 400 POTWs (3 percent of the total number of POTWs) and this method accounts for about 16 percent of the total amount of sludge disposed of. This means that incineration of sludge is more commonly used at large wastewater treatment plants than at medium or small plants.

Compost products using sludge may divert another 3 percent of generated sludges on the average, but there is wide geographic variation because many of the programs are short-term or demonstration projects. Market volatility also contributes to the fluctuating sludge diversion figures.

Solids stabilization by anaerobic digestion is the single most common sludge management practice among POTWs, regardless of size or location; over three quarters of plants larger than five MGD use it. That percentage is even higher if computed from the total gallons treated. Plants smaller than five MGD using other stabilization methods appear to favor lime stabilization — or no treatment at all.

REGULATORY OUTLOOK

Regulation of POTW sludge management has historically been within the purview of state agencies. More recently, federally mandated sludge land disposal practices were promulgated under the joint authority of the Resource Conservation and Recovery Act (RCRA) and Section 405(d) of the Clean Water Act (CWA). In February 1987 Congress enacted the Water Quality Act of 1987, which amended portions of the CWA, including Section 405. Those changes imposed new standard-setting requirements, set deadlines, and established sludge permitting and state program requirements. The EPA issued final regulations in 1993 (40 C.F.R. Part 503) that regulate the use and disposal of sewage sludge. The definition of sewage sludge includes any material that is derived from sewage sludge such as composted sewage blended with another material. The EPA's regulations establish pollutant limits, management practices, operational standards, monitoring frequency, recordkeeping, and reporting.

The EPA has recognized that there are distinct uses and disposal methods for sewage sludge and has classified sewage sludge into different categories, each with its own set of standards. These classifications are:

- Land application — sewage sludge applied to the land (which includes sewage sludge sold or given away in bulk or in a bag or other container for application to the land).
- Land disposal — sewage sludge placed on a surface disposal site (including sludge placed in a monofill).
- Incineration — sewage sludge fired in a sewage sludge incinerator.

The EPA's regulations concerning land application of sludge are significant because land application is, in many cases, still the most cost-effective method available to local governments. The regulations link the characteristics of sludge to the options for land application — the higher the quality the more options are available. It is likely that sludge generators will find it in their interest to more closely manage the quality of the sludge they produce. The connection between the presence of certain pollutants (especially the metals that are specifically listed in the EPA's sludge regulations) and the cost of sludge disposal will become even stronger and sludge generators may find it cost effective to tighten up their wastewater systems to reduce the presence of these pollutants in their sludge. This approach is consistent with a stronger emphasis on beneficial use of resources such as sludge, instead of a disposal-based approach such as landfilling or land disposal. Public support for a reuse ethic in management of wastes has consistently grown stronger.

Sewage sludge that passes all the tests, including the most demanding pollutant levels and pathogen reduction standards, is classified as "exceptional quality" and has few restrictions for land application or use of the sludge. The available options include:

- Agricultural land
- Forests
- Public contact sites
- Reclamation sites

- Rangeland
- Pastures
- Lawn or home gardens

Requirements for monitoring and reporting are also less stringent than for lower quality sludges.

Depending upon the ability of the sludge to meet the various combinations of pollutant levels, pathogen reduction, and processing for vector attraction, the regulations specify the allowable land application options, annual and cumulative loading rates, monitoring requirements, and reporting requirements. Generally, as the quality of the sludge decreases, the regulations become more restrictive.

The management of land resources also benefits from the reuse of sludge through a carefully managed program. Soils used for agricultural production are highly stressed and replenishment of organic matter is beneficial. Sludge application can also offset some of the cost of fertilizer, further enhancing the benefits of land application.

Another important factor in the balance among different sludge disposal options is that landfills and land disposal sites are becoming scarcer and more costly. Many states have banned yard waste from landfills, recognizing that there are alternative means for managing yard waste that don't deplete scarce and costly landfill space. Although such bans have not yet been extended to sludges, it is clear that, where viable options exist for diverting wastes from landfill, they will become more attractive. The economics of landfill disposal will also reinforce this trend.

The regulations at 40 C.F.R. § 257, Criteria for Classification of Solid Waste Facilities, and 40 C.F.R. § 258, Solid Waste Landfills, also address the co-disposal of sewage sludge with household and municipal wastes. The EPA's co-disposal goal is to assure consistency in its regulation under two different regulatory schemes — RCRA and CWA.

Other federal regulations that may also play a significant role in the municipal sludge manager's planning process include the Clean Air Act (CAA), the Marine Protection, Research, and Sanctuaries Act (MPRSA), the Toxic Substances Control Act (TSCA), and the Ocean Dumping Act of 1988. The latter act effectively prohibits coastal sludge disposal after December 31, 1991. Others will restrict emissions from thermal systems, probably including drying and composting operations, and will govern storage, hauling, and monitoring practices.

CONCLUSION

Looking to the future, there are two issues that may receive increasing attention: decreasing the limits for cadmium in sludge and reducing potential for contaminating groundwater from nitrates. The cadmium issue is related to export of agricultural products and the need to maintain access to foreign markets that seek to assure that cadmium levels in food products are low. Nitrates are seen as having a potential for contaminating groundwater supplies but nitrates in sludges are associated with organics and have a lower leaching potential than nitrates in chemical fertilizers. Thus the beneficial use of sewage sludge may receive additional emphasis.

Overall, the changes in federal regulations require closer management of sewage sludge. Land application remains a good option but using it requires higher levels of assurance through testing and recordkeeping. Reducing pollutants in sewage sludge will become more attractive in order to maintain the land application option. Controlling the final sludge product from the beginning of the process may receive more emphasis. Municipalities are likely to increase their standards for industries discharging into municipal wastewater systems in order to reduce pollutants that ultimately find their way into the sludge. Whichever method a municipality chooses to improve sludge management, this issue will remain in the forefront of municipal concerns.

CHAPTER **12**

The Safe Drinking Water Act

Matthew D. Lee and Susanna M. Higgins

Water has often been called the universal solvent. Abundant and chemically versatile, water comprises from 70 to 90 percent of almost every living organism. The value of water to humanity is incalculable. Of utmost importance is our need to drink water to support and maintain proper bodily functions. Our physiologic requirement for a steady supply of wholesome water makes us vulnerable to adverse effects of contaminated water. Drinking water contaminated with pathogenic organisms or toxic compounds can be disastrous. Contaminated water has been linked to many diseases, such as cholera, typhoid, and neurological dysfunctions.

Sources of contamination are not always obvious. Many factors can contribute to unsuitable drinking water quality, such as indigenous metals in the soils; runoff from agriculture containing fertilizers and pesticides; improper use of household wastes such as cleaning products, oil, and garden chemicals; and naturally occurring radioactive materials.

The public is becoming more concerned about contamination of water and the government's ability to address it. The last decade has witnessed a dramatic increase in the sale of bottled water and household water-processing units. Some experts speculate that, by the year 2000, the federal government will require each home to be equipped with its own water-processing unit.

The Safe Drinking Water Act (SDWA), 42 U.S.C. §§ 300(f) *et seq.*, was enacted in 1974 to establish regulations for the quality of tap water. The Act currently requires:

- National primary and secondary standards for drinking water quality.
- Monitoring and reporting requirements for public water systems.
- Regulations for underground injection of fluids.
- A ban on the use of lead materials in public water systems and structures that transport drinking water.
- Monitoring of unregulated drinking water pollutants for possible inclusion in the standards.

1-56670-098-1/95/$0.00+$.50

As groundwater pollution has increased, the regulations for drinking water have become more stringent. This puts added pressure on municipal water quality departments to meet the regulatory requirements for contaminant levels while meeting the increasing demands of a growing population.

The SDWA directs the EPA to regulate the safety of "public water systems," which includes systems providing piped water for human consumption with at least 15 service connections, or which regularly serve at least 25 people for a minimum of 60 days each year. The national standards issued by the EPA are called maximum contaminant levels (MCLs). These standards are stated in terms of how many parts per million (ppm) of a given chemical are permissible in water delivered to customers at the tap. In setting MCLs, the EPA decides what level of contamination will not harm human health, and then decides whether a public water system can meet that standard, given available technology and cost.

In most states, the SDWA regulations are enforced through a cooperative partnership between the federal and state governments. Where states have been delegated "primacy" from the EPA, they have the authority to administer and enforce the requirements of the Act while the EPA provides guidance and technical assistance, sets the standards, and provides some financing for certain programs. In the remaining states, the EPA implements the SDWA.

The SDWA should not be confused with federal water pollution statutes such as the CWA. Generally speaking, the key difference is that the SDWA applies to the quality of water at the tap, while the CWA apply to water in lakes, streams, and rivers. In most homes, the SDWA is the last line of defense against water contamination that could endanger health.

The SDWA includes regulations governing where drinking water treatment facilities may be sited. Before construction of a new treatment facility or an expansion of an existing facility may commence, the owner/operator must notify the state and, to the extent possible, avoid locating the new or expanded facility at a site that is subject to a significant risk from earthquakes, floods, fires, or other disasters that have the potential to destroy or damage a public source of drinking water. Also, facilities should not be sited within the floodplain of a 100-year flood or, if located near a shoreline, below any recorded high tide level.

NATIONAL PRIMARY DRINKING WATER REGULATIONS

The MCLs establish the concentration of a chemical or contaminant (in parts per million) that the EPA has decided is acceptable for human consumption, supported by the numerous physicochemical studies conducted since the early 1900s. These standards, specifically applicable to water intended for human ingestion, are collectively referred to as the National Primary Drinking Water Regulations. MCLs exist for organic and inorganic chemicals, volatile organic chemicals, turbidity, radioactivity, and microbiological contaminants.

The maximum level of contamination considered safe for human health is of utmost importance to the EPA in establishing these primary standards. The

EPA decides whether or not a public water system can achieve these standards by applying the **best available technology (BAT),** that is, the most effective technology, treatment techniques, or other means the EPA finds acceptable. Included in this determination are the technology's efficacy under field conditions and cost considerations.

The EPA is continually augmenting the requirements of the SDWA, and these changes are making compliance more rigorous for public water systems. For example, several sweeping changes were promulgated during 1991, 1992, and 1993. Those changes include:

- Establishment of new or revised MCLs increasing the number of included contaminants from 34 to 63 (Table 1 summarizes all current MCLs).
- New analytical methods and laboratory performance requirements.
- Added secondary standards for silver and aluminum.
- Use of bottled water, point-of-use, and point-of-entry devices.
- New language regarding health effects to be included in public notices.
- New requirements for states relative to recordkeeping and reporting.

The regulations implementing the primary standards describe the sampling protocol and analytical methods required for each contaminant. Alternate analytical techniques may be employed if the state, with the EPA's concurrence, gives written permission to do so. Samples may be considered only if they have been analyzed by a state-approved laboratory. Exceptions to this rule are analyses typically performed in the field for turbidity, free chlorine residual, temperature, and pH, which can be performed by any qualified person acceptable to the state.

REPORTING, PUBLIC NOTIFICATION AND HEALTH ADVISORIES

Perhaps the most demanding components of the primary drinking water regulations are those dealing with reporting, public notification, and recordkeeping. The reporting requirements mandate the submission of monitoring results, MCL violations, and public notices. If at any time the MCLs are exceeded, or if a sample is not taken as required, the water department must notify the state within 48 hours. An invalid sample is considered a failure to monitor.

Any time there is a violation of the drinking water standards or treatment technique, the public water system owner or operator must give public notice. Depending on the classification of the violation as a Tier 1 or Tier 2 (Tier 1 is more critical) the water system can be required to give public notice through publication in a daily paper, by mail, or by radio and television. Certain other violations, such as deviance from the established testing procedures, also require public notification. Whenever any public notice is issued, a copy of each type of notice must be submitted to the state as specified by the reporting requirements. The regulations also prescribe "health effects language" to be used in the public notice.

Table 1 Summary of Current MCLs and SMCLs

Contaminant	MCL (mg/l)	SMCL(mg/l)	Comments
Inorganic Chemicals			
Aluminum	Not applicable	0.05–0.2	
Arsenic	0.05	Not applicable	
Asbestos	7 MFL	Not applicable	Million fibers per liter longer than 10 m
Barium	2.0	Not applicable	
Cadmium	0.005	Not applicable	
Chloride	Not applicable	250	
Chromium	0.1	Not applicable	
Color	Not applicable	15 color units	
Copper	Treatment technique	1.0	EPA specifies treatment techniques that optimize corrosion control
Corrosivity	Not applicable	Noncorrosive	
Fluoride	4.0	2.0	
Foaming agents	Not applicable	0.5	
Iron	Not applicable	0.3	
Lead	Treatment technique	Not applicable	EPA specifies treatment techniques that optimize corrosion control
Manganese	Not applicable	0.05	
Mercury	0.002	Not applicable	
Nitrate (as N)	10	Not applicable	
	1	Not applicable	
Total nitrate and nitrite (as N)	10	Not applicable	
Odor	Not applicable	3 threshold odor number	
Ph	Not applicable	6.5–8.5	
Selenium	0.05	Not applicable	
Silver	Not applicable	0.1	
Sulfate	Not applicable	250	
Total dissolved solids	Not applicable	500	
Zinc	Not applicable	5	
Microbiological Contaminants			
Total coliforms	Presence	Not applicable	If more than 40 samples are taken, only 5% may be total coliform positive
Giardia lamblia	Treatment technique	Not applicable	Install treatment processes that remove or inactivate at least 99.9% of the microbes
RPC	Treatment technique	Not applicable	Same
Legionella	Treatment technique	Not applicable	Same
Viruses	Treatment technique	Not applicable	Same
Turbidity	1.0–5.0 NTU	Not applicable	Nephelometric turbidity units
Organic Chemicals			
Acrylamide	Treatment technique	Not applicable	EPA limits the amount of acrylamide in polymer

Table 1 *continued*

Contaminant	MCL (mg/l)	SMCL(mg/l)	Comments
Benzene	0.005	Not applicable	
Carbon tetrachloride	0.005	Not applicable	
O-Dichlorobenzene	0.6	Not applicable	
para-Dichlorobenzene	0.075	Not applicable	
1,2-Dichloroethane	0.005	Not applicable	
1,1-Dichloroethylene	0.007	Not applicable	
cis-1,2-Dichloroethylene	0.07	Not applicable	
trans-1,2-Dichloroethylene	0.1	Not applicable	
1,2-Dichloropropane	0.005	Not applicable	
Epichlorohydrin	Treatment technique	Not applicable	EPA limits the amount of epichlorohydrin in polymer
Ethylbenzene	0.7	Not applicable	
Monochlorobenzene	0.1	Not applicable	
PCBs	0.0005	Not applicable	
Styrene	0.1	Not applicable	
Tetrachloroethylene	0.005	Not applicable	
Trihalomethanes	0.10	Not applicable	
Toluene	1.0	Not applicable	
1,1,1-Trichloroethane	0.2	Not applicable	
Trichloroethylene	0.005	Not applicable	
Vinyl chloride	0.002	Not applicable	
Xylenes	10	Not applicable	
Pesticides			
Alachlor	0.002	Not applicable	
Aldicarb	0.003	Not applicable	
Aldicarb sulfoxide	0.004	Not applicable	
Aldicarb sulfone	0.002	Not applicable	
Atrazine	0.003	Not applicable	
Carbofuran	0.04	Not applicable	
Chlordane	0.002	Not applicable	
2,4-D	0.07	Not applicable	
1,2-Dibromo-3-chloropropane	0.0002	Not applicable	
Endrin	0.0002	Not applicable	
Ethylene dibromide	0.00005	Not applicable	
Heptachlor	0.0004	Not applicable	
Heptachlor epoxide	0.0002	Not applicable	
Lindane	0.0002	Not applicable	
Methoxychlor	0.04	Not applicable	
Pentachlorophenol	0.001	Not applicable	
Toxaphene	0.003	Not applicable	
2,4,5-TP	0.05	Not applicable	
Radionuclides			
Gross alpha particle activity	15 pCi/l	Not applicable	
Gross beta particle activity	4 mRem/Year	Not applicable	
Photon radioactivity	4 mRem/Year	Not applicable	
Radium 226 and 228	5 pCi/l	Not applicable	

The SDWA prohibits the use of lead pipes in public water systems. It is now illegal to use anything but "lead-free" pipe, solder, or flux when installing or repairing a piping system that serves a covered water system. The regulations require municipalities to notify residents and report to the state if lead levels rise above a specified maximum.

RECORDKEEPING

Recordkeeping is vital to fulfilling statutory requirements — and may help mitigate penalties for noncompliance. The regulations require records of bacteriological and chemical analyses, actions taken to correct violations, sanitary surveys of the system, and variances or exemptions granted to the system. The department should also keep telephone logs, letters, or other forms of communication with state and local agency officials. Well-organized records of all training certificates, operation certifications, quality assurance procedures, lab inspection results, water quality reports, and communications should also be maintained.

NATIONAL SECONDARY DRINKING WATER REGULATIONS

The National Secondary Drinking Water Regulations control contaminants that primarily affect the aesthetic qualities and public acceptance of drinking water. When contaminants are present at considerably higher concentrations than the **secondary maximum contaminant levels (SMCLs),** however, health implications may also exist. Under the SDWA, the secondary regulations are not federally enforceable, and state agencies with jurisdiction over public water systems are not required to adopt these secondary standards. The standards are guidelines for the states and represent reasonable goals for drinking water quality. Table 1 contains a summary of the SMCLs.

Provided that public health and welfare are not adversely affected, states may establish higher or lower SMCLs appropriate to local conditions such as unavailability of alternate water sources or other compelling factors.

The secondary drinking water regulations recommend monitoring SMCLs at intervals no less frequent than those applied to the inorganic chemical contaminants listed in the primary regulations. Suggested methods of analyses for these contaminants can be found at 40 C.F.R. § 143.4(b).

One confusing aspect of the secondary drinking water regulations is the public notification requirement for fluoride. The primary standards establish the MCL for fluoride at 4.0 mg/l. The secondary standards establish the SMCL for fluoride at 2.0 mg/l. In the case of fluoride, public notification is required whenever the SMCL is exceeded.

Exposure to fluoride levels above 4.0 mg/l for an extended period of time may cause skeletal fluorosis, a crippling bone disorder. For children under nine years of age, exposure to levels above 2.0 mg/l may cause dental fluorosis, a brown staining and/or pitting of the permanent teeth. Therefore, public notification is required when fluoride levels in the drinking water exceed the SMCL. This is the only secondary drinking water regulation for which a community water system cannot be exempt.

Recently, some scientists have become concerned with the concentration of aluminum in drinking water and its possible link to Alzheimer's disease, a neurological disorder causing, among other things, confusion and memory loss. Aluminum in the form of alum (aluminum sulfate) is commonly used as a clarifying agent in water treatment. The EPA has set a new standard for aluminum at 0.05 ppm. However, the standard is only a secondary (nonmandatory) standard until the issue can be studied further.

UNDERGROUND INJECTION CONTROL PROGRAM

The SDWA provides for the protection of underground sources of drinking water by regulation of underground injection. Some facilities use underground injection to dispose of hazardous and other liquid wastes in isolated geologic formations. The depth of the wells can vary from 300 feet to thousands of feet. The construction and use of any underground injection well requires a permit issued under the underground injection control (UIC) program.

The regulations for different types of injection wells vary. Injection wells are classified as follows:

Class I	Wells that inject hazardous waste or other industrial and municipal fluids beneath the lowest formation containing, within one quarter mile of the well bore, an underground source of drinking water (USDW).
Class II	Wells that inject fluids for enhanced recovery of oil or natural gas and for storage of hydrocarbons, which are liquid at standard temperature and pressure.
Class III	Wells that inject fluids for extraction of minerals.
Class IV	Wells used by generators of hazardous or radioactive wastes to dispose of the material, generally above a formation containing, within one quarter mile of the well bore, a USDW, or an aquifer.
Class V	Wells not included in the first four classes.

The construction, operation, and maintenance of any Class IV well is specifically prohibited, except for wells used to reinject treated contaminated groundwater into the same formation from which it was drawn. Such reinjection must, however, be approved by the EPA pursuant to requirements and provisions for cleanup of releases under the Comprehensive Environmental Response, Compensation, and Liability Act of 1980 (CERCLA) or the Resource Conservation and Recovery Act (RCRA).

Class V injection wells are used by municipalities for a variety of uses. These uses include stormwater control, sanitary waste disposal, and cooling water return wells. Sanitary waste disposal wells include cesspools and septic systems that serve greater than 20 people per day. The EPA requires users of Class V injection wells to inventory the use with the regional EPA office.

Permits for injection wells specify requirements for proper use, maintenance, and installation of monitoring equipment; type, intervals, and frequency of monitoring sufficient to yield representative data; and applicable reporting requirements based upon the impact of the regulated activity. Owners or operators of injection wells must submit inventory information to the state, as required. Any monitoring, regulatory noncompliance, malfunction of the injection system, or other information that indicates a potential for contamination of a USDW must be reported within 24 hours of the discovery.

The applicable UIC program is either a state program approved by the EPA, a federal program administered by the EPA, or a combination of the two, depending on the class of well. The UIC programs for each of the states, territories, and possessions are set forth in 40 C.F.R. Part 147.

SOLE SOURCE AQUIFER PROTECTION

The purpose of 40 C.F.R. Part 149 is to provide criteria for identifying critical aquifer protection areas. Under § 1424(e) of the SDWA, the EPA may designate certain aquifers as sole or principal source aquifers. These aquifers are recognized sources of significant amounts of water that are particularly vulnerable to contamination because of the area's hydrogeologic characteristics. The Edwards Underground Reservoir in the San Antonio, TX, area is an example of a designated sole source aquifer. Any activities that could potentially damage a sole source aquifer are prohibited by the regulations.

Any department planning construction should identify the location of nearby aquifers and determine whether any aquifer is — or potentially could be — a designated sole source aquifer. Construction that could damage or significantly alter a sole source aquifer is prohibited under federal regulations. Be sure to check your state regulations, as the limitations may be even more stringent. In many cases, any actions that could alter or damage any sources of surface water or groundwater are prohibited.

WELLHEAD PROTECTION PROGRAM

The 1986 amendments to the SDWA also established the Wellhead Protection Program (WHP) to protect groundwater supplies and wellfields that are sources of public water supply systems. Under Section 1428 of the SDWA, states must develop their own plans.

Local governments are encouraged to become involved in the WHP of their state to secure future drinking water supplies. It may be less costly to prevent contamination than to clean up contamination. It is also beneficial to enter the program so that potential sources of groundwater contamination may be identified early in the process and appropriate remedial activity may begin.

LOCAL GOVERNMENT APPLICABILITY

Obviously, the municipal division for which the bulk of the drinking water regulations were written is the department of water quality. The public water system must adhere to the strict regulations governing this sensitive area, such as those concerning permits, monitoring, recordkeeping, and compliance assessment. Beyond the federal regulations, which are typically endorsed by an approved state agency, state regulations may impose additional requirements.

The electric department may also be subject to the drinking water regulations, depending on its methods of operation. Regulation would come primarily from the Underground Injection Control (UIC) program. If an electric department employs an injection well for process waters (cooling tower water, boiler blowdown), it is subject to the UIC program, as administered by either the federal EPA or an approved state agency. Again, state programs may be more stringent and should be investigated.

In some instances, the electric department may be injecting domestic sewage generated on-site into a well. This practice also requires compliance with the applicable UIC program regulations. In some municipalities, the water department and the electric department are combined. However, the regulations apply for each individual department and are probably best handled as though two separate departments existed.

Often parks and streets departments will utilize drywells for stormwater control. These drywells are considered Class V injection wells by the EPA, and as such should be registered with the EPA inventory. Injection wells used to dispose of swimming pool water are similarly regulated.

CONCLUSION

As more chemical compounds are created and as research on the effects of hazardous substances to human health progresses, the EPA continues to revise and amend the rules and regulations of the Safe Drinking Water Act frequently. Municipal departments should assess their compliance regularly to avoid strict penalties and poor community relations.

CHAPTER 13

Air Quality Management

D. Edward Settle, Michael S. Robinson, and Linda M. Long

Centuries of history have recorded the human effort to manage air quality for the destruction or preservation of life. Four thousand years ago, ancient India used smoke screens and toxic fumes in battle. Twenty-four hundred years ago in the Peloponnesian War, the Spartans besieged the cities of Athens by burning sulfur and pitch, producing sulfur dioxide which is extremely irritating to the eyes and respiratory tract. In 1775, a medical doctor discovered that the inhalation of particulate matter in chimney sweeps (soot) caused cancer. Between 1948 and 1953, smog caused the deaths of over 4,200 people in Pennsylvania, London, and New York.

Shortly after the New York smog incident, the U.S. government began managing air quality with the Air Pollution Control Act of 1955. The law, now referred to as the Clean Air Act (CAA) and codified at 42 U.S.C. § 7401 *et seq.*, has been amended several times. Relevant regulations are found at 40 C.F.R. Part 50 and following. However, no matter how the law and associated regulations change as the years pass, its underlying purpose remains to protect public health and welfare.

With this in mind, local government employees with the responsibility for environmental compliance must always ask whether an activity has the potential for directly or indirectly affecting air quality. Activities that might affect air quality could be specifically regulated or exempted from regulation. However, finding the specific regulation or exemption can be a challenge.

This chapter provides a general discussion of the federal air quality regulations and describes many of the municipal activities that could be regulated under the federal program. Since states, territories, and even counties can and often do implement regulatory programs that are more stringent than the federal program, and no two state or local programs are exactly alike, a comprehensive discussion of state and local programs is beyond the scope of this chapter.

Keep in mind these considerations: (1) federal, state, and local regulatory programs are constantly changing and require forward-thinking, proactive

1-56670-098-1/95/$0.00+$.50
© 1995 by CRC Press, Inc.

vigilance to maintain compliance and (2) just because an activity isn't regulated, municipalities are not necessarily protected from liability if the activity has detrimental effects on public health and welfare.

THE FEDERAL AIR REGULATIONS

Air regulations are one of the most complex issues a municipality encounters on a day-to-day basis. Possible considerations range from emissions from maintenance activities to operation of a city-owned electric system. An overview of the federal regulations and short definitions of applicable terms reflect only a small portion of existing legislation. Compliance with air regulations often requires the assistance of consultants trained in relevant technologies and up-to-date on the newest requirements.

The primary purpose of the CAA is "to protect and enhance the quality of the Nation's air resources so as to promote the public health and welfare and the productive capacity of its population." Through research, the government determines which of the various air pollutants cause acute or chronic health effects and environmental damage. Once the government determines that a certain pollutant can be detrimental to our lives and our habitat, the "acceptable" concentration in the air we breathe is determined and established as a standard for air quality. The determination of acceptability may be based on factors such as the number of projected deaths per one million people, the inhibited growth of agricultural crops, the potential for bioaccumulation in the ecosystem, a person's visual perception of an outdoor scene, or the necessity and economic benefit of the activity that causes the air pollution.

NATIONAL AMBIENT AIR QUALITY STANDARDS

The EPA has established National Ambient Air Quality Standards (NAAQS) based on certain "acceptability" factors not unlike those identified above. The EPA has developed NAAQS for six "criteria" pollutants which are shown in Table 1.

The NAAQS consist of primary standards to protect public health and secondary standards to protect public welfare. Public welfare includes the natural ecosystem (*e.g.*, forests, soil, water, crops, and vegetation), man-made materials (*e.g.*, buildings and statues), climate, visibility, transportation, and general economic welfare. Both primary and secondary standards are equally binding on sources of air pollution covered by the regulations.

The NAAQS apply to all states and territories of the U.S. — they are the same for Los Angeles, New York, Anchorage, Miami, and Guam. The mechanism for assuring compliance with the NAAQS is the state implementation plan (SIP) which is reviewed and approved by the EPA for each state. How-

Table 1   National Ambient Air Quality Standards

Pollutant	Averaging Interval	Standard ($\mu g/m^3$)
Nitrogen oxides	Annual	100
Sulfur dioxide	Annual	80
	24-hour	365
	3-hour	1,300
Particulates	Annual	50
	24-hour	150
Carbon monoxide	8-hour	10,000
	1-hour	40,000
Ozone	1-hour	235
Lead	$\frac{1}{4}$-hour	1.5

ever, some states have established ambient air quality standards that are more stringent than the NAAQS, and activities in those states must comply with the more stringent state standards.

OTHER AIR QUALITY STANDARDS

While the NAAQS apply specifically to the six criteria pollutants, the air quality concentrations of other pollutants may be regulated by different means and for different purposes. Other air quality standards that may affect a local government include:

- U.S. Occupational Safety and Health Administration (OSHA) permissible exposure limits intended to protect workers in the workplace.
- American Conference of Governmental Industrial Hygienists threshold limit values (TLVs) for worker protection.
- EPA risk-specific concentrations (RSCs) for trace metal emissions from sewage sludge incineration projects.
- States' "no threat levels" or "acceptable ambient concentrations" for various toxic air pollutants.

NEW OR MODIFIED SOURCES OF AIR POLLUTION

Proposed new sources of air pollution and proposed modifications to existing sources may subject a facility to one of the many regulatory programs. New source performance standards can restrict emissions from such a facility. The types of pollutants emitted can require compliance with the program regulating hazardous air pollutants. The size and location of a new source or modification can require new source review under the prevention of significant deterioration or nonattainment area programs. New sources may also be required to purchase "allowances" under the acid rain program. Even a small new source or modification can be subject to minor source permitting requirements depending on the state's regulations. Each of these programs is described in more detail below (see also Figure 1).

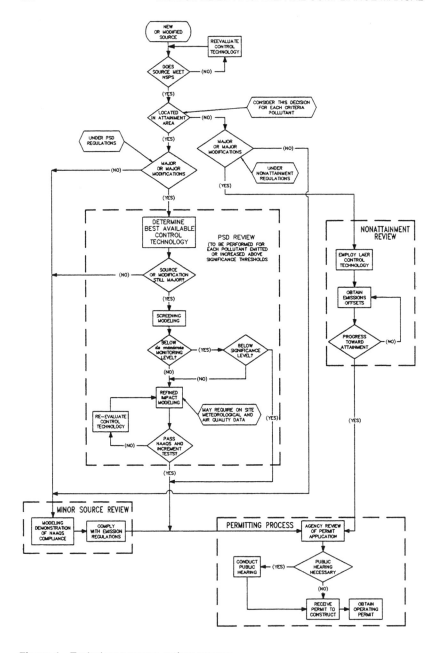

Figure 1 Typical new source review process.

New Source Performance Standards

If a new facility will emit to the atmosphere, it will be subject to air emission control standards if it meets certain size and emission level criteria. In addition, a modification of an existing facility may be subject to the same standards, even if it currently does not have any air emission limitations. The types of pollutants that are regulated include particulates, nitrogen oxides, sulfur dioxide, organic compounds, and many others. These air emission standards are referred to as new source performance standards (NSPS). The NSPS limit emissions from individual industries or processes that fall under specified groups called source categories. A source is defined as a facility or process that emits air pollutants. Examples of source categories of interest to local governments include:

- Fossil fuel-fired steam generators
- Municipal waste combustors
- Sewage sludge incinerators
- Stationary gas turbines
- Storage vessels for petroleum liquids

A modification under the NSPS regulations is any physical change or change in the method of operation of an existing facility that increases the amount of any regulated air pollutant for which a standard applies (40 C.F.R. § 60.2). An extensive overhaul of an older source could constitute a reconstruction under the NSPS program and subject the overhauled source to the NSPS regardless of any change in the amount of air pollution emitted.

Hazardous Air Pollutants

The CAA requires the EPA to develop emission standards for pollutants that do not have NAAQS. The law requires National Emission Standards for Hazardous Air Pollutants (NESHAPs or HAPs) for 189 pollutants with high risks.

Two categories of sources are regulated under the HAPs program — major sources and area sources. A major source has the potential to emit 10 tons per year of any listed HAP or 25 tons per year of any combination of HAPs. The major source categories include, but are not limited to, activities associated with fuel combustion (potentially excluding electric utility steam-generating units), gasoline distribution, and waste treatment and disposal (such as municipal landfills and publicly owned treatment works). Industrial process cooling towers are listed under the miscellaneous process category. An area source is any stationary source of HAPs that is not a major source. Area sources include facilities such as dry-cleaning establishments and asbestos-processing operations.

New and existing major sources must apply the maximum achievable control technology (MACT) for the source category in question. MACT is similar to the determination of best available control technology under the prevention of significant deterioration program as described below in that it may take into consideration the cost of achieving the emission reduction, non-air quality environmental effects, and energy requirements. For new sources, or those sources that begin construction, modification, or reconstruction after an applicable emission standard is proposed, MACT is at least as stringent as the emission control achieved in practice by the best controlled similar source.

Prevention of Significant Deterioration

The "PSD" program is intended to "prevent the significant deterioration" of air quality. The regulations established under the PSD program focus on two primary aspects of a source: emissions control and air quality impacts. Although the source owner or operator must justify the adequacy of the emissions control and the acceptability of the air quality impacts related to the source, a permit to construct a facility will not be issued until the reviewing agency concurs.

The complicating factor in the entire PSD review process is that it must be performed on a pollutant-by-pollutant basis. A facility that is a major source of sulfur dioxide and nitrogen oxides but a minor source of particulates would undergo the PSD review process for sulfur dioxide and nitrogen oxides but not particulates. The requirements for PSD review also depend on whether the area where the source is located has "attained" certain standards for particular pollutants.

A modification to an existing facility may also subject it to the PSD regulations. If the modification itself would exceed the 100 or 250 ton per year thresholds (depending on the source type), then the modification is subject to PSD review. If the existing facility is a major source with emissions exceeding 100 or 250 tons per year (again depending on the source type), a modification of the facility would be considered major under PSD regulations if it results in an increase in emissions above specified significant emission rates. Table 2 gives the significant emission rates for the pollutants as listed in the PSD regulations (40 C.F.R. § 51.166).

Once it is determined that a new source or modification will be subject to the PSD provisions, all pollutants emitted above the significant emission rates in Table 2 become subject to PSD review. Thus, if a fossil fuel-fired boiler is a major source and the owner installs another boiler that has potential emissions of sulfur dioxide exceeding 40 tons per year, the sulfur dioxide emissions and ambient air quality impacts from the new boiler would be subject to PSD review before construction of the new boiler could begin.

Best Available Control Technology

Under the PSD regulations, a new or modified source must apply the best available control technology (BACT) for the pollutants emitted in excess of the

Table 2   Significant Emission Rate

Pollutant	Tons Per Year
Carbon monoxide	100
Nitrogen oxides	40
Sulfur dioxide	40
Particulate matter (PM)	
Total PM	25
PM10[a]	15
Ozone (volatile organic compounds)	40
Lead	0.6
Asbestos	0.007
Beryllium	0.0004
Mercury	0.1
Vinyl chloride	1
Fluorides	3
Sulfuric acid mist	7
Hydrogen sulfide	10
Total reduced sulfur	10
Reduced sulfur compounds	10
Municipal waste combustor organics	$3.5\ e10^{-6}$
Municipal waste combustor metals	15
Municipal waste combustor acid gases	40

[a] PM10 is particulate matter with an aerodynamic diameter less than 10 microns.

significant emission rates. BACT is the maximum control on emissions of each regulated pollutant that is achievable taking into account energy, environmental, and economic impacts. This analysis is performed on a case-by-case basis. For example, BACT control on a combustion turbine can be steam injection to reduce nitrogen oxides to 25 parts per million or the combination of steam injection and selective catalytic reduction to reduce nitrogen oxides to 5 parts per million. The selection of either of these control methods as BACT for a specific facility would depend upon energy, environmental, and economic impacts evaluated for the specific application under consideration.

Air Quality Analysis

In addition to the BACT analysis, each PSD application for a major source or modification of a major source must evaluate the source's potential impact on air quality. The analysis must be conducted for each criteria pollutant that is emitted in significant amounts. Volatile organic compounds, precursors to the criteria pollutant ozone, are typically excepted since the dispersion modeling required is both complicated and expensive.

Nonattainment Area Provisions

The EPA classifies a particular geographic area as a nonattainment area (NAA) according to whether the extent of pollution in the area is marginal, moderate, serious, severe, or extreme. A new major source in a nonattainment area must employ the strictest control technology for that pollutant, termed the lowest achievable emission rate (LAER). LAER is defined as the lowest amount of air emissions achieved in practice from a facility of the same type. In determining what LAER is for a facility, the cost of installing a specific technology for emissions control cannot be used as a reason for not selecting that technology, unless the facility could not be built if such control technology is applied.

Sources wishing to locate in a nonattainment area must compensate for their emissions by a decrease in pollution from other sources. This compensating decrease is referred to as an "offset." The permitting agency will often require emission offsets to be acquired at a ratio greater than one to one. The ratio will depend on the severity of the nonattainment classification or the distance between the proposed source and the source of the offset emissions. The magnitude of the offset ratio will also be chosen so that progress can be made in attaining the NAAQS.

The permitting process for a new source in an area that is nonattainment for one or more pollutants is demanding. It requires consideration of the NAA provisions as well as the PSD provisions for those pollutants for which the area is designated attainment. Obtaining emissions offsets may be cumbersome if not impossible, and demonstrating progress toward attainment is difficult. Locating a major source in a nonattainment area should be avoided, if possible.

Minor Source Permitting

If a proposed new source is a minor source of air pollutants (below the thresholds identified in the PSD and NAA new source review programs), the permitting is far less complicated. It is for this reason that many owners and operators submit to federally enforceable limitations on hours of operation or emissions to avoid the more complicated process.

New Source Acid Rain Requirements

The CAA Amendments of 1990 superimposed another layer of control over most fossil fuel-fired electric generating facilities under the acid rain provisions. The core rules implementing the acid rain provisions of the CAA are found at 40 C.F.R. Part 72. These rules differ from previous regulations by taking a market-based approach to controlling emissions.

In addition to previously established limitations in pounds per million BTU or pounds per hour, the provisions require a facility to have an allowance to emit sulfur dioxide. An allowance is an authorization to emit one ton of sulfur dioxide in one year. These allowances can be sold, traded, and banked for use in future years. Since the total number of allowances was capped at 8.9 million tons per year to achieve the overall 10 million ton reduction in emissions required by law, new facilities will not be allocated allowances but will require allowances to operate. Allowances can be purchased from publicly held auctions or other utilities, or transferred from other facilities that have been retired. The first public auction of allowances was held March 29, 1993 at the Chicago Board of Trade.

With few exceptions, all units subject to the acid rain program must install, certify, and begin operating a continuous emissions monitoring system at the start of commercial operation for new units or by January 1, 1995 for existing units. The system must incorporate continuous monitoring of sulfur dioxide, opacity, nitrogen oxides, and volumetric flow at a minimum. All records of monitoring results, plans, and certification tests must be retained for three years after they are generated.

EXISTING SOURCES OF AIR POLLUTION

When referring to new source performance standards or prevention of significant deterioration provisions, sources that were constructed before the effective date of the rules are often referred to as "grandfathered" sources and traditionally have been exempted from the regulations. However, there are several regulatory provisions that could subject an existing facility to new requirements and even require a facility to modify its operations or add new equipment to comply with the requirements.

Hazardous Air Pollutants

There are three provisions of the HAPs program that should be of particular interest to a municipality. First, any activities involving asbestos, such as demolition of a building or fire department training activities, are subject to the asbestos provisions of the HAPs program. For more information, refer to Chapter 9. Second, any specified source categories under the modified HAPs program, such as sewage sludge incinerators, must apply the maximum achievable control technology (MACT) to control emissions of the hazardous air pollutants. Third, activities involving the storage and use of hazardous chemicals, such as the use of chlorine in water treatment, may require the preparation of a risk management plan.

Maximum Achievable Control Technology

New and existing major sources subject to the HAPs regulations must apply the MACT for the source category in question. Activities associated with fuel combustion, gasoline distribution, and waste treatment and disposal could be subject to the MACT requirements. Industrial process cooling towers are listed under the miscellaneous process category, and the EPA has the authority to regulate many more source categories. For existing sources, MACT is

Table 3   Regulated Hazardous Pollutants
           Requiring Risk Management Plans

Substance	Threshold (lbs.)
Anhydrous ammonia	10,000
Aqueous ammonia	20,000
Bromine	10,000
Chlorine	2,500
Hydrochloric acid	15,000
Hydrogen sulfide	10,000
Sulfuric acid, mixture with sulfur trioxide	10,000
Butane	10,000
Ethane	10,000
Methane	10,000
Propane	10,000
Pentane	10,000

determined by the average emission limitation achieved by the best performing 12 percent of existing sources in a category with 30 or more sources, or the average emission limitation achieved by the best performing 5 sources in a category with fewer than 30 sources.

Risk Management Plans

Pending new rules will establish requirements for the prevention of accidental releases of regulated hazardous substances and the minimization of the consequences of such releases. The EPA is developing regulations to provide guidance for release prevention, detection, and response. The regulations will apply to sources that produce, process, handle, or store hazardous substances above established threshold quantities. They will be required to prepare and implement a risk management plan to detect and prevent or minimize accidental releases of such substances from the stationary source, and to provide a prompt emergency response to any such releases in order to protect human health and the environment. The current list of regulated substances consists of 77 toxic substances and 63 flammable substances. Table 3 shows those substances that are of particular interest to local governments.

Existing Source Acid Rain Provisions

The overall acid rain program is discussed above under the discussion of new or modified sources of air pollution. However, not only do the provisions of 40 C.F.R. 72 affect new facilities, but many existing facilities are subject to the provisions and are required to obtain allowances. (An allowance is an authorization to emit a single ton of SO_2 in a single calendar year.) Similar to other regulatory programs, states have the authority to develop additional, more stringent regulations. Some of the states that are most affected by acid rain, including Massachusetts, Minnesota, New Hampshire, and New York, have adopted their own acid rain legislation that is not displaced by the federal law.

Operating Permit Program

The EPA has developed regulations providing for comprehensive state air quality operating permit programs. The regulations are found at 40 C.F.R. 70. The intent of the regulations is to bring uniformity and consistency to the operating permit programs in each state and to incorporate most aspects of the CAA, including ozone protection, acid rain, air toxics, and compliance with the various programs, under new source review.

The permit application requirements are comprehensive, in order to characterize the current status of the source with all CAA provisions. The information required for a complete application includes general source information, a process description, emissions information, air pollution control requirements, applicable requirements, alternative operating scenarios, compliance plans and certification, and acid rain requirements. Since a new permit is required every five years, the permit application must be prepared every five years.

To comply with state emissions inventory requirements as well as the operating permit program, a municipality must first identify all owned or operated sources. This process should include facility inspections to locate and identify all potential emissions points, including both point and fugitive sources. Emission sources can include any facility, process, or activity or the construction or alteration of any facility, process, or activity from which air pollutants are emitted. Therefore, all facilities, processes, and activities such as combustion units, fuel storage tanks, chemical storage tanks, cooling towers, coal and ash handling operations (including fugitive emissions from haul roads and storage piles), sorbent handling operations, solvent use, miscellaneous painting activities, laboratory hoods, maintenance activities, etc. should be reviewed for sources. Additionally, any proposed new units or sources and any new or retrofitted emissions control equipment should be identified and included. Once sources are identified, operational data should be gathered and reviewed, including identification of emissions control equipment with associated removal efficiencies and any emissions monitoring data available.

MOBILE SOURCE REGULATIONS

There are three primary areas of interest to local governments in reference to mobile source requirements. First, municipally owned vehicle fleets can be affected through the maintenance of vehicle emissions control equipment and compliance with requirements for centrally and alternative-fueled vehicles. Second, a municipality may be involved in mass transportation planning including buses and trains and the new progressive approach of telecommuting or flexible work schedules. The employee trip reduction (ETR) program is one of the requirements that would fall in this category. Third, air quality planning could be a local requirement. Some local governments have appropriated money to pave roads or offer alternative heating devices to reduce particulate levels from gravel roads and wood stoves.

Fleet Vehicles

New automobiles are designed to verify the proper functioning of the air pollution control devices, which must work for 100,000 miles. It is a violation of federal law to disconnect the air pollution control devices on vehicles, even if the vehicle can pass an emissions inspection without the devices. An individual can be fined up to $10,000 per occurrence for removing pollution control devices.

Many states and metropolitan areas have inspection and maintenance programs to make sure that vehicles are adequately maintained to keep pollutant emissions below specified levels. Enhanced inspection and monitoring equipment and procedures are required for many metropolitan areas.

Local governments operating vehicle fleets in areas with poor air quality are required to purchase new, cleaner vehicles beginning in the late 1990s. Many fleet owners may be encouraged, if not required, to purchase vehicles powered by alternative fuels. Alternative fuels could include methanol, ethanol, or natural gas. A covered fleet is defined in the regulations as a fleet of 10 or more motor vehicles under common ownership, excluding law enforcement and other emergency vehicles. The phase-in requirements for fleets require light-duty vehicles in a centrally fueled fleet to consist of at least 30 percent clean-fuel vehicles and alternative-fuel vehicles beginning in 1998 and up to 70 percent by 2000. For heavy-duty trucks, at least 50 percent of the fleet must be clean- or alternative-fuel vehicles beginning in 1998. There are credits that the state can issue to fleet operators with early participation.

Mass Transportation

Mass transportation needs are addressed in a number of ways. Cities have a responsibility to develop a mass transit system consisting of buses, trains, and subways. Those areas with very poor air quality must develop policies to promote the use of the mass transit system. Also, van pools and high occupancy vehicles, typically carrying two or more people, may be provided incentives. Parking surcharges in the downtown areas can discourage unnecessary auto use. Some parking garages in cities with poor air quality offer a discount to those drivers who carry a passenger with them.

The ETR program includes some of the more progressive approaches to dealing with poor air quality such as telecommuting and flexible work schedules. The ETR program applies to any person, firm, educational institution, municipal agency, nonprofit agency, or other entity that employs at least 100 people at a single worksite and is located in an area with very poor air quality, *i.e.*, a severe or extreme ozone nonattainment area. Applicable metropolitan areas include Los Angeles, Baltimore, Chicago, Houston, Milwaukee, New York, Philadelphia, and San Diego.

Air Quality Planning

From mass transportation provisions and route layouts to planning for new roads, each city has a responsibility to keep air quality in mind. Economic growth in an area can result in increased use of automobiles and buses, triggering the need for additional highways and side streets. Prior to taking any action, the city should coordinate with the state air quality division to determine which regulations apply to the proposed activity. For example, construction of a highway or development of a mass transit system could require review under the provisions of new source review found in 40 C.F.R. Part 52.

MUNICIPAL ACTIVITIES AFFECTED BY REGULATIONS

Some of the local government activities that may be subject to regulation under air quality programs are shown in the matrix presented in Figure 2. The matrix covers many major activities and many major regulatory programs, but is not a complete picture of all local government activities. It also does not reflect state or local regulations. Individuals managing compliance with the regulations will find it necessary to check federal, state, district, and county regulations on every issue.

SMALL STATIONARY ENGINES

Local governments typically use small internal combustion engines for various purposes. These combustion engines can include emergency generators, compressors, space heaters, pump stations, fire pumps, and others. Although most of these engines are relatively small in terms of power output and emissions, many states require that they be permitted once they exceed criteria established with respect to size, hours of operation, or emissions. Additionally, some of these stationary engines may have high enough emissions to be subject to operating permit program requirements. A 1-megawatt diesel engine can emit more than 100 tons of nitrogen oxides per year and be subject to these rules if there are no federally enforceable limitations on its operation.

You should review all municipally owned facilities to identify small stationary internal combustion engines. Common facilities include police and fire departments, water treatment plants, and wastewater treatment plants that may use diesel generators for emergency electrical generation, while water and wastewater treatment plants might also use combustion engines for pumping during power outages. Municipal facilities may also use small internal combustion engines for providing space heat, compressed air, and so on. Once the stationary internal combustion sources are identified, you can determine whether they require a state air permit and whether they will be affected by the operating permit program.

STORAGE TANKS AND DISPENSING OPERATIONS

Storage and dispensing of petroleum fuels and other types of volatile organic liquids create emissions of VOCs and HAPs, primarily from "breathing" losses and "working" losses. Breathing losses are caused by the expulsion of vapor due to changes in temperature and barometric pressure, while working losses are caused by the expulsion of vapor from tank filling and emptying operations. VOC emissions from petroleum storage tanks and volatile organic liquid storage tanks are regulated by federal NSPS, while HAPs emissions from these storage tanks will be regulated under NESHAPs for source categories. In addition to technology standards set for these tanks under HAPs regulations, storage of certain hazardous substances exceeding threshold quantities will soon require municipalities to prepare risk management plans. Sources that are subject to either NSPS or NESHAPs are also subject to the provisions of the operating permit program.

SOLID WASTE TREATMENT, STORAGE, AND DISPOSAL

The treatment, storage, and disposal of solid waste involves collecting, transferring, landfilling, composting, recycling, and incinerating. The mobile source emissions dealing with the collection of solid waste are discussed briefly under the Mobile Sources heading. Composting is generally regulated only through state or local programs, where odor control is an issue. In California, even transfer stations and recycling operations can be required to have air permits. This discussion focuses on landfills and incinerators.

Landfills

Landfill operations may be regulated under the PSD and NAA programs as well as by NSPS, NESHAPs, and the operating permit program. The current PSD regulations do not specifically refer to the regulation of landfill gas. However, with the proposed NSPS for landfill gas emissions, landfill gas may become a listed PSD regulated pollutant. The PSD regulations could conceivably apply to emissions of VOCs that can be emitted from a landfill. NAA provisions can apply to the VOC emissions from landfills.

Solid Waste Combustion

The combustion of municipal solid waste is regulated under PSD, NAA, NESHAPs, and NSPS, and there is considerable overlap among these pro-

Activity	Prevention of Significant Deterioration	Nonattainment Area Provision	Minor Source Provisions	New Source Performance Standards	National Emission Standards for Hazardous Air Pollutants	Operating Permit Program	Risk Management Planning
Airport Construction/Operation	•	•	•				•
Chilling, Refrigeration, Air Conditioning							
Compressing/Pumping		•	•		•	•	
Electric Generation	•	•	•	•	•	•	•
Emergency Generation		•	•	•	•	•	•
Employee Commuting (100 or more)							
Fire Department Training			•				
Fire/Police Hazmat Storage							•
Flaring/Process Heating		•	•		•	•	•
Fleet Maintenance							
Fleet Purchasing							

Figure 2 Matrix of municipal activities and potential air regulations (• = potential federal/state/county local regulations).

Activity	Prevention of Significant Deterioration	Nonattainment Area Provision	Minor Source Provisions	New Source Performance Standards	National Emission Standards for Hazardous Air Pollutants	Operating Permit Program	Risk Management Planning
Mass Transit Planning			•				
Sewage Sludge Handling & Incineration	•	•	•	•	•	•	•
Solid Waste Combustion	•	•	•	•	•	•	•
Solid Waste Handling			•				
Solid Waste Landfilling	•	•	•	•	•	•	
Space Heating		•	•			•	
Street Sanding/Salting			•				
Street Sweeping/Maintenance			•		•		
Wastewater Treatment		•	•			•	•

Activity	Acid Rain Provisions	Employee Trip Reduction Program	Vehicle Emissions Control	Alternative and Centrally Fueled Vehicle Requirements	Regional Air Quality Planning	Ozone Depletion Provisions
Airport Construction/Operation		•			•	
Chilling, Refrigeration, Air Conditioning						•
Compressing/Pumping						
Electric Generation	•		•	•		
Emergency Generation						
Employee Commuting (100 or more)		•				
Fire Department Training						
Fire/Police Hazmat Storage						
Flaring/Process Heating						
Fleet Maintenance			•	•	•	
Fleet Purchasing		•	•	•	•	

Figure 2, cont. Matrix of municipal activities and potential air regulations (• = potential federal/state/county local regulations).

Activity	Acid Rain Provisions	Employee Trip Reduction Program	Vehicle Emissions Control	Alternative and Centrally Fueled Vehicle Requirements	Regional Air Quality Planning	Ozone Depletion Provisions
Fuel/Chemical Storage and Displacing				•		
Mass Transit Planning			•	•	•	
Solid Waste Combustion	•		•			
Solid Waste Handling			•	•		•
Solid Waste Landfilling			•			
Space Heating						
Street Sanding/Salting			•	•	•	
Street Sweeping/Maintenance		•	•	•		
Wastewater Treatment						
Water Treatment						

Figure 2, cont.   Matrix of municipal activities and potential air regulations (• = potential federal/state/county local regulations).

grams. A municipal waste combustor (MWC) capable of charging more than 250 tons per day of waste is subject to PSD review if emissions of a PSD-regulated pollutant exceed 100 tons per year. An MWC of capacity smaller than 250 tons per day is subject to PSD review if emissions of a PSD-regulated pollutant exceed 250 tons per year. MWC organics, metals, and acid gases are listed PSD-regulated pollutants with specified significant emission rates (see Table 2). Therefore, for example, emissions of sulfur dioxide and hydrogen chloride from an MWC should be added together and compared to the significant emission rates to determine PSD applicability. Applicability of NAA new source review for an MWC is dependent on the status and severity of the nonattainment area and the amount of emissions from the MWC unit.

Both existing and new large MWC facilities with plantwide charging capacities exceeding 250 tons of municipal solid waste or refuse-derived fuel per day became subject to new emissions regulations in 1991. Emissions limits for existing units restrict emissions of particulates, dioxins, furans, sulfur dioxide, hydrogen chloride, and carbon monoxide. The minimum controls that may be required for each unit include good combustion practices, a spray dryer or dry sorbent injection, and an electrostatic precipitator. In addition to all of the pollutants with emissions limits for existing units, new units must meet emissions limitations for nitrogen oxides. The basis for controlling emissions from new units includes good combustion practices, spray dryer, fabric filter, and ammonia injection. Annual stack tests and continuous emissions monitoring systems are required, with an additional monitor for nitrogen oxides. The EPA must revise the standards for new and existing units to include mercury, lead, and cadmium. The EPA also must promulgate standards by September 1, 1995, for new and existing MWC units with plantwide charging capacities between 40 and 250 tons per day.

WATER AND WASTEWATER TREATMENT FACILITIES

Wastewater treatment plants are regulated under NSPS regulations that establish requirements for sludge incineration. Recently air emissions-related regulations have been imposed on water and wastewater treatment plants. Volatile air emissions, including VOCs and HAPs, from processes such as wastewater treatment and sludge handling operations are now regulated. Additionally, in response to pending regulations concerning the prevention of accidental releases of hazardous substances, many municipal water and wastewater treatment facilities may be required to prepare risk management plans.

Sewage Sludge Incineration

Sewage sludge incineration can be regulated through PSD, NAA, NESHAPs, and NSPS. The general PSD and NAA provisions are described above. A sewage sludge incinerator is subject to PSD review if emissions from the facility are projected to exceed 250 tons per year. A sewage sludge incinerator's classification as a major source under the NAA provisions will depend on the status and severity of the nonattainment area and the quantity of emissions from the incinerator.

A new or existing sewage sludge incinerator is subject to the Part 503 requirements including pollutant limits, management practices, and monitoring requirements. Subpart E applies to the generator of the sewage sludge as well as the owner and operator of the incinerator. Thus, a generator must prepare the sludge to meet the requirements specified in the permit for the incinerator. Limits for emissions of arsenic, beryllium, cadmium, chromium, lead, mercury, and nickel from a sewage sludge incinerator are established based on dispersion modeling or performance testing or both.

Wastewater Treatment and Nonattainment Areas

Certain municipal wastewater treatment plants with emissions above specified minimum levels and located in nonattainment areas may be required to apply Reasonably Available Control Technology (RACT) to limit VOC emissions from operations such as wastewater treatment and sludge handling. This requirement can result from a state's efforts to attain and maintain compliance with ambient air quality standards by requiring existing sources to retrofit pollution control equipment.

Wastewater Treatment and HAPs

Many municipal wastewater treatment facilities will likely be affected by new HAP emissions regulations, as the EPA's initial list of categories of major and area sources of HAP emissions includes publicly owned treatment works. A draft MACT standard for wastewater treatment is expected to be issued by the EPA in 1995. Note that, whatever the MACT standard, control of air emissions from municipal wastewater treatment will be affected by the industry's ability to pretreat its wastewater discharges. MACT standards set for various industries should reduce the amount of VOCs and other pollutants in the municipal wastewater stream. In any case, it is advisable to gather as much information as possible relating to the air emissions at municipal wastewater treatment facilities in order to develop a compliance plan. This effort can be tied in with emissions inventory requirements.

Water and Wastewater Risk Management Plans

Many municipal wastewater treatment plants may be required to prepare risk management plans due to the types of chemicals commonly stored at these facilities. To prevent accidental releases of regulated substances, the EPA will promulgate regulations and guidance for release prevention, detection, and response. The regulations will be effective three years after promulgation or three years after the date on which a substance in quantities greater than threshold amounts at the source is listed as a regulated substance, whichever is later. Regulated substances commonly found at water and wastewater treatment facilities are shown in Table 3 along with their threshold quantities.

Gas Flares and Other Sources

Water and wastewater treatment plants may have other air pollution sources such as emergency generators and pumps, methane flares, and heaters. Some of these sources may require permits and calculation of emissions for purposes of meeting emissions inventory requirements.

MOBILE SOURCES

Municipal vehicles can include maintenance vehicles for electric, water, and sewer; parks and recreation vehicles; road sweepers; sanding and salting trucks; mass transit buses and support vehicles; and police department and fire department vehicles. Additionally, you may have a fleet of automobiles for city staff. Although law enforcement and emergency vehicles are exempt from some of the fleet vehicle requirements, each local government should evaluate its vehicle fleets and the regulations to assure compliance.

MAINTENANCE ACTIVITIES

Since street maintenance activities such as sweeping, sanding, and salting operations and maintenance of dirt and gravel roads have potential air impacts, they may be subject to air emission regulations. Additionally, street painting and paint booths may also be regulated. There are currently no federal regulations that cover these operations, but state regulations are common.

FIRE AND POLICE DEPARTMENT ACTIVITIES

Fire departments typically conduct training exercises to prepare firefighters for an actual event. Specific federal requirements do not exist for such exercises; however, many states either exempt such activities or have specific regulations governing them.

Fire and police departments may have occasion to store hazardous materials taken during a raid or similar incident. Such hazardous materials may subject the fire and police departments to specific requirements under the federal or state air regulations. If the stored materials are listed in the accident release prevention regulations and present in quantities exceeding the thresholds, a risk management plan may be required for the storage area.

AIRPORT OPERATIONS

The air regulations can encompass many of the operations at a municipal airport. For example, an airport might have emergency generators and fuel storage tanks subject to the regulations. Constructing a new airport may also be subject to the federal new source program under 40 C.F.R. Part 52. The new source regulations for airports are highly specialized and are not discussed in detail in this chapter. If a city is planning the construction of a new airport, those regulations should be reviewed for applicability.

CHILLERS, REFRIGERATION, AND AIR CONDITIONING

The EPA regulates pollutants that are suspected of depleting stratospheric ozone. These pollutants include chlorofluorocarbons, hydrochlorofluorocarbons, and others. The regulations restrict the use and discharge of these pollutants for certain activities. Releasing the pollutants into the environment is considered illegal and such action could result in fines or imprisonment for the individual carrying out such action. Municipal property that could be subject to the ozone depletion regulations could include ice rinks, large refrigeration units, and air conditioning units. A municipality that maintains its own vehicles could be subject to the regulations when repairing a vehicle's air conditioning system.

ELECTRIC GENERATING STATIONS

Electric generation is subject to various air emission regulations depending on the size of the facility, the location of the facility, and the amount of pollution it emits. An electric generating station could be subject to prevention of significant deterioration provisions; nonattainment area requirements; new source performance standards (NSPS); acid rain provisions; hazardous air pollutant emissions standards; accidental release program requirements; and the Part 70 operating permit program.

CONCLUSION

The air regulations are complex and have many far-reaching effects on a municipality's activities. From the generation of electricity to the purchase of vehicles that operate on alternative fuels, the individual responsible for maintaining the municipality's compliance with air regulations has a number of complex issues to consider concurrently.

PART III

Compliance and
Risk Management Issues

Establishing Environmental Compliance Programs

John M. McNurney and David R. Meyer

Local governments are on the front line of environmental problems for several reasons. First, a local government wears two hats with respect to environmental issues: it is both a functional entity which is a significant source of pollution and a regulator which must protect its environment for the benefit of its citizens. Second, local governments represent and act at the pleasure of their constituents, who increasingly demand protection of the community's natural resources and strict environmental compliance. Third, local government operations are regulated by federal and state environmental agencies, and sometimes by municipal ordinance, and applicable requirements have multiplied exponentially in the last decade. These facts place local governments at the center of numerous environmental conflicts that demand immediate attention. Municipalities, with their multiple identities, including polluter, representative of the populace, regulatee, and regulator, have special incentives to develop and maintain an effective environmental compliance program and must do so under the watchful eyes of the press and their citizens.

There are a number of reasons a compliance program makes good sense. First, the design and implementation of compliance programs enable a local government to demonstrate a clear commitment to the public by making every effort to protect health and the environment. Municipal operations such as landfills and wastewater treatment plants are an integral and important part of the communities where they operate. In this era of heightened public concern about environmental protection — especially with respect to toxic pollution — local governments pay a high public relations price for noncompliance. Furthermore, as a regulator, cities must set an example for local businesses.

A second reason for having an effective compliance program is to minimize expensive legal liabilities. Violations of the law involving hazards to public health and pollution of natural resources can lead to enforcement actions by regulatory agencies involving hundreds of thousands of dollars in civil penalties. In the worst cases, management can even face criminal penalties.

The local government can be ordered by a court to clean up the contamination, at a cost of millions of dollars, for even relatively small quantities of toxins that have, for instance, contaminated groundwater supplies. Such violations give ammunition to citizens who use potentially contaminated natural resources as grounds for a lawsuit seeking damages under state laws, claiming that the pollution adversely affected their health or damaged their property.

The EPA and most state agencies encourage the initiation of systematic environmental compliance programs including audit procedures. These agencies realize that they cannot possibly review the performance of all the regulated industries under their jurisdiction and that internal compliance programs are a real, long-term solution to effective environmental compliance. Because of their wish to encourage the development of such programs, government officials conducting an enforcement review of a given city may take the existence of such a program into consideration in determining whether and how to assess penalties for violations of the law. In short, if a city sets up a good program it may get significant credit for it if the city is ever inspected for compliance by the government. In fact, the EPA has increasingly written assessment and compliance programs into its consent agreements with alleged violators and the EPA may be willing to decrease penalties in exchange for such provisions.

A final benefit of an effective compliance program is that it may help a city convince an insurance company to write insurance for future environmental impairment liability. Difficulties in obtaining insurance for such liability is one of the most pressing problems facing cities, counties, and towns today.

An effective compliance program for a local government logically consists of four key activities:

- Determine the city's environmental compliance goals.
- Assess where your local government stands on compliance.
- Attain compliance.
- Maintain compliance.

DETERMINING ENVIRONMENTAL COMPLIANCE GOALS

The compliance goals of each local government will vary, depending on the overall policy objectives and the availability of resources. These parameters will also fluctuate in accordance with changes in the elected governing body and national and local economic conditions.

There are several possible goals of municipal compliance programs:

- Protecting human health and the environment as responsible public officials.
- Enhancing the local government's public image.
- Avoiding or limiting liability under federal and state laws.
- Setting up an effective internal management structure to maintain compliance.
- Obtaining insurance.

Activities can be designed to range from taking only those steps absolutely necessary to comply with current regulations to risk reduction activities that are not mandated by law. Obviously, locating yourself at the first end of the spectrum can be cheaper at first, but you risk higher, long-term costs in the form of cleanup liability or expensive retrofits. The other extreme (nonmandated activities such as compliance with guidelines or anticipated requirements) may have high short-term costs, but long-term risks are substantially reduced.

The commitment of management, including both appointed and elected officials, affects the selection of a compliance strategy. Each decision must be supported by incentives, resources, and adequate organization. Incentives include verbal and written policies to inform employees that environmental compliance is an important part of their jobs. They should also include positive and negative reinforcement communicated to employees through periodic performance reviews. Compliance programs need both human and financial resources. At a minimum, qualified personnel must be assigned to coordinate compliance efforts among municipal departments, maintain records, and constantly evaluate performance.

ASSESSING COMPLIANCE STATUS

Assessing where you stand is often the trickiest part of beginning an effective program. Most local government managers have made some effort to talk with personnel about the importance of environmental compliance and to implement some procedures for assuring compliance. However, new developments in environmental laws and regulations happen so frequently, and are often so complicated, that these initial efforts may quickly become outdated. Also, a city may be concerned that their compliance is not what it should be, but may not know how to address the problem and get its organization into better shape in this area.

The first step in assessing where a city stands is to review some key compliance requirements and then arrive at a judgment about how the city compares. The following questions give some idea of where to start in the evaluation of a city's status:

- Where does the community landfill its garbage? Was industrial waste co-disposed there? What must be done to bring the landfill into compliance with EPA regulations?
- Is there a municipal airport? What kind of activities are lessees conducting on the land? Remember cities are fully liable for problems lessees create.
- Does local government have any problems with asbestos in the civic or convention center or in local schools?
- Does the city audit property before purchase? Has a government or private party ever given the city a gift of land?

- Are both fire and police hazmat teams fully trained, especially to coordinate with each other? Does each team member have protective equipment that is well-maintained?
- Are there underground tanks to store fuel? Have notices been filed with state authorities? Have plans been made to upgrade them?
- Who is in charge of responding to spills of oil or hazardous substances, and what procedures do they follow in such emergencies?
- Do local government operations generate hazardous wastes? Have municipal officials checked the status of all materials thrown away?
- Does the city dispose of wastes such as used oil or discarded solvents in full compliance with federal and state requirements? How are disposal contractors chosen? Who reviews contracts to make sure they protect the city from liability for future cleanup costs?
- Is there an ongoing program for monitoring the local government's compliance with water discharge and air emissions permits?
- Where are records of compliance with respect to each of these activities? Are they complete? If the city had to show those records to a government official tomorrow morning in order to demonstrate compliance with the law, how would he or she react?

If a city is not satisfied with answers to any of these important questions, or does not completely understand what employees are doing with respect to each one, there may be compliance problems.

A second set of questions to ask in assessing the state of compliance involves the skills of the personnel in charge of such efforts:

- Who is officially in charge of ongoing compliance efforts? Who supervises this individual?
- Who is in charge of maintaining records of compliance? If more than one person is in charge of the various aspects of environmental compliance mentioned above, how does this team coordinate?
- Has someone been assigned to take charge of such emergency events as an unforeseen chemical spill?
- Do senior managers understand the importance of environmental compliance, and are they working to educate employees about such requirements? Is there sufficient personnel so that these employees have time to include the activities necessary for compliance with environmental regulations among other normal activities? If not, is it possible to add new personnel or reorganize existing personnel to get more resources for environmental compliance activities?
- Who is in charge of disposing of hazardous wastes? What steps is that person taking to make sure that these waste materials are properly handled and disposed of after they leave the facility?
- Who coordinates compliance among branches of city government? Are people working effectively with others in the city engaged in similar activities?

The more goals an assessment program is to fulfill, the more ambitious compliance activities should be. The public may be more impressed by a comprehensive formal program. Elected officials may also have more confidence in such a program. Some insurance companies will only consider formal assessments performed by trained outside professionals when underwriting insurance policies.

IDENTIFYING AN APPROPRIATE COMPLIANCE PROGRAM

After identifying the goals of a program and evaluating the nature and scope of internal management challenges, consider the three basic types of compliance programs:

- *Informal internal assessment.* This type of program involves use of a city's own employees to figure out where problems are and what can be done to correct them. The employees may carry out these functions on an informal basis, reporting verbally to management about their progress. Employee training is a crucial component of this type of program.
- *Formal internal environmental assessment.* This type of program generally involves the preparation of written questionnaires, which are systematically answered on the basis of a careful review of the local government's activities, and possible omissions of activities required under the law. Once the questionnaire is completed, a formal written report is prepared which contains recommendations to management of steps to be taken to solve problems. The questionnaire and report can be prepared and completed by management, or by personnel under the supervision of management. Once again, employee training is crucial.
- *Consultation with outside professionals.* This type of program involves hiring outside experts to analyze the city's compliance with environmental laws and regulations. These experts visit the local government's facilities, interview key personnel, and review relevant records. They then prepare a final report with recommendations and, depending on contractual arrangements, may work with the city on an ongoing basis to develop programs to improve compliance. Bringing in outsiders to conduct an assessment of a local government's compliance may be advantageous, depending on the program goals identified by management.

The key factor affecting the choice of what type of compliance assessment program will best suit a city's needs — that is, whether to go the self-assessment route or hire outside consultants — is the nature and scope of internal management organization and personnel capabilities.

If the local government is small and has very limited resources, the most realistic choice may be self-assessment. On the other hand, if the city is small, and officials suspect major compliance problems, an outside consultant may be necessary in order to avoid the problems that arise when the assessment is done by the same employees who must improve their performance. In such situations, management may not have the time or the resources to conduct the assessment process itself.

Even for larger cities, there are definite advantages and disadvantages in the self-assessment route. Larger cities are likely to have more personnel to devote to the assessment process and can therefore avoid the problem of having personnel evaluate their own performance. With large staffs, managers may be able to audit one another. However, if there are several people involved in compliance efforts, and they are not well coordinated, management may wish to bring in an outside expert to assist by conducting an assessment and organizing subsequent in-house reviews.

Once again, selecting the type of program that best suits a city's needs involves a variety of factors including goals, resources, and available personnel. As all of these factors are weighed and a final decision is reached, city officials should remember that an assessment without action to solve the problems that are discovered is worse than no assessment at all. Before launching an assessment program, a city must make sure it has the resources and top management commitment to back it up. Municipal officials should take the time to sell the value and importance of the program to city management to get the necessary resources.

SEEKING OUTSIDE ASSISTANCE

It sometimes makes sense to seek outside help to assess compliance because a report prepared by an outsider may have greater credibility with employees and impress upon them the importance of compliance efforts. An outside report may also help convince elected officials to allocate sufficient funds for full compliance efforts.

Two types of professionals generally provide assessment services. First, engineers with an expertise in environmental compliance issues can help assess the status of facilities and recommend the implementation of both procedures and technologies to bring activities into compliance with the law. Second, attorneys with an expertise in environmental laws and regulations can help determine whether a city is following the requirements set forth in the complex maze of federal and state regulations, and can evaluate the city's contracts and agreements related to compliance and risk of liability.

If an attorney is involved in conducting the assessment, the results may be protected by attorney/client privilege. The privilege makes correspondence with a lawyer confidential so that clients can have full and effective representation. This confidentiality means that, if an enforcement action begins, a municipality will usually not need to turn over the results of the assessment to the government. Of course, the attorney/client privilege does not remove a city's obligation under some federal laws to report known violations, especially permit violations.

All of this discussion should not be interpreted to mean that there is only one good way to go about setting up an effective internal — or external — compliance program. Some local governments have established a formal assessment process, independent of their normal operations. Other local governments weave environmental concerns into their daily operations without resorting to an independent, formal assessment process. Either approach can be equally effective. The selection must depend on the "personality" of a city and what resources are available.

Despite all these clear benefits of an effective compliance assessment program, one crucial point must be kept in mind. No one should begin a compliance program and fail to follow through with the actions that are necessary to remedy problems discovered during the assessment. If a city launches an effort to find out whether it is complying with the law, discovers problems with compliance, and then fails to do anything about them, the situation in any future enforcement action will be much worse. Lack of knowledge about compliance problems is never a defense to an enforcement action by the EPA or a state agency. However, knowing that there are problems and failing to do anything about them can mean tougher civil penalties and can even lead to criminal penalties in some cases.

ACHIEVING COMPLIANCE

Once an internal or external assessment has determined that there are areas in which a local government is not in full compliance, it is essential to identify a means for bringing it into compliance. Compliance is typically achieved through the following steps:

- Identify alternatives.
- Evaluate the alternatives, considering costs, a reasonable schedule, and the risks of noncompliance.
- Develop a plan for funding and conducting the necessary work.
- Carry out the plan with specific review sessions to confirm progress of the work.

First, achieving compliance is not just a matter of spending more money. The job requires a top-to-bottom commitment by management to free up personnel, to carry out required activities, to reorganize work assignments, and to make tough management decisions about the appropriate people who must be given authority to organize the compliance effort.

Second, in many cases, it will be clear just what must be done to achieve compliance. For instance, failure to label hazardous wastes properly can be corrected by testing and labeling questionable drums. However, if more complex problems are identified, it may be appropriate to explore a full range of options. In such cases, it may be a good idea to increase the city's base of knowledge by comparing notes with other cities in a similar situation or using a consultant with experience in the proper technical area.

Third, a compliance program must include a schedule that recognizes the urgency of rectifying hazards to human health and the environment, and that minimizes to the greatest extent possible future liability and penalties. Clearly, more funds should be made available and a shorter schedule should be followed in instances where human health is at risk, where noncompliance is likely to be detected early, or where fines and liabilities may be large.

Finally, a compliance plan is likely to result in the minimization of potential problems. Not only is such an effort good business, but, if an enforcement action is begun, documentation of timely progress toward compliance can be useful in negotiating a settlement with the agency.

The importance of keeping careful, complete, and accurate records of all compliance activities cannot be overemphasized. A city cannot prove it is in compliance or moving toward compliance without a careful written record of the efforts it has made to ensure that fact.

Too often, local governments launch ambitious compliance efforts, but ignore this essential aspect. Employees inspect facilities, test, and take precautions in handling material, but never write down a description of any of these activities. If the local government's operations are ever investigated by regulatory officials, this lack of written records means that — from an enforcement perspective — the local government will not only be denied credit for its efforts, but could face penalties for apparently failing to take action required under the law.

Because municipalities operate in the public eye, and many records are subject to sunshine laws or other disclosure requirements, some employees may tend to avoid creating paper trails. Management must educate employees to overcome these instincts when documenting environmental compliance.

MAINTAINING COMPLIANCE

Maintaining compliance relies on the establishment of standard procedures for constantly checking compliance and correcting deviations. Both assessment results and compliance goals change over time. The situation in various city departments will change as services and facilities are added or dropped. Policy goals are revised as appointed and elected officials are replaced. Federal and state environmental regulations have become both stringent and complex, and there is little sign these trends will change.

Monitoring and maintaining compliance requires management commitment as well as financial resources. Even small problems can be expensive to correct, but failing to correct them can cost far more over the long run.

One of the first steps in maintaining compliance over the long run involves setting up an effective chain of command within the city, and instituting periodic performance reviews by top management. Most cities have some structure for reviewing employees' performance and giving periodic pay raises.

Management should consider conscientious pursuit of environmental compliance as an element of such performance evaluations.

Second, to implement an internal program, management must put in place routine procedures for evaluating compliance for all city departments. For example, departments may conduct monthly or semi-monthly staff meetings, and environmental compliance should be a regular item on that agenda. In small cities, personnel can be asked to make regular reports to their management on their success in completing assigned portions of the compliance program.

Apart from giving personnel appropriate incentives to make environmental compliance a priority, the key to maintaining compliance is routine, periodic reviews of the local government's overall compliance situation. Unless a city reviews compliance periodically, a situation can develop where violations begin to occur.

Achieving an ongoing commitment to maintaining compliance will not be easy. Especially for small cities, the press of daily business can push environmental concerns onto the back burner. However, as in so many areas of local government operations, problems put off today are double trouble tomorrow.

CHAPTER 15

Environmental Compliance: Management and Staff Considerations

Todd W. Filsinger

The 1980s brought heightened public and governmental awareness of a wide variety of environmental issues. Scientific research on the depletion of the ozone layer, the greenhouse effect, air quality, and soil and groundwater contamination has brought environmental protection to the forefront of business and government agendas. The mandate from society to operate in an environmentally responsible manner is growing each month. This strong public sentiment has led to stiffer environmental regulations and increasingly severe penalties for noncompliance.

Effective environmental compliance programs are an increasingly important part of local government compliance strategies, and management systems must be in place to assure compliance at each appropriate municipal departmental level. There are several management considerations inherent in establishing a successful environmental compliance program.

PROGRAM DEVELOPMENT

A proactive local government leadership develops its own environmental compliance program or establishes a separate compliance department, hedging its risks before disaster happens. Prudent operation of *all* municipalities, both now and for the foreseeable future, must include an environmental compliance program.

To develop an effective in-house environmental compliance program, several goals and objectives are of utmost importance. A formal, organization-wide written environmental compliance policy should be adopted. The policy should set specific, practical goals that are realistically achievable, and spell out the risks of noncompliance. These policies and procedures should be clearly communicated from upper management to individual departments and employees.

1-56670-098-1/95/$0.00+$.50
© 1995 by CRC Press, Inc.

An effective program must also track compliance with environmental permits and approvals. Employees should be able to assess the magnitude of legal or financial risks from current operations and proposed changes. Accessible, complete, and current files are imperative. Staff in charge of the program must have sufficient authority to act and to require compliance from all divisions and departments. Accordingly, the environmental officer must be so placed in the hierarchy that it is clear he or she enjoys top management support and can deal effectively with department heads.

PROGRAM MANAGEMENT

Several management functions must be considered in developing an environmental compliance program. Some of these are further discussed in Chapter 14.

A number of basic principles of good organization have been developed and tested during recent decades. Many of these principles, including purpose, mission, goal objectives, and communications, are directly applicable to organizing and developing an environmental compliance department. If your local government is large enough, you may have several employees charged with environmental compliance responsibilities. For smaller cities and towns, environmental responsibilities may be assigned to a committee of department heads, or even to a single person. Regardless of the size of the unit, the same management principles apply when the unit is working to gain the cooperation of all departments.

Your compliance program must have a clear purpose. While the environmental unit's reason for being may seem obvious, a clearly defined statement of purpose or mission statement should be developed and communicated to employees throughout the department.

Each employee within the environmental department should have a clear concept of how his or her role contributes to the achievement of overall objectives and goals of the department. Employees should not only be apprised of the group's basic purpose and high-level objectives, they should help develop departmental objectives and goals that support the overall mission. Duties and responsibilities should be clearly defined and described in written position descriptions, as a lack of clear definition increases the likelihood of conflicts. Employees in other departments should also understand the purpose of the environmental unit and how their own jobs affect the achievement of overall environmental compliance.

STAFFING ENVIRONMENTAL COMPLIANCE PROGRAMS

The size and staffing of an environmental compliance program will be specific to the organization and will depend on the many variables distinguishing one organization from another. Some factors influencing the size of the environmental staff are in-house expertise, size of service territory, number of employees, type of operation, the level of regulation, and current policies and procedures. The environmental compliance staff must be large enough to carry out its functions in a timely manner.

If your environmental unit will perform audits, it may require a larger staff because of its simultaneous involvement with numerous departments and personnel. If an external auditing program is needed, there is the additional requirement that the department be involved with other organizations.

One of the most common complaints among environmental managers is the limited size of their staffs. In general, most large municipal operations that currently have compliance programs have relatively small staffs representing less than one percent of total municipal employees, and many smaller municipalities have only one environmental staff person. It is also critical to focus on the qualifications of individuals staffing the unit. The environmental coordinator should have significant previous regulatory experience with environmental compliance. Giving the job to a low-paid staffer with no experience is a sure path to compliance problems.

KEY ELEMENTS OF AN EFFECTIVE PROGRAM

The success of an environmental compliance program is not necessarily contingent on the management structures, but rather on the acceptance of the program within the city. The ultimate success of an environmental compliance program can be categorized in the context of:

- Commitment
- Communication
- Cooperation

COMMITMENT

One of the most important aspects of a successful environmental program is the city's commitment to the program. A program cannot survive merely as a response to regulatory pressure. The city, from the governing body down to the line personnel, must be committed to environmental compliance. Simply creating an environmental division can give rise to numerous and unnecessary barriers resulting from resistance to organizational change.

Thus, as the environmental concept is implemented or expanded, it is crucial to receive input from all levels and to get a sincere commitment from the local government's governing body and management staff. This commitment can initially be secured through interactive work sessions and/or meetings and through facilitated consensus building sessions. Other suggested mechanisms to achieve commitment are surveys, monthly meetings with each department, environmental task forces, and advisory bodies that cross all division boundaries.

COMMUNICATION

An important aspect of a successful environmental compliance program is communication. Communication includes one-on-one conversation, communication of ideas through training, written communication, and recordkeeping. An environmental department should be structured so that it facilitates continuous and consistent communication throughout the organization.

The first step in the communication process should be the development of a mission statement for the city's environmental process. The mission should not be a top-down mandate, but rather should reflect the views of all the city departments. The mission statement should be clearly communicated through all levels of the organization, both verbally and in written form. It is generally effective to publish the mission statement so that the city, the employees, and the citizens of the community understand the goals and direction of the city's environmental commitment.

Simply enforcing environmental compliance is no longer enough. Employee training is a crucial means of communicating the tools necessary to assist members of the staff to successfully implement an environmental program. This training can provide personnel with an understanding of the risks and solutions associated with environmental issues. Training can help facilitate external and internal communication, effective methods of dealing with environmental regulation and policy changes, awareness of potential liabilities, and problem recognition.

COOPERATION

Many local governments have not had proactive environmental programs in the past. Thus, the implementation of an aggressive program is generally a significant change within the organization. Change often results in resistance. It is very important to understand the dynamics within an organization as change is introduced. It is not uncommon for various departments to participate in power struggles with respect to environmental responsibilities. Many times personnel will claim ownership of the responsibilities within their sphere of influence and are adverse to sharing information with outside departments for fear they will lose responsibilities. Often employees will conceal critical information to strengthen their individual positions. The effect of the internal power struggle can be devastating for the overall organization. As a result, it is important to have the entire organization fully involved in the process of implementing change. The formation of environmental task forces or advisory groups consisting of personnel from various departments and the ability of critical personnel to participate in the process and to contribute to the effort will be vital to acceptance of the change.

Another key to ensuring cooperation throughout the organization is the selection of "champions" of the environmental effort. Effective leadership within the ranks will be vital. It is important that individuals in the organization who will provide leadership for the program are "on board" early.

PROGRAM DESIGN

For each area of regulatory compliance (hazardous waste, pesticides, etc.), the following activities should be considered:

- Developing policy and procedure
- Implementation
- Maintaining the programs and updating them as regulations change
- Inspecting and auditing the various divisions, including external audits if applicable, and instituting follow-up action based on the audit results
- Training department heads and employees in environmental compliance theory and practice

These programs can be organized within the environmental department in a number of ways; however, to enhance objectivity, auditing should be kept separate from other compliance activities. Two of the basic functions of the environmental department are the environmental services function and the auditing function.

ENVIRONMENTAL SERVICES

The environmental services division develops policies and procedures and trains all employees. The division is also responsible for ensuring that each local government department uses standardized environmental procedures that comply with federal, state, and local regulations.

Each operating division should establish a documented training program, whether administered by staff or by an outside firm. Periodic refresher training is also recommended to keep procedures and requirements fresh in employees' minds, and to incorporate any changes in procedures or regulations.

AUDITING

The audit function serves to review the compliance of the various municipal divisions with the procedures established by the environmental services division. Auditors also recommend changes in procedures to bring the various departments into compliance and follow up to assure that the recommended changes have been made. Auditing reveals strengths and weaknesses in management systems as a whole, giving management the opportunity to address problems early.

Many local governments contract with outside consultants to perform auditing functions. For further information on the benefits of an audit and what your municipality can gain from one, review Chapter 14.

PROGRAM ORGANIZATION

An environmental compliance program must fit into a municipality's over-all organization in a manner that allows it to operate effectively through existing lines of authority and communication. We have seen environmental departments organized in several distinct ways:

- Environmental staff are employees of various operating departments, report-ing directly to the head of the department to which they are assigned. In addition, a champion of the overall environmental program reports to the city manager. This champion may be an individual or a task force or advisory group that oversees the city's program and handles public relations.
- An environmental coordinator position within each division handles specific functions for the department.
- The environmental department is a separate entity at the same level as other departments reporting to the city manager, with the director having the same level of authority as the director of public works, director of utilities, etc.
- The environmental department is a division of another department (such as the utility department), but the environmental director reports directly to the city manager or department director.

Whatever organizational structure is chosen should promote free exchange of information among divisions. Many local governments with effective envi-ronmental programs have hired employees and directors who are dedicated to environmental preservation. As this attitude spreads throughout an organiza-tion, the environmental department's job becomes easier. To secure commit-ment by department managers, the environmental manager should meet with each department and division, explain the program, seek their ideas for imple-mentation, clearly define the costs and benefits, and explain how the environ-mental program applies to their department operations.

CONCLUSION

Local governments should consider establishing an environmental depart-ment to ensure their compliance with federal, state, and local regulations. The costs of operating such a unit may well be less than the cost of the penalties for noncompliance.

The creation of an environmental department can and should be presented as a forward-looking, coordinated effort, not as a knee-jerk response to a regulatory threat. This approach will gain the support of officials and management, as well as commitment from the community to support environmental issues.

CHAPTER **16**

Risk Communication in the Context of Environmental Planning

Susan K. Lawson

People instinctively fear the unknown. When the unknown concerns hazardous materials or other threats to public health and safety, what people don't know can hurt everyone. Over the last two decades, there has been a growing public suspicion of technology and its side effects. Highly publicized environmental disasters like Three Mile Island, Love Canal, and the Valdez oil spill have fueled this public distrust and increased skepticism about the government's willingness and ability to protect the public from serious threat.

Many communities that once viewed public works facilities, power plants, and manufacturing plants as sources of valued services and jobs now feel vulnerable to the possibility that these same facilities could pose an unassessed or, worse, an undisclosed threat. In fact, people are most outraged when they perceive that they are being deceived or incompletely informed about hazards in their midst. A community that feels that it has reason to suspect a cover-up by industry or local government officials may react far more strongly than the potential threat warrants. Moreover, once distrust has set in, the damage to a municipality's credibility may be difficult to repair.

At the same time, public officials who must respond to an angry public may also experience frustration and resentment as they try to convey complex technical information in an emotionally charged atmosphere. An official's obvious discomfort, defensiveness, or even shyness can aggravate, rather than calm, a tense situation.

Public officials can address these challenges by adopting a proactive attitude toward communication with the public they serve. In the past, it was not uncommon for public agencies to talk *at* the public, rather than communicating *with* citizens about potential hazards. All too often, whether the project is a water treatment facility or an asbestos removal project, the prevailing attitude has been to "protect" citizens, divulging only the minimum required — and no sooner than necessary.

1-56670-098-1/95/$0.00+$.50
© 1995 by CRC Press, Inc.

Now, in the wake of several disasters, there is a growing understanding that technology cannot always protect the communities it serves and that communities have a right to know both the benefits and risks associated with a given installation. In this atmosphere, officials are finding they can better address public concern, instill confidence, and rebuild trust by conscientiously informing and involving residents from the earliest stages of a project or a release.

An open approach should include proactive, forthright communication about environmental and health risks and can include programs to both educate the public and offer concerned citizens an opportunity to participate in related discussions and decisions. In a number of national and state agencies, proactive public communication is now recognized as a formal component of project and facility management.

Though nothing can guarantee public acceptance, a well-designed, ongoing, two-way communication process can increase the chances for a confident, informed public response if an emergency should occur. Even more, successful communication requires a cool head under pressure, a genuine empathy for public concerns, and an appreciation for a community's residents' right to be aware of conditions that can affect their homes and families. Above all, it takes a respect for citizens' ability to absorb complex information and their readiness to respond constructively when fully informed. In many instances, openness about hazardous chemicals isn't just good sense. It is required by the Emergency Planning and Community Right-to-Know Act. See Chapter 4 for more information.

COMMUNICATING RISK EFFECTIVELY

"Risk communication" refers to the need for communicating about environmental hazards with the general public. Recent research on risk communication confirms that efforts to communicate about hazard and emergency conditions are most effective when they follow some basic principles of good overall communication. Successful risk communication also requires some basic respect for the vulnerability and outrage that people can feel when they must trust others to manage a risk that may threaten their family and friends.

DEALING WITH THE PUBLIC'S REAL CONCERNS

Frequently, decision makers with a sound technical understanding of a hazard are frustrated when residents focus on a seemingly minor concern, often ignoring more critical issues. However, such "trivial" concerns are often closely related to citizens' sense of well-being (environmental or personal) and can form the basis for heated opposition. Variables affecting these concerns can include a resident's proximity to a facility, similar experiences in the community, overall sensitivity to environmental hazards, or recent news coverage of national events.

The key to building trust and confidence in your message is to take the time to understand and focus on the public's concerns. Some of the most common community concerns can be characterized in two categories:

- Environmental and quality-of-life issues:
    Concerns about hazardous environmental and health impacts from air emissions, groundwater contamination, or accidental releases.
    Frustration with the levels of uncertainty associated with defining many hazards.
    Resentment that one community may be asked to bear the burden of hazards that benefit neighboring communities.
- Mistrust of the planning process:
    Concern that citizens are being excluded from decisions that directly affect them.
    Misunderstandings about why a facility is necessary and why a specific location has been chosen over alternative ones.

The most effective communications programs will deal with both dimensions.

ENVIRONMENTAL AND QUALITY-OF-LIFE ISSUES

One of the greatest risk communications challenges is the need to say "we just don't know for sure." Recent publicity about the uncertainties associated with hazardous materials and wastes has contributed to public resistance and trepidation. As one example, people have become quite concerned about the potential health hazards of air emissions and residue ash from waste-to-energy facilities. The concern is amplified when the exact nature and extent of the threat is unknown. Dioxins, for example, are frequently mentioned in accounts of hazardous air emissions, but the truth is that maximum safe dioxin levels still have not been established. Without the reassurance of definitive government safety data, already grave concerns may be magnified.

In an atmosphere of uncertainty and skepticism, issues that may seem secondary to an official with technical insight can become the focus of disputes. This situation can become further confused when project opponents do not concentrate on the more controversial issues. Siting an incineration facility is a good example. Obviously, the most forceful resistance often emerges from people living in proximity to the proposed site, but their concern may focus as much on the facility's impact on their daily lives as on the long-term health risks. Don't be surprised to find as much furor about the adverse effects of odor, traffic congestion, and noise issues as about the hazards of dioxin or other potentially toxic emissions. The key is to avoid making any assumptions, to listen carefully, and to make sure you understand which mix of threats and impacts are perceived as most significant to that community's sense of well-being.

MISTRUST OF THE PLANNING PROCESS

In addition to issue-based resistance, the public has a growing mistrust of the planning process itself. Historically, many local government officials have allowed public review only *after* decisions were finalized. Today, as public concern increases with regard to both environmental hazards and the right to influence all public agency decisions, citizens demand to be heard early and often during a municipality's decision making process. These demands can become particularly urgent when people feel that the outcome of a decision will affect the well-being of their family or neighbors. When those demands are frustrated, citizens who are excluded from decisions that affect them personally may generate enough community resistance to obstruct an entire project.

THE KEY TO CREDIBILITY: RELEASING INFORMATION

Technically, much of the concise information about a public project has always been public information. However, the public typically has taken little interest in digging the relevant volumes out of agency libraries, and, more often than not, municipalities have not actively distributed or announced the contents of reports. However, as people take a more active interest in public safety issues, their demand for facts and figures will increase.

A commitment to release concise information promptly is key to maintaining credibility in the public eye. Further, a knowledgeable official can reassure anxious residents by actively reporting on either progress or setbacks. When specific information isn't available, it is critical to let people know when it will be — or why it won't. Whenever possible, release information quickly, preferably accompanied by a public statement that puts the information into context, explaining the results to date and reviewing future plans.

Regular communication of this type benefits the spokesperson as much as the public, especially if an agency establishes the habit before any emergencies occur. Such an approach allows you to build some level of rapport with the community. That familiarity and comfort level will put you in good stead if an emergency should arise. Your credibility — and your local government's — will be enhanced by your ability to remain collected in tough situations.

DON'T PLAY YOUR CARDS TOO CLOSE TO THE VEST

In some cases, it may seem appropriate to guard information for release "at the right time." The case for guarding information or releasing reports selectively is often based on the assumption that, to reduce anxieties and ensure public support, the public must be given a carefully tailored impression of the situation.

Such manipulative strategies can only strengthen the sentiment that public agencies are withholding vital information. Further, when information is withheld, chances increase that the media or project opponents will fill the information void with open speculation. By taking the initiative, acting promptly and openly, you are more likely to ensure that information will be accurately reported in an appropriate context.

Information on environmental or public health impacts is especially sensitive. The public is suspicious of anything that looks like a coverup on issues that affect them, and will be unwilling to accept justifications for delay. Further, withholding or selectively releasing information can make public officials seem condescending, implying that the everyday citizens can't be trusted to understand the risk assessment process or the technical concepts involved.

Most citizens are fully capable of grasping scientific concepts, procedures, and results, and, if people are not kept informed, concerned groups will fortify their assumptions with materials — not necessarily accurate — that support their particular agendas. Not only is confusion a likely product of withholding information, so are frightening rumors and news leaks that have weak technical foundations and no official context.

ESTABLISHING PUBLIC TRUST

In addition to keeping citizens well-informed, public officials are finding that, in order to fortify public confidence and earn informed community consent, agencies must also offer citizens reasonable access to decisions and the decision makers. Such an approach can go a long way to defusing distrust or outrage. It acknowledges that people deserve a reasonable degree of control over the risk they are being asked to assume. Involving informed citizens in decisions that affect the community offers the additional benefits of enhancing the final plan with citizen insights and increasing the likelihood that resulting efforts will receive needed community support and trust for the long run.

BUILDING EFFECTIVE DIALOGUE

The commitment to involve citizens in decisions is based on a commitment to hold a constructive dialogue with those affected by those decisions. A dialogue is a two-way communication: an agreement to speak and an agreement to listen. Dialogue cannot guarantee public acceptance of a project and it is not a new trick to "sell" the risk. However, a dialogue sincerely pursued can reduce unproductive tensions and produce a fertile environment for public understanding of — and constructive response to — potential risk.

Community dialogue is as much an attitude as it is an activity. In many cases, such a dialogue requires public officials to put aside their preconceptions about the community's traditional role in public policy making and risk management. In particular, officials must put aside their judgments about the "legitimacy" of public concerns: public concerns are *always* legitimate and these concerns will form the foundation for long-term public resistance or consent.

To promote effective dialogue and build credibility, decision makers must make several commitments:

- *Understand that risks will not be accepted because of what you know, but because of what the public feels.* Citizens' concerns are often very personal. Sometimes their mistrust of officials and the planning process is more at issue than the stated concerns. In such an emotionally charged environment, you need to win their confidence before trying to address public issues with scientific data or technical explanations.
- *Listen actively and respectfully to the concerns and perceptions of residents.* Officials with a technical understanding of the project run the risk of discounting emotional public responses as trivial or illegitimate, claiming that people "just aren't concerned about the right things." The key is to put yourself in the shoes of someone who will be affected by the project and to understand that, in many cases, the concerns of residents are deeply personal and emotionally charged.
- *Avoid defensiveness.* Officials may feel that they are being personally attacked or ignored by anxious residents. A defensive person cannot really hear what people are saying and may be perceived as arrogant or insincere. By carefully listening to what people are saying, decision makers will have a much better chance to gain the public confidence they will need to address the real cause of public fears, and gain the community's informed support.
- *Be forthcoming with information. Present information clearly and concisely — and get the facts straight.* An open exchange of ideas and information will foster public trust and enhance the dialogue. Public officials should disclose information early and present it as concisely and accurately as possible. To avoid perceptions that you are evading issues, publicly correct inaccuracies as soon as possible. Translate bureaucratic reports into plain English (or other languages as appropriate).
- *Think before you speak and do not be afraid to say "I don't know, but I'll find out."* In an emotionally charged public forum — and especially in an emergency situation — it's far too easy to "shoot from the hip." Read a prepared statement if necessary, answer questions briefly, honestly, and dispassionately — and if you don't know, say so. Facing a news camera can be a powerful temptation to display expertise. Resist it.
- *Be patient.* In most cases, such an open approach to public information is very new. Understandably, people may be very skeptical at first. Further, understand that you are not likely to satisfy every single person's concerns and doubts. However, given time and evidence, most people's skepticism will likely fade into productive public involvement and, in many cases, informed community support.

PUBLIC EDUCATION AND PARTICIPATION

It can take a little time for people to sort out what the issues are and how these issues affect them, their community, and the country. However, once they understand, citizens will be more likely to appreciate the difficult decisions facing public officials responsible for risk assessment and management. They will also be more likely to contribute to that effort in a constructive and insightful manner. Thus, informing and involving the public are the two cornerstones of effective risk communication.

Though it is beyond the scope of this chapter to provide a detailed how-to manual for specific programs, the following is an overview of the types of programs and materials that have proved helpful in keeping concerned citizens well-informed and constructively involved in the management of the community's environmental hazards.

PUBLIC EDUCATION

The first cornerstone deals with informing through public education efforts. The most effective public education programs are instituted early in the planning process, allowing the public time to absorb basic issues and concepts before major decisions are addressed. At first, some of the audience may be relatively unsophisticated about the potential for risk of a proposed project. However, it is important to recognize that some will bring a wealth of related knowledge and all will bring a rich understanding of what is important to their family and their community.

Of course, just because citizens are informed doesn't mean that they will always agree with you. However, informed citizens are more likely to understand the variables affecting your decisions and be more open to a respectful discussion of the options for managing those variables.

The most challenging concept for all parties involves the understanding that, regardless of how carefully we plan and how fastidiously we pursue those plans, we cannot eliminate 100 percent of the risks associated with many technologies. Though this is not a complex idea, it can be a frustrating reality to accept. In this context, all communities and their public officials are faced with difficult tradeoffs between the benefits and risks of a given project or operation. Time is often needed before a community comes to terms with the uncertainties that come into play in a given situation. Further, each community can be expected to weigh the tradeoffs in a unique way that makes it difficult to predict the final choices. Regardless, one of the responsibilities inherent in any risk education program is to help a community understand the following:

- Hazardous materials are a national and a local problem that is associated with many of the technologies we have come to rely on for basic services and products.
- My community and I are part of the problem and should be part of the solution.
- We can use generally accepted risk management alternatives to address only portions of known hazards. We can't eliminate all risks.

- There are no 100 percent safe ways to manage toxic materials. Given our unique situation, we must make some difficult choices among potential hazards, economics, and public health and safety. We must recognize that some tradeoffs will always be necessary.

WHAT MAKES AN EFFECTIVE EDUCATION CAMPAIGN?

First, take time to plan the approach and include time in the plan for evaluating education efforts over the course of a project or event. Start by identifying the target audiences, what information to present, what techniques and media to use, and what materials to develop.

Target audiences could include neighbors of the existing or proposed facility or operation, environmental issues groups, and others who are likely to be or become interested in specific project impacts. Don't overlook parties who are concerned with related issues, such as economic development and general health issues. Residents of other areas may be targeted too, if they will be affected — downstream or downwind, for example.

The educational techniques and media selected will depend on what information is being communicated and to whom. Public education programs often feature a number of different campaigns, distributing increasingly detailed information to specific audiences. Further, efforts to inform and educate will be most effective if delivered through a mix of materials and forums that present the information at different levels of detail. All materials should be clearly written and contain straightforward examples to illustrate concepts and the points being made. Further, this mix can be altered, based on the needs and interest levels of different target audiences. Basic campaigns will often include the following approaches:

- *Central Information Source.* Any public education campaign should include a designated source where interested parties can get their questions answered and review related materials, such as reports and summaries. The key is to set aside adequate space and staff time to respond promptly.
- *News Coverage.* News coverage is a staple for any public education campaign and hazardous materials are considered a very newsworthy topic.
- *Printed Literature.* Brochures, pamphlets, and fact sheets are staples of public education. They can help cover key issues in a convenient, concise format. Do not overlook the effectiveness of multilingual translations for some target audiences.
- *Informational Meetings and Workshops.* This personal approach can be very effective and can help build rapport with target communities. However, informational forums can only complement — not replace — forums designed to gather citizen input on decisions. Make sure that presentation materials (slides, videos, displays) are updated as the project progresses.
- *Advertising.* In general, extensive advertising is most cost-effective when decision makers want to deliver a message that would not otherwise receive adequate press coverage. Further, advertising in the newspaper can be less expensive than extensive mailings to every resident.

- *Site and Facility Visits.* One of the most powerful ways to address residents' concerns is to give them a chance to see for themselves, both before a facility is built and after it is operating. Since this approach can be very time-consuming and cost-intensive, it is best to plan these trips very carefully, ensuring that visitors include the most involved and influential community leaders.

PUBLIC INVOLVEMENT

The second cornerstone of an effective risk communication program is involvement — public participation. Whereas public education is a one-way communication intended to inform residents about issues and decisions that affect them, public participation programs are designed to *involve* residents in those same decisions. Such an approach is most appropriate for project development. However, a standing (advisory) committee can be a very effective part of emergency planning strategies.

History shows that public participation is not really optional. If there is public concern about a project, people *will* get involved. However, if the public has to force its way into the decision-making process through protests or legal actions, the outcome will suffer, not to mention all parties concerned.

As discussed earlier, effective public involvement programs are designed to involve affected parties in a constructive two-way dialogue with decision makers. In order to offer satisfaction to all parties, this outreach must provide meaningful access to the decision-making process. As such, it is critical that decision makers:

- Approach the public as a "partner" in weighing the options and struggling with the tradeoffs that are inevitably associated with these decisions. Such an approach calls for all parties to offer respect and an open mind.
- Offer access to the debate early enough that all parties can develop some mutual understanding and that citizen input can be seriously considered in final decision making.

There are risks and benefits associated with opening a public dialogue. First, public dialogue will usually involve some conflict, reflecting differences of opinions, as well as suspicions about the sincerity of the process. However, conflict is also an opportunity to identify underlying issues, resolve differences, increase mutual understanding, and build public confidence in decision makers. Further, allowing the public into the decision making process will inevitably change the face of the project. Such changes can be seen as improvements if they also create a project that will be more readily supported by the community it serves. Finally, effective dialogue can take time and must be carefully planned, allowing both parties a chance to gain trust, listen to the other side, and build effective solutions out of differences.

DESIGNING A PUBLIC PARTICIPATION PROGRAM

A comprehensive public participation effort should be carefully designed to complement the planning process. As previously stressed, access to the planning process should begin *early* and should be scheduled at key decision points throughout. Related considerations include:

- Schedule forums early enough to allow input to be incorporated into subsequent decisions in a timely and meaningful manner. Remember that the schedule should allow decision makers enough time to respond to the input *before* decisions are made.
- Provide a mix of forums, balancing "representative" forums with access for the general public. For example, an advisory group's activities may include hosting open public meetings throughout the planning area as a way to collect resident comments.

Access is the byword of public participation. It is paramount that decision makers let people know how and when they can get involved and how their input will be incorporated into the decision-making process. Decision makers must establish realistic expectations and must *not* promise what they can't deliver. People should be very clear about how broad or limited public access will be and what level of impact they can expect from their input.

Deadlines and meeting dates should be explicitly and repeatedly publicized. Remember that different people will take an interest in the process at different points and it should be relatively easy for them to find out how to get involved.

To ensure that the public participation process is meaningful and to sustain public trust, a formal procedure for responsiveness should be established and publicized. Again, the key is to allow people to set reasonable expectations about how their input will be incorporated into the decision-making process. The trick is to balance a need to respond with the need to proceed on decisions. The format for responsiveness can range from formal written response (as is required by some regulatory hearing processes) to orally answered questions and debate during a public meeting. At a minimum, it is prudent to attach all forms of public comment (testimony, letters, statements) as an appendix to subsequent decision statements. Further, as decision makers deliberate in public meetings, it is important to reference how public input is being considered.

Finally, it is critical that the involvement process honor the needs of all participants, including the decision makers. Decision makers are people, too. Keep in mind that public participation programs must be designed as tools for decision makers, not an arena for angry citizens to bludgeon those who bear the burden of responsibility. Further, since hazardous materials management often involves several levels of decision makers, public input should be packaged in a manner that can be effectively delivered to each level. The point is to ensure that public input is delivered in a timely manner and in a form that will give each decision maker a meaningful perspective on public data and sentiment.

Thus, it is important to promote support and cooperation for a participation program among decision makers by including them in the design and review of the proposed strategy. Further, all decision makers should be kept apprised of public input throughout the planning process, regardless of when they will play an active role. The goal is to give all parties reason to relax and look forward to public input as a means to improve project development and promote community partnership in sustainable risk-management solutions.

CHAPTER **17**

Environmental Considerations in Real Estate Transactions

William J. Mundt and David R. Meyer

A great deal of concern has arisen in recent years about contaminated land and the associated trail of liability when the land changes owners. The biggest concern is fear of enormous cleanup costs. This fear has become all too real in the few short years since environmental liability was first associated with real estate transactions.

Local governments face the same issues that affect the private sector in commercial and industrial real estate transactions. Superfund liabilities associated with contaminated land may expand to include the new owner, whether the transaction is completed by deed, sale, or gift. Chapter 1 provides greater detail on how these liability provisions work, and also describes some exceptions and defenses that may be available to local governments. This chapter addresses the practical issues of identifying and dealing with environmental problems in real estate transactions.

NATURE OF TRANSACTIONAL RISKS

There are two key questions to ask in real estate transactions: (1) could my city become liable for cleanup costs for this property? and (2) could environmental problems on this site make it impossible or too expensive for my city to complete the project for which the property is desired?

SITE CONTAMINATION

Parties to real estate transactions should understand that government agency policies are driven by the regulatory requirements of federal and state environmental laws that define site cleanup criteria, and that ownership of a contaminated site may cause the owner to become financially responsible for the remediation of the property even if the damage was caused by others.

1-56670-098-1/95/$0.00+$.50
© 1995 by CRC Press, Inc.

While "midnight dumping" on "virgin," undeveloped properties may occur from time to time, most property contamination results from historical or current uses of the site. Because the previous use of a property can be difficult to judge from existing conditions, historical review of a site is critical to an environmental site investigation. Common examples of prior or current site uses that can cause significant environmental damage include industrial, commercial, and manufacturing activity; sites with underground storage tanks (*e.g.*, gas stations); and sites on which illegal or permitted dumping has occurred.

Contaminated land could involve problems with soil, surface water, or groundwater. Building contamination may involve contamination to porous surfaces or the presence of friable asbestos or hazardous wastes. Properties requiring the most expensive cleanups usually exhibit some form of soil or groundwater contamination from hazardous substances. Significant levels of contaminants in the soil not only present a health threat via inhalation or direct contact, but also pose a threat to aquifer contamination due to potential leaching of the pollutants into the groundwater. Since groundwater is used by approximately 50 percent of the U.S. population for drinking water, the public's interest in protecting this resource and cleaning up contaminated aquifers is strong. Federal and state standards for drinking water quality, protection of groundwater resources, and the mechanisms for compliance are established by the water quality regulations of the federal government and the individual states. Even low concentrations of contaminants in the groundwater beneath a site can cause a great deal of concern about the potential cleanup responsibility the property may present to the new owner.

The regulatory status of a property may affect the owner's ability to use the property as intended, because acquisition of environmental permits and resolution of compliance issues may be required prior to developing the site or continuing facility operations. If the property is contaminated, it may be impossible to break ground or do construction for fear of triggering another release. If permits are required for a project, the permitting authorities may impose expensive conditions requiring cleanup which may not have been represented in the project budget.

LEGAL RISKS AND LIABILITIES

The concept of ownership has varying definitions, but there are three categories with potential significance under the environmental laws: *title* (right to dispose of property), *occupancy* (right to use property, such as a lease), and *control* (right to affect the use of or derive a benefit from the property, such as an easement). There is a surprising amount of overlap among these categories, and it is possible for more than one entity to be adjudged the "owner" or "operator" of a piece of property under Superfund, regardless of the name on the deed.

Provisions of the Clean Water Act (CWA), Resource Conservation and Recovery Act (RCRA), and Superfund have been broadly construed to include any or all parties who maintain an interest in a contaminated property or in an operation that generates, uses, processes, or discharges hazardous substances to the environment as "owners" or "operators." "Interest" can include fee simple ownership, site management and operation, or derivation of a benefit from site use. Other interests may include trusts, easements, or estates. In many instances, local governments participate in land swaps and acquire rights by easement, dedication, or right-of-way. Cities, counties, and towns must look carefully at the nature of their interest, and the nature of the proposed use, to determine whether these acquisitions could subject them to environmental liability.

DISCLOSURE REQUIREMENTS

A number of state laws and local ordinances mandate disclosure of environmental problems as part of a property transfer. Most of these laws provide for disclosure of prior site uses including the management of hazardous wastes on the property or, in some states, certification that contamination has not occurred. Sometimes, a cleanup plan may be required before contaminated property can transfer.

Noncompliance with the pretransfer disclosure laws may result in civil penalties and strict liability for all cleanup costs. The transferee or buyer may also be entitled to recovery of damages. Therefore, when engaging in real estate transactions, local governments must evaluate specific state laws requiring pretransfer disclosures and cleanup responsibilities. This evaluation is best made *prior to* initiating the transaction.

STRUCTURING TRANSACTIONS

The old saying "knowledge is power" might be more appropriately translated as "knowledge could save you millions" when it comes to the risks involved in acquiring real estate without inquiring into the potential for site contamination and other environmental issues. Practically everyone involved with real estate transactions has heard horror stories of municipalities, corporations, or individuals who needlessly incurred environmental liability through the acquisition of property.

Proper management of a real estate transaction should include investigation of the potential environmental liabilities associated with the property. The risks identified during a site investigation must be further translated into legal, regulatory, and civil liability risk. Such liabilities may be derived under provisions of specific laws such as Superfund, RCRA, CWA, SDWA, and the Toxic Substances Control Act (TSCA), or tort principles such as nuisance, negligence, trespass, and strict liability. The information gained from environmental site investigations may assist in determining the feasibility of the transaction and may provide information valuable in structuring the agreement with the buyer or seller. Information about site assessments is provided in the last section of this chapter.

Environmental contamination is not always a "deal breaker." In some cases this scenario may happen, especially if extensive site cleanup is found to be cost prohibitive, or if an inflexible seller or buyer is involved in the transaction. However, there are a number of steps a local government can take, either as a seller or buyer, to secure a stronger financial position and safeguard against liability while still completing the transaction.

If a site investigation discloses contamination, completion of the transaction may require prompt action to restrict or contain the further spread of contamination, and implement a cleanup plan. In addition, by exercising prudent forethought and proactively mitigating environmental damages, a landowner may improve his or her negotiating position with the regulatory agencies responsible for overseeing any cleanup. It is important, however, to involve an environmental attorney in negotiating such a transaction. The mechanisms discussed in this chapter may vary in usefulness and structure depending on local law.

Some methods that local governments may use to protect themselves as purchasers include the use of representations and warranties, such as

- Seller's compliance with appropriate environmental laws and regulations.
- Existence of pending environmental notices or claims, lawsuits, enforcement actions or investigations, and consent orders regarding the subject property.
- Existence of any environmental permits, zoning approvals, or licenses.
- Existence of any solid or hazardous waste or hazardous substances that have been stored, treated, disposed of, or managed on the subject property.
- Knowledge of any preexisting site conditions, site uses, or impending changes or events on-site that could materially affect the value or use of the property.

Conversely, a seller may attempt to negotiate an "as is" clause, which essentially transfers full responsibility for the reduction in value or assorted liabilities of the property condition to the buyer. Obviously, such a clause is quite undesirable to the buyer and could be a strong hint that something may be wrong with the property under evaluation.

Certifications by principal parties to a transaction are often used to guarantee the environmental condition of a property as determined by the site investigation. Another protective method a buyer may use is to simply insist that the seller clean up the property prior to closing. Such a provision may involve an analysis of other potentially responsible parties who may also be liable for cleanup costs.

Adjustment of the purchase price is a very simple method of compensating the buyer for known liabilities. In such a case the cost for site cleanup may be estimated, producing a range of "likely" to "worst case" factors to be used in establishing a fair adjustment. This is an especially difficult process to undertake, given the risks and uncertainties involved in determining the fair market value for contaminated properties for which the extent of contamination may not have been fully determined. The buyer must be careful in negotiating such price breaks due to the legal impacts involved and should evaluate such a position carefully on a case-by-case basis.

Another possible structure establishes guarantees for remedial action provided by the seller. Obviously, such guarantees are only as good as the company or entity that makes them, and guarantees should only be accepted if you are fairly certain the guarantor will be around to make good on them. Indemnity clauses that apportion liability and establish how certain contingencies will be handled may also be useful. Sellers may make use of covenants that restrict future use or access to the property if there is reason to be concerned that certain types of uses could cause releases of hazardous substances to the environment.

Mechanisms also exist to provide liability protection for the seller after financial closure. From the seller's perspective, additional covenants that impose limitations on the purchaser's post-transaction activities (prohibiting excavation, or use of the property for a playground) may be effective in controlling future liabilities that could be attached to the seller. Other covenants might include duties of the purchaser to conduct monitoring, inspection, and property maintenance. Another option available to the seller is a covenant that restricts the use of hazardous substances on the site in the future. Also, the seller may attempt to secure the buyer's commitment to prevent discharges or exposure to contaminated materials. Other protections include prompt notifications to the seller of claims or other situations that may give rise to environmental liabilities; and retaining the right to enter the property to conduct visual, nonintrusive inspections. Finally, a seller may try to secure a buyer's commitment to a performance deed of trust on the property. This is a promissory guarantee designed to hold the purchaser to the agreed-upon covenants and to ensure the availability of money to fund any future environmental claims.

It may be beneficial to both seller and buyer to consider whether the inclusion of explicit dispute resolution mechanisms in the transaction agreement would be helpful. Given the inherent uncertainties in accounting for environmental risks and liabilities, disputes may arise concerning causes of contamination, time of occurrence, amount involved, or response measures required. Dealing with such matters in court may prove costly and time consuming. Therefore, arbitration or mediation may prove more expedient and less painful than a lengthy court proceeding.

TYPICAL ELEMENTS OF A SITE INVESTIGATION

The risks associated with site contamination can be significantly reduced by conducting pretransfer environmental site investigations that research these concerns. A prepurchase environmental site assessment (ESA) can also be used to help establish an "innocent landowner" defense under Superfund. This defense is discussed further in Chapter 1. The scope of an environmental investigation may vary not only with the potential for problems to exist at a site, but also according to the needs of the client requesting the services. If "due diligence" efforts (required for the innocent landowner defense) are a planned element of the real estate transaction, solicitors of these services should be skeptical of cursory or incomplete investigations.

ESAs are often described as "Phase I" or "Phase II" assessments. The Phase I ESA examines a property for any associated environmental contamination that could result in financial liability for the owner. An ESA is normally conducted for the buyer prior to closure and transfer of the real estate or at the request of the seller or lender. The primary objective of a Phase I ESA is to identify environmental conditions that suggest that an existing release, a past release, or risk of a release of any hazardous substances or petroleum products has occurred or may occur in structures on the property or into the soil, surface water, or groundwater of the property.

The Phase I ESA typically consists of three basic parts: (1) data acquisition, (2) a site visit to the property, and (3) a written report of findings. The information presented in the report should identify the potential environmental liabilities that exist as a result of previous or ongoing contamination of the property from on-site or off-site origins, which may result in financial responsibility to the owner. Normally, any recommendations regarding additional work, such as a Phase II investigation, are included. The purpose of a Phase II ESA is to qualify and quantify contamination in suspected areas through the sampling of soils, surface water, and groundwater, or other media of concern as required. A Phase I ESA does not usually include sampling. If cleanup of a site is necessary, Phase III operations may be designed to achieve site remediation and long-term solutions to bring the property to a condition suitable for the intended purposes of the owner.

DATA ACQUISITION

Information gathered during interviews and records reviews will assist in evaluating the environmental conditions of the property. Examples of information that should be collected include history of land use and previous operations at the site, current site uses, previous site characterizations, and relevant geological and hydrogeological data. Proximity to other off-site areas of concern should be evaluated by an examination of relevant EPA, state, or county databases that list known or suspected contaminated sites, spills, landfills, and hazardous waste generators. For example, the most common databases available for locating documented contaminated sites are the National Priorities List (NPL), the Comprehensive Environmental Response, Compensation, and Liability Information System (CERCLIS) list, and equivalent lists at state environmental or water quality agencies. The environmental departments within county health agencies are also a common source of environmental information.

Investigative methods typically include review of public and private records, including maps, aerial photographs, and site-specific geologic or hydrologic data and interviews with the client, current owner/operator, employees of operating facilities on the property, neighbors, and public officials, as appropriate. In most cases, the client and current owner will be asked to provide the consultant with available information regarding prior owners and current and prior uses of the property, copies of data and drawings, and the cooperation of the client and their representatives (*e.g.*, their advisors and engineers).

For a complete investigation, available files regarding both the subject property and nearby adjacent properties at appropriate federal, state, and local agencies should be obtained through Freedom of Information Act requests or reviewed at the agency offices. This information should be evaluated for potential environmental impacts on the property.

SITE VISIT

The purpose of the site visit is to visually examine the property and existing structures for evidence of contamination and historical or current site uses that suggest contamination could be present. This is accomplished through observation of the grounds and terrain, identification of surface conditions such as topography, drainage, surface water, soil, vegetation, and locations of accumulated debris, tanks, drums, and buildings. Particular attention should be paid to disposal areas, spills, stains, dead wildlife/vegetation, evidence of burial, pits, and other situations that suggest potential areas of concern. Conditions inconsistent with the historical land use should also be noted.

Interior examination of on-site buildings is also part of the site visit. For public buildings, the physical inspection should include accessible common areas as well as a reasonable number of accessible tenant areas. Indications of potential concerns include but are not limited to stains, corrosion areas, drains and sumps, containers, unusual odors, equipment that may contain polychlorinated biphenyls (PCBs), or the potential presence of asbestos, radon, and lead-based paint. If the ESA is being conducted for a commercial or industrial site, an understanding of facility processes is certainly beneficial in recognizing potential concerns such as chemical supply areas, management practices for hazardous wastes, potential spill areas, and use of storage tanks.

The conditions and current uses of adjoining properties and the surrounding area should also be observed and noted during the site visit. This is normally accomplished through observation along the subject property's perimeter areas and public thoroughfares within an appropriate area. It is important to keep in mind the potential impact to the subject property from these off-site areas while assessing the orientation of streams, gradients, and other potential migration pathways toward the property.

Written Report

The written report contains the findings of the investigation, describing suspected areas of contamination or environmental concern, including a discussion of potential contamination of the property from off-site areas. Necessary documents, figures, and photographs that support the opinions and conclusions offered in the report are included. Depending upon the wishes of the client, recommendations may be made as to whether additional work such as a Phase II investigation is warranted. If offered, the recommendations should justify the reasons for conducting further investigations, and provide a concise plan for the recommended range of sampling and additional investigations during the Phase II study.

While the results of an ESA should reduce the uncertainty regarding the potential for site contamination, in no case should any consultant portray an ESA as completely exhaustive or as guaranteeing that a property is absolutely "clean" and free of hazardous materials or other environmental risks. It is impossible to ever be 100 percent certain that a property is completely clean.

Site Conditions Suggesting Further Investigations

The necessity of conducting additional investigations is related to the degree of risk you are willing to accept. It is not imperative to conduct intrusive Phase II investigations if you are comfortable with an identifiable risk. For example, the buyer may be willing to accept a worst-case cost estimate for cleanup of a small spill without soil sampling if the potential for groundwater contamination appears unlikely. However, prospective buyers should also understand that Phase II investigations may someday be viewed by the courts as a necessary component of the "innocent landowner" defense if the Phase I study has revealed the potential for significant contamination. Buyers should also bear in mind that the innocent landowner defense will not protect against problems not disclosed by an incomplete investigation. Some examples of situations in which Phase II investigations might be warranted include:

- Information that suggests that historical site uses could have contributed to site contamination.
- Site uses, facility processes, procedures, or waste management practices that demonstrate a significant potential to cause contamination.
- Observed or historical evidence of on-site spills or soil stains.
- Conditions within on-site structures that warrant sampling (such as the potential presence of asbestos or prior/current use of hazardous substances).
- Observed or historical evidence of on-site disposal of solid waste from on-site or off-site areas including (but not limited to) process wastes, sludges, fill soils, dredged soils, ash, refuse, debris, or construction materials.
- Documented or suspected off-site sources of groundwater contamination that are hydrogeologically upgradient to the property.
- Documented or suspected off-site surface contamination having a surface migration pathway to the property.

Current Industry Standards for Environmental Site Assessments

While the scope of ESA services performed by environmental and engineering consultants must reflect the needs of the client, the most conscientious professional consultants prefer to provide an effort that will inform the client of the potential environmental liabilities associated with the property while also satisfying the requirements of the innocent landowner defense under CERCLA. Although the federal government has not yet defined a minimum standard for what should be included in a due diligence assessment, numerous articles, books, and guidance materials have been written by many qualified individuals and organizations on the ESA process. Some of these information sources are:

- *Standard Practice for Environmental Site Assessments: Phase I Environmental Site Assessment Process*, prepared by the American Society for Testing and Materials (ASTM, 1993).
- *Preacquisition Site Assessments, Recommended Management Procedures for Consulting Engineering Firms*, prepared by ASFE/The Association of Engineering Firms Practicing in the Geosciences (ASFE, 1989).
- *Guidelines, Environmental Site Assessments*, published by The Consulting Engineers Council of Metropolitan Washington (CEC/MW, 1989).
- *Guidance to Environmental Site Assessments*, produced by the Association of Ground Water Scientists and Engineers (AGWSE, 1992).

These standards were developed to promote generally accepted site assessment practices and to provide a comprehensive explanation of the tasks that must be conducted during an ESA. Currently, the ASTM standard is probably the most widely recognized attempt to standardize the ESA process for commercial real estate transactions and it is widely expected to be persuasive to courts in establishing an innocent landowner defense. However, neither the ASTM standard nor any other protocol has been acknowledged by the courts as a guarantee of "all appropriate inquiry" under CERCLA. Except for the very earliest stage of data gathering, the ASTM standards require that ESAs be undertaken by "environmental professionals." For most local governments, this will mean hiring an outside consultant. You will want to make certain that the consultant you select is familiar with the ASTM and other standards, and is qualified to help you judge the degree of investigation required to meet your goals.

THE ENVIRONMENTAL COMPLIANCE ASSESSMENT

An environmental compliance assessment (ECA) consists of an investigation of existing operations at a site and a review of permits and compliance with applicable environmental laws and regulations. In the case of a real estate transaction for an existing facility, an ECA identifies concerns associated with facility operations that may transfer to the new owner. For undeveloped sites, an ECA may provide an indication to a buyer whether the planned use of the property is feasible. Additional detail about environmental compliance audits is included in Chapter 14.

CONCLUSION

In order to effectively protect themselves from the gauntlet of environmental liabilities and regulations that abound in today's real estate and business environment, local governments must take preventive measures. None of the measures discussed in this chapter can be expected to fully eliminate the environmental risks associated with real estate transactions. However, numerous steps can be taken to significantly reduce the potential environmental liabilities inherent in acquiring or disposing of real estate or other property rights such as leases and easements. These steps include environmental investigations and agreements structured to protect against environmental liabilities.

CHAPTER 18
Insurance

Russell F. Smith III

The ever-rising costs associated with liability for environmental contamination make it necessary for local governments to seriously consider insurance coverage. However, insurance for environmental liability is offered by few companies, and tends to be extremely expensive where it does exist. Many local governments are "running bare," meaning that they have decided to forego the expense of such insurance and take the risk of paying future claims out of their normal operating budgets. The environmental insurance that is available, environmental impairment liability (EIL) policies, offers "claims-based" coverage, which generally means that the injury must occur and the claim must be made *within the policy period*. It is often difficult to qualify for EIL coverage because this insurance is contingent on a detailed evaluation of the insured's facilities and environmental practices.

This chapter will discuss insurance coverage that local governments may not even know they have, and some of the things you should keep in mind when possible claims arise.

In the past, many local governments held Comprehensive General Liability (CGL) insurance policies. Many courts have found that coverage remains under old policies for current claims related to environmental contamination that may have occurred years ago, because these policies were written to cover "occurrences." These so-called occurrence-based policies provide coverage for damage that occurred during the policy period, even if the claim against the policy is filed today. Such policies can provide coverage for contamination that happened years before the discovery of the contamination and the tendering to insurers of claims for defense and indemnification regarding the site cleanup.

As you read this chapter, please keep in mind that there are many complex issues involved in insurance coverage determinations. One of the most important factors to keep in mind is that insurance cases are decided under state, not federal, law. Decisions concerning the coverage provided by almost identical policies can vary from state to state. The contents of your insurance policies can only be analyzed with reference to the law of the relevant state.

1-56670-098-1/95/$0.00+$.50
© 1995 by CRC Press, Inc.

It is beyond the scope of this chapter to provide a full discussion of insurance coverage decisions and trends in each of the various states. What we can tell you, however, is that federal and state court decisions interpreting insurance contract provisions have found that there *is* coverage for many kinds of environmental harm. Furthermore, many of these cases required insurance companies to provide coverage under policies issued years, even decades, ago. It is, therefore, a good idea to locate all potentially relevant municipal insurance policies (dating back as far as they exist). If you become involved in a Superfund or other case involving environmental liability, read the policies carefully with the facts of your case in mind, and take whatever steps the policies require to protect your rights to make a claim.

INTERPRETATION OF INSURANCE POLICIES

Determining the coverage provided by a particular insurance policy can be difficult. In undertaking such a task several things should be kept in mind. First, each policy is in some ways unique; even though the basic policy is written in a standard form, it usually contains critical amendments and modifications tailored to fit the risks posed by the insured's individual situation. Judges interpreting whether there is coverage for a particular situation must evaluate what the parties intended when they signed the insurance contract, and must examine the underlying policy and all amendments and riders carefully. The language itself is the starting point for this analysis, but where that language is unclear and the parties disagree about what the words mean courts often give the benefit of the doubt to the insured party.

Second, the policy's application to a particular situation will depend on a close review of facts about the underlying pollution case. Courts deciding insurance disputes have a more complicated job than courts applying Superfund's strict, no-fault liability scheme, because fault by the insured can affect insurance coverage.

THE HISTORY OF POLLUTION COVERAGE AND EXCLUSIONS

In the next several paragraphs, we will describe standard form policies and the terms generally used in them. It bears repeating that you have to read your own policies carefully to determine the provisions they contain. It is particularly important to read any amendments, endorsements, or other attachments to a policy, since they will often significantly modify language in the standard form.

As we mentioned above, coverage for environmental claims is most often sought under past CGL policies that protect the insured against liability for injury to other people or their property. Actually, the standard CGL policy imposes two obligations on the insured, the duty to indemnify and the duty to defend the policyholder. Over the past two decades, the insurance industry revised CGL policy language several times in an effort to limit exposure to "long-tail risks," *i.e.*, risks such as hazardous waste site cleanups or chemically caused illnesses that typically take years to discover. Until 1966, which was roughly the time when pollution risks were recognized as a problem for insurers, the insurance companies insured against risks "caused by accident," without defining the term. Although the insurers now maintain that they intended to insure only sudden and unexpected — and *not* gradual and foreseeable — events, the courts generally interpreted the word "accidental" broadly, finding coverage for losses resulting from either gradual or sudden pollution. Therefore, for example, the seepage of pollutants from a city-owned lagoon into groundwater could be considered accidental, regardless of how long it has continued or how slowly it occurred.

In 1966, the insurance industry modified the language in standard policies to clarify that the industry did not intend to cover intentional pollution. As a result, most CGL policies that were issued between 1966 and 1986 are occurrence based; they protect the insured from liability resulting from an occurrence during the policy period, regardless of when the claim is filed. The occurrence is the act that results in property damage or personal injury, such as the discharge of chemicals. Generally, policy language would define occurrence as "an accident *or unexpected event*, including continuous or repeated exposure to conditions, which results in property damage neither expected or intended from the standpoint of the insured" (emphasis added). The term "occurrence" is broader than the term "accident," as it covers both gradual *and* sudden discharges of contaminants.

By essentially giving in on the "gradual" vs. "sudden" debate, the insurers claimed they intended to cover more losses, and they charged higher premiums for this expansion. At the same time, however, the policies were clarified to emphasize the insurers' intent to shift the focus of the courts to whether the loss caused by pollution was expected or intended. The insurance companies apparently believed that most pollution, gradual or sudden, was somehow deliberate enough that coverage would be denied because of this condition.

To the insurance industry's dismay, many courts have interpreted the occurrence language to mean that there *is* coverage for essentially *any* pollution event resulting in injury or property damage, unless it was very plain that the injury or loss *was* expected or intended. Furthermore, it is generally accepted that an intentional *act* that results in unintentional *contamination* is included in the definition of occurrence. For example, in one case a company legally sent two shipments of hazardous wastes to a licensed disposal facility. The disposal facility was operated improperly and the hazardous wastes contaminated the environment. The court held that the company certainly neither "expected or intended illegal and harmful dumping of its toxic waste" and thus the disposal was an occurrence. In another case, vandals opened the valve on an oil tank, causing a release of oil into a river. The spill was considered to be an occurrence under the tank owner's CGL policy, because the owner clearly did not intend the release.

In 1973 insurers again moved to cut back on coverage for pollution-related loss. They began inserting into CGL policies language that expressly excluded coverage for property damage or personal injury arising out of the discharge of pollutants into the environment unless the discharge was "sudden and accidental." Many of the recent court opinions turn on interpretations of this "pollution exclusion clause." In particular, they focus on the meaning of the phrase "sudden and accidental." In some cases judges have found that the phrase is ambiguous and, therefore, under traditional rules of insurance contract interpretation, interpreted it in favor of the policyholder. Some of these courts have gone so far as to find that the words are nothing more than a restatement of the definition of occurrence, and consequently find coverage for any unexpected and unintended personal injury or property damage. As a result, insurance coverage has even been found to be sudden and accidental in an instance where a landfill was seeping contaminants for a number of years and in a case where a long-term leak from an underground storage tank polluted groundwater.

In contrast, several other courts have found that the words "sudden and accidental" are clear, and must be understood to have their everyday meaning. The word "sudden" in particular is interpreted by these judges to have a temporal sense, precluding coverage for contamination that occurs gradually. For a discharge to be "accidental" there must be no indication that the polluter was aware of the problem and failed to take steps to correct it. Under this reasoning a court found that gradual seepage from a landfill into groundwater over a six-year period is not a sudden occurrence. Another held that a highway death that resulted from diminished visibility due to smoke escaping from an aluminum recycling plant is not accidental, since the plant released the gas on a regular basis and had received prior complaints.

One court that ruled that the words "sudden and accidental" were not ambiguous refused, nonetheless, to give effect to the pollution exclusion clause, and permitted the insured to recover its costs associated with cleaning up the environmental contamination. This case turned on the representations that insurance companies and their representatives made to state insurance regulators. The insurance industry is regulated by state law. When insurers wish to offer new types of coverage or modify the conditions of coverage that they have already received permission to offer, they are generally required to obtain approval from the insurance agency of the state or states in which they are subject to regulation.

In this case the court reviewed the representations made to the New Jersey insurance commission concerning the impact that the inclusion of the pollution exclusion clause would have on coverage under the standard CGL policy. The court found that the insurance commission had been told that the clause would have little impact upon the scope of the coverage such policies. In fact, if the clause is read as insurers have argued that it should be, all coverage for damage caused by gradual pollution would be eliminated. Since such damage was covered by CGL policies prior to the introduction of the pollution exclusion clause, and since numerous claims had been made for reimbursement related to environmental contamination, the court ruled that insurers had misrepresented the effect of the modification to coverage under CGL policies. It concluded that, because of these misrepresentations, the pollution exclusion clause could not be enforced as a bar to coverage for unintended gradual contamination.

The litigation over insurance coverage under CGL policies for environmental harm has focused closely on interpreting the specific contractual terms used in the policy. Frequently litigated key words and phrases include "occurrence" and "sudden and accidental," discussed above. Two other key issues are whether there has been "property damage" within the meaning of the policy definition and whether an EPA claim for reimbursement of cleanup funds or the costs of responding to an EPA cleanup order amounts to damages that the insurer is obligated to pay out.

The courts' efforts to determine whether cleanup costs are reimbursable damages under a standard policy has involved some of the more arcane and confusing legal reasoning in the insurance coverage area. While it is difficult to summarize these court opinions, essentially the issue the courts must decide is whether cleanup costs payable to the EPA or another government agency qualify as reimbursable damages as that term is traditionally understood when used in insurance contracts. The courts go both ways, sometimes requiring insurance companies to cover cleanup costs and sometimes finding that costs are not damages and therefore not covered. Only legal advice tailored to your specific policy and legal jurisdiction can answer the question of whether your local government is likely to prevail in a coverage dispute, particularly one that involves this "damages" issue.

As we mentioned above, the insurance industry finally developed an "absolute pollution exclusion" which effectively eliminated occurrence-based coverage for environmental claims, leaving specially tailored EIL policies the only alternative. Note, however, that this exclusion may not have been inserted into policies until a few years after that date. Therefore, policies issued in the late 1980s should still be carefully examined.

FINDING YOUR POLICIES AND MAKING CLAIMS

It is a good idea to hunt down all of your old policies that might apply to environmental cleanups well before you need them, and before they are destroyed in accordance with your local government's normal document retention practices. Locating these policies now will make it easier to notify your insurance companies of environmental claims if the need arises. To determine the full scope of potential coverage, you should check your entire portfolio of all past insurance policies, not just your general liability policies and your

environmental impairment policies. Depending on your particular circumstances and the types of policies you have held, you may be covered by policies
that would not seem to be related to environmental issues. For example, there
may be coverage under some first-party property insurance, or "all-risk" policies. In addition, some auto insurance policies cover transportation accidents
involving spills of hazardous substances. You may have landlord/tenant or
contract coverage that applies to the contamination of facilities or disruption of
business relationships because of environmental problems. There may also be
umbrella or excess insurance to cover liability over the maximum coverage of
the primary insurance coverage.

If you cannot find the policy itself, it is still helpful to discover the number
of the policy, since the number will usually indicate the type of policy, if not
the exact language, and the insurers themselves may have samples on file.
Ideally, you want to be able to identify any potential source of insurance for the
entire period during which occurrences may have taken place for which your
local government is potentially liable. If you find gaps in your insurance
history, you should be aware that there are companies that specialize in
searching for insurance policies. They can help you prove your case even if you
have only fragmentary records of past coverage.

One important place to look for insurance coverage is in the contracts you
may have held with disposal companies or environmental contractors. Those
companies may have contracted to indemnify you or to hold insurance covering their involvement with your operations. Even if you are unable to find the
policies held directly by your city, you may find evidence of the policies in
accounting records where the request for payment or payment of insurance
premiums are recorded. You may also find evidence of policies in the minutes
of meetings where insurance coverage was discussed and/or approved.

NOTIFYING YOUR INSURANCE COMPANIES

Your notification obligations are defined by each policy. There are usually
two kinds of notification to the insurer required under standard CGL policies,
both primary and excess: (1) notice of occurrences and (2) notice of claims.
You are usually required to notify your insurance company of an occurrence
as soon as practicable. For example, if there is a spill of a hazardous substance
at your facility, you have to tell your insurer right away, even if no action is
taken against you by the EPA or the state. (You should not, of course, delay
cleanup or compliance with state and federal notification requirements while
you are notifying your insurers.) If you do not notify the insurance company,
it may try to disclaim coverage under your policy when you file a claim later.
With respect to excess carriers, ordinarily you must notify them once you know
that the costs arising from an occurrence or a subsequent claim could exceed
your primary insurance coverage. A better practice is to notify your excess

carriers as soon as you are aware of a claim and minimize the possibility of a dispute over whether notice was timely.

If there is a claim made against you, such as in a lawsuit or a notification that you have been named a potentially responsible party (PRP) at a Superfund site, you must inform your insurance companies immediately. An issue that has been raised by insurers is whether an EPA or steering committee notice letter constitutes a sufficient claim to trigger your obligation to notify the insurance company and its obligation to assume your defense. Some courts say that an EPA letter notifying you of your potential responsibility is enough; some say that it is not. The safest course is to send by certified mail to all your insurers, both primary and excess, a written notice about any occurrence or possible claim. The notice should go to all sources of potential coverage, and you should also notify your insurance agent. *You should not wait until you have located and researched the precise language of past policies.* Rather, notice should be sent to protect your rights as soon as you become aware of potential claims against you. The only possible drawback to this strategy is that the insurer may decide to file a lawsuit right away to get a court to declare its obligations under the insurance policy. However, you do not really have a choice in complying with notice requirements in a timely fashion, and the insurance company is not likely to go to court the minute it receives notice of a claim.

After the initial notification, you must give the company additional notice, before you incur any expense, such as reimbursing the EPA or paying for a site study. The reason for this notice is that most CGL policies have a provision under which the insurer may try to deny coverage for costs you assumed voluntarily. The insurance company can and often will notify you in writing that it will not contest the expenditures. Although you may not have any legal obligation to continue keeping the insurer informed once coverage is denied, it is a good idea to do so, since it will make it more difficult for an insurer that is later found to have provided coverage to challenge your actions as unreasonable.

Once you notify the carrier of the claim, you will probably receive a detailed request for information. An important consideration in responding to such a letter is that insurance companies are supposed to make decisions on whether they will undertake to defend you based solely upon whether the allegations in the complaint or other claim against you provide a basis for coverage under the policy. If there is a basis for coverage they must provide a defense even if the claim appears to be groundless. Until it actually agrees to defend you, the company may try to get you to give it additional information to use as a basis for denying coverage.

Although the general rule is that the insurance companies have to defend against a claim if it is even conceivable that the claim falls under the policy, a few courts have looked at the costs of defending Superfund cases and have found it unfair to require the insurers to assume the insured's defense before the coverage issues have been determined where it is pretty clear that the policy language would preclude coverage.

The safest course is to have a lawyer control the flow of information to the insurance company, even the initial claim letter. Obviously, you cannot change the facts about your involvement at a site and your potential liability. How they are presented and characterized to your insurer, however, can be critical in the coverage case, as issues of fault and intent and other matters are often relevant in insurance claims. Furthermore, a lawyer can monitor the insurance company's investigation of your claims, which is generally subject to state law time limitations and requires a good faith inquiry into the claim.

LITIGATION OVER COVERAGE FOR ENVIRONMENTAL CLAIMS

After it receives your notification, your insurance company may send you a "reservation of rights letter" while it continues to investigate your case, and then may eventually send you a letter notifying you that it is denying coverage. The "denial letter" should specify the grounds on which the denial is based.

At some point, you may end up in court with your insurance company. As the above discussion indicates, this area is heavily litigated and it is important that all relevant court opinions that address the applicability of policy exclusions and the scope and interpretation of key policy terms discussed above are carefully researched.

Of course, there are many other issues that are raised by insurers. For example, a common term in CGL policies excludes coverage for claims arising out of pollution on property you own or over which you have exclusive control (that property might be insured under property or other insurance). Some courts have, however, found that environmental contamination claims involve the cleanup and protection of groundwater that is generally considered the property of the state and not the individual land owner. The whole issue of when an occurrence took place involves a determination of whether the important trigger is the time of disposal of the hazardous substance, the time of the injury, the time of discovery, or some combination of the three. Which trigger is selected is often critical to the insured's right to maintain its claim against the insurer. Insurance companies may raise public policy arguments concerning the detriment to society that will result if they have to pay out on the old liability and other policies. If, as is frequently the case, there is more than one insurer, there may be issues about which one is responsible for a particular time period or a particular loss.

Even if the insurer does not formally deny coverage, at some point you and your lawyer may decide it makes sense to go to court to get a declaration of your rights under the policy. If, however, there are facts in dispute — *e.g.*, you and the insurer disagree over the nature of contamination at the underlying site — a judge may decide it cannot issue the judgment without a full trial. Even if you avoid a trial, filing an insurance case will require your lawyer to spend time and money investigating the facts and writing legal pleadings, and it could take several months or even years to get a ruling. Even if you win, you may never recover the costs of securing your rights under the policy or policies, since in most circumstances you are not entitled to recover attorneys' fees from the insurance companies and those fees spent in obtaining a declaration of your rights under the policy would not be considered defense costs for which the insurance company is responsible under the insurance contract.

Additionally, some insurers will file a suit against you for a declaration of their obligations, rather than simply denying coverage, in order to protect themselves against future claims that they have denied coverage "in bad faith." Bad faith refusals to defend and indemnify can be penalized by the courts because it is a fundamental principle of insurance law that insurers have a fiduciary relationship with their insureds. A successful bad faith claim can result in the insurer being required to pay the insured's cost of litigating the coverage dispute. Insurers may also choose to file first so that they can have some control over which court will decide the case. Since the same policy could be interpreted in opposite ways under the laws of different states, filing in the most favorable jurisdiction can determine the outcome of the case.

CONCLUSION

As is probably clear from this chapter, the questions surrounding insurance coverage for environmental liabilities are complex, and cannot possibly be completely answered in a single chapter. The law varies from state to state, policy to policy, and case to case. As this chapter demonstrates, however, there are steps you can take now (such as locating all your old insurance policies) which may help your local government if claims of environmental liability are raised in the future.

Index

A

Acid rain, 159, 164–167, 178
ACMs, see Asbestos-containing materials
Acutely hazardous waste, 22, 26, 27, 29–32
  pesticides as, 112, 113
Air conditioning, 178
Air pollutants, see also Clean Air Act (CAA)
  criteria, 158, 159, 163
  existing sources for, 165–167
  hazardous, 161–162, 165–166, 170, 178
  mobile sources for, 167–170, 177
  sources for, 159–165
    existing, 165–167
    mobile, 167–170, 177
Air Pollution Control Act, see Clean Air Act
    (CAA)
Airport operations, 178
Air quality, 157, see also Clean Air Act (CAA)
  analysis of, 163
  criteria for, 49
  planning for, 169
  standards for, 158–159
American Society for Testing and Materials
    (ASTM), 217
Annual reports, 31
Applicator certification for pesticides,
    108–109
Aquifer protection, 154
Area Contingency Plans, 88
Asbestos cement pipe, 116, 128
Asbestos-containing materials (ACMs),
    115–128, 163, 166
  abatement of, 118, 121, 123–125
  assessment of, 121, 122, 124
  cleanup of, 117, 123–124
  compliance programs on, 183
  disposal of, 117, 128
  encapsulation of, 117, 123
  enclosure of, 117, 123

friable, 115–125
  real estate transactions and, 210
guidance document on management of, 116
identification of, 117–118
inspection of, 118, 120–123
labeling of, 125
management of, 116–118, 121–123
NESHAPs and, 116, 118–121, 126
nonfriable, 116, 118, 120–122, 124, 125
operations and maintenance pans for
    facilities with, 124–125
prevention of emission of, 118
real estate transactions and, 210, 215, 216
regulated, 118–121
reinspection of, 121–123
removal of, 117, 123, 124, 127
repair of damaged, 117, 123
risk communication and, 197
in schools, 116, 121–125
Worker Protection Rule on, 116, 119,
    126–127
Asbestos-In-Schools Rules, 116
Ash, 42
As is clause, 212
Assessment monitoring, 53
ASTM, see American Society for Testing
    and Materials
Attorney-client privilege, 186
Audits, see also specific types
  compliance, 195–196
  defenses in, 16–17
  property purchase, 15–17, 183

B

"Bad faith", 227
Banning of pesticides, 106, 111
BAT, see Best available technology
Batteries, 39
BCT, see Best conventional technology

Best available technology (BAT), 133, 149, 162–163
Best conventional technology (BCT), 133
Best management practices (BMPs) plan, 132, 138
Best practicable technology (BPT), 133
Biennial reports, 29, 31, 35
Bioaccumulation of pesticides, 107
BMPs, see Best management practices
Bond rating test, 101
BPT, see Best practicable technology
Burning for energy recovery, 83

C

CAA, see Clean Air Act
Carbon monoxide, 159, 175
Cathodic protection systems, 93, 95, 98
CERCLA (Comprehensive Environmental Response, Compensation and Liability Act), see Superfund
CERCLIS, see Comprehensive Environmental Response, Compensation and Liability Information System
CGL, see Comprehensive general liability
Characteristic hazardous waste, 21, 23–25, 30, 83
Chemical Referral Service Hotline, 24
Chillers, 178
Chlorine gas, 69
Civil liability, 30
Claims notifications, 213
Clean Air Act (CAA), 49, 61, 72, 157, 158–169, see also Air pollutants; Air quality
    acid rain and, 159, 164–167, 178
    air conditioning and, 178
    airport operations and, 178
    chillers and, 178
    criteria pollutants under, 158, 159, 163
    fire departments and, 177
    fleet vehicles and, 168
    maintenance activities and, 177
    mass transportation and, 168–169
    maximum achievable control technology under, 161–162, 165–166, 176
    municipal activities affected by, 169–178
    NAAQS and, 158–159, 164, 170, 175
    NESHAPs and, 175, 176
    new source performance standards under, 159, 161, 165, 170, 175, 178
    permits under, 73, 78, 167, 169, 170
    police departments and, 177

prevention of significant deterioration program under, 162–165, 170, 175, 178
    refrigeration and, 178
    sludge management and, 145, 175–176
    small stationary engines and, 169–170
    solid waste and, 170–175
    storage tanks and, 170, 178
    wastewater treatment plants and, 175–177
Clean Water Act (CWA), 50, 61, 72, 148, see also National Pollutant Discharge Elimination System (NPDES)
    effluent standards under, 138
    emergency notifications under, 69, 75–76
    oil management and, 81, 84–85
    penalties under, 140
    permits under, 73, 78, 131, 133, 135
    real estate transactions and, 210, 211
    reporting requirements under, 137
    sludge management and, 141, 144
Coast Guard National Response Center, 61, 62, 70, 71, 74, 76–78, 111
Combustion of solid waste, 170–175
Commercial solid waste, 45
Common carriers, 30–31
Communications, 194
    effective, 198–202
    risk, see Risk communication
Community consent, 201
Community education, 202–207
Community emergency coordinators, 62, 78, 79, 111
Community information, 200, 202, see also Risk communication
Community involvement, 202–207
Community participation, 202–207
Community relations, 201, 204
Community resistance, 200
Community right-to-know, 11, 57, see also Emergency Planning and Community Right-to-Know Act (EPCRA); Risk communication
Community support, 202
Community trust, 201
Compliance, see also specific types
    achievement of, 187–188
    assessment of status of, 183–185, 217–218
    auditing in, 195–196
    commitment to, 193–194
    communications and, 194
    cooperation in, 194–195
    design of programs for, 195–197
    development of programs for, 191–192

establishment of, 181–189
goals for, 182–183
identification of appropriate, 185–186
maintenance of, 188–189
management considerations in, 191–196
organization of programs for, 196
outside assistance in, 186–187
policy on, 191
staffing for, 191–196
Composting, 40, 41, 143, 145, 170
Comprehensive Environmental Response, 61
Comprehensive Environmental Response, Compensation and Liability Information System (CERCLIS), 8
Comprehensive general liability (CGL) insurance, 219–226
Conditionally exempt generators, 22, 26, 29–31, 35, 83
Confidentiality, 186
Contingency plans, 29, 34, 87, 88
Cooperation, 194–195
Corrective action, 52–53, 97–98, see also specific types
Corrosion protection for USTs, 93–96
Corrosivity, 23
Cost recovery, 7
Covenants, 213
Credibility, 200
Criminal liability, 30
Criteria pollutants, 163
CWA, see Clean Water Act

D

Data acquisition, 214–215
Deeds of trust, 213
De minimis settlement, 10
Demolition, 116–121, 126, 165
Dewatering of sludge, 142, 143
Dioxins, 175
Direct dischargers, 131, 133, 139
Discharge permits, see Permits
Disclosure in real estate transactions, 211
Disease vector control, 48
Disposal contracts, 11–14
Dispute resolution mechanisms, 213
Do-it-yourselfers (DIYs), 84
Drinking water quality, 147, see also Safe Drinking Water Act (SDWA)
Drinking water treatment plants, 20, 69, 131, 175–177
Due diligence, 214, 217
Dust, 42, 83

Duty to defend, 220
Duty to indemnify, 220

E

ECA, see Environmental compliance assessment
EIL, see Environmental impairment liability
Electric power generators, 91, 92, 178
Electric utility generating plants, 20, 57, 178
Emergency generators, 91, 92, 178
Emergency notifications, 69–79, see also Risk communication
under CWA, 69, 75–76
under EPCRA, 57–59, 61–62, 70, 75, 77–79
under HMTA, 75
mechanics of, 74–75
of oil spills and leaks, 89
of pesticide spills, 111
under RCRA, 70, 72, 75–77
records of, 75
under SDWA, 149–152
under Superfund, 69, 70–75, 77, 78
under TSCA, 69, 72, 76
Emergency planning, see Emergency response planning
Emergency Planning and Community Right-to-Know Act (EPCRA), 57, 198, see also Community right-to-know; Emergency response planning; Risk communication
compliance with, 58
emergency notifications under, 57–59, 61–62, 70, 75, 77–79
inventory reporting and, 62–67
record requirements of, 67
reporting requirements of, see Emergency notifications
requirements of, 59–62
tier I information under, 66
tier II information under, 66–67
Emergency power generators, 91, 92, 178
Emergency reporting requirements, see Emergency notifications
Emergency response, 11
Emergency response committees, 57–59
Emergency response personnel, 62
Emergency response planning, 30, 57–68, see also Emergency Planning and Community Right-to-Know Act (EPCRA)
development of, 60
implementation of, 60

local, see Local emergency response committees (LERCs)
requirements for, 59–61
state, see State emergency response committees (SERCs) for USTs, 92
Emergency situation preparedness and prevention, 28, 29, 32, 34
Eminent domain, 16
Employee training, 28, 29, 30, 33, 34, 63
for compliance programs, 194, 195
for oil management, 85, 89
Energy recovery, 40, 83
Environmental assessment, 185, 186
Environmental compliance, see also specific types
achievement of, 187–188
assessment of, 183–185, 217–218
auditing in, 195–196
commitment to, 193–194
communications and, 194
cooperation in, 194–195
design of programs for, 195–197
development of programs for, 191–192
establishment of, 181–189
goals for, 182–183
identification of appropriate, 185–186
management considerations in, 191–196
organization of programs for, 196
outside assistance in, 186–187
policy on, 191
staffing for, 191–196
Environmental compliance assessment (ECA), 183–185, 217–218
Environmental departments, 192, 196
Environmental impairment liability (EIL) insurance, 219
Environmental liability, 181, 188
Environmental planning, 197–207
Environmental services divisions, 195
Environmental site assessments (ESAs), 212–217
EPA identification numbers, 26–30, 36
for large-quantity generators, 34
oil management and, 84
provisional, 37
for small-quantity generators, 31–32
EPCRA, see Emergency Planning and Community Right-to-Know Act
ESAs, see Environmental site assessments
Exception reports, 29, 33
Explosions, 57
Explosive gases, 48–49
Extremely hazardous substances, 60, 61, 64, 66, 73, 74, 77

F

Federal Emergency Management Agency (FEMA), 81–82
Federal Insecticide, Fungicide, and Rodenticide Act (FIFRA), 105, 109
FEMA, see Federal Emergency Management Agency
Fertilizers, 147
FIFRA, see Federal Insecticide, Fungicide, and Rodenticide Act
Filters, 84
Financial assurance, 43, 50, 53–54
for USTs, 92, 98–103
Fire departments, 57–59, 62–65, 67, 78, 165, 177
Fires, 57
Fleet vehicles, 168
Found waste, 20, 36–37
Fund balance, 102
Furans, 175

G

Gas condensate, 50
Gases, 42, 48–49, 51, 69, 170, see also specific types
Gas flares, 177
Generators, see also specific types
conditionally exempt, 22, 26, 28–31, 35, 83
large-quantity, 26, 28–30, 34–35
small-quantity, see Small-quantity generators
Groundwater corrective action and monitoring, 52–53
Guarantees
real estate transactions and, 213
of USTs, 99–100, 102

H

Harmful quantities of oil, 85
Hazard Communications Standard, OSHA, 63, 64
Hazardous air pollutants, 161–162, 165–166, 170, 178
Hazardous Materials Transportation Act (HMTA), 75
Hazardous substances, 10–14, 16, see also Hazardous waste; specific types
compliance programs and, 184
CWA requirements on, 132
disposal of, 106

emergency response planning for release of, see Emergency response planning
EPCRA and, 65–67
extremely, 60, 61, 64, 66, 73, 74, 77
handling of, 106
insurance and, 224
in landfills, 71
list of as EPCRA requirement, 65–67
OSHA and, 63
RCRA and, 73, 76
real estate transactions and, 211–214, 216
release of
  defined, 61
  emergency notifications of, see Emergency notifications
  emergency response planning for, see Emergency response planning
spills of, 70
storage of, 106
Superfund covered, 73
Hazardous waste, 7, 11, 19–37, see also Hazardous substances; Hazardous waste; specific types
accidents with, 69
acutely, 22, 26, 27, 29–32, 112, 113
  pesticides as, 112, 113
ash as, 42
characteristic, 21, 23–25, 30, 83
cleanup of, 5–7
  federal law on, see Superfund
compliance programs and, 184, 187
disposal of, 7, 11–14, 28, 29
  options for, 28, 30–31, 33, 34
found, 20, 36–37
handling of, 32, 34
identification of, 20–25, 28, 29, see also EPA identification numbers
insurance and, 221
land-banned, 24–25, 33
in landfills, 47, 48
liquid, 50
listed, 21–23, 25, 30
management of, 28
minimization of, 25–29, 33, 35
packaging of, 35–36
pesticides as, 105, 108, 112, 113
pretreatment of, 132
RCRA and, 76, 77
real estate transactions and, 210–212, 214, 215
release of, 6, 11, 17
SDWA and, 153

sole active ingredient rule on, 22
storage of, 28, 29, 32, 34
"technical", 22
transport of, 30–31, 35–36
Hazardous waste manifests, 25, 29, 31, 35, 36
Health advisories under SDWA, 149–152
HMTA, see Hazardous Materials Transportation Act
Hotlines, 23–24, 76, see also specific types
Household solid waste, 14, 45, 47, 54
Hydrogen chloride, 175

I

Ignitability, 23
Impoundments, 7
Incineration, 40–42
CAA and, 170
risk communication and, 199
of sewage sludge, 175–176
of sludge, 143, 144, 165, 175–176
Indemnity clauses, 213
Indirect dischargers, 131–132
Industrial dischargers, 133, 134, 137
Industrial solid waste, 45
Industrial stormwater, 136
Information availability, 67
Injection wells, 154
In-kind contributions, 10
Innocent landowner defense, 16, 17, 214, 216, 217
Insurance, 219–227, see also specific types
claims on, 223–224
comprehensive general liability, 219–226
environmental impairment liability, 219
history of, 220–223
interpretation of, 220–223
liability, 100
  Comprehensive General, 219–226
  environmental impairment, 219
litigation over, 226–227
pollution exclusion clause in, 222, 223
self-, 99
Interim Policy, 10
"Interim Prohibition", 93
Interstitial monitoring, 95
Inventory control for USTs, 95, 98
Inventory reporting requirements, 62–67

J

"Joint and several" liability, 5–7

L

Labeling
  of asbestos-containing materials, 125
  of pesticides, 105–110, 112, 113
LAER, see Lowest achievable emission rate
Lagoons, 7
Land application of sludge, 144, 145
Land-banned wastes, 24–25, 33
Land disposal of sludge, 144
Landfills, 7, 22
  CAA and, 170
  closure of, 43, 45, 50–53
  corrective action for, 43, 45, 47
  coverage of existing and new, 44–45
  design of, 43, 45–47, 50, 51
  financial assurance for, 43, 50, 53–54
  gases in, 170
  hazardous substances in, 71
  legal requirements for, 43–54
  liners for, 42, 46, 50
  location of, 45–46
  monitoring of, 43, 45, 47, 50, 51
  operation of, 43, 47–50
  post-closure care of, 43, 50–53
  sludge management and, 143
  solid waste, see Solid waste landfills
Land titles, 210
Large-quantity generators, 26, 28–30, 34–35, 76
Leachate, 42, 46, 49, 50, 51
Lead, 147, 150, 152, 159
Lead-acid batteries, 39
Leaks, 69, 89, 95–96, 98
LERCs, see Local emergency response committees
Letters of credit, 100
Liability, see also specific types
  civil, 30
  criminal, 30
  environmental, 181, 188
  "joint and several", 5–7
  "no-fault", 6
  in oil management, 89
  real estate transactions and, 209–211
  Superfund, 5–7
    disposal options and, 30
    protection from, 8–17
    real estate transactions and, 209
  third-party, 98
  for USTs, 98
Liability insurance, 100, see also specific types
  comprehensive general, 219–226
  environmental impairment, 219

Liquid hazardous waste, 50
Listed hazardous waste, 21–23, 25, 30
Litigation, 226–227
Local emergency response committees
    (LERCs), 57–60, 63–67
  emergency notifications and, 70, 74, 78, 79
  pesticide spills and, 111
  Superfund and, 70, 74
Local government financial test, 101
Lowest achievable emission rate (LAER), 164

M

MACT, see Maximum achievable control
    technology
Management plans for solid waste, 40
Management systems, 191–196
Manifests, 25, 29, 31, 35, 36
Marine Protection, Research, and Sanctuaries
    Act (MPRSA), 145
Mass transportation, 168–169
Material Safety Data Sheet (MSDS), 60, 63,
    64–67
Materials recovery facilities, 41
Maximum achievable control technology
    (MACT), 161–162, 165–166, 176
Maximum contaminant levels (MCLs), 148,
    149, 150
MCLs, see Maximum contaminant levels
Media relations, 204
Medical professionals, 62
Methane, 48
Minimum content requirements, 39
Minor source permitting, 164
Mixtures, 60, 63, 65, 67, 74, 83
Mobile sources, 167–170, 177
Monitoring, see also specific types
  assessment, 53
  groundwater, 52–53
  interstitial, 95
  of solid waste landfills, 43, 45, 47, 50, 51
  of underground injection control program,
    154
  of underground storage tanks, 95
  vapor, 95
MPRSA, see Marine Protection, Research,
    and Sanctuaries Act
MSDS, see Material Safety Data Sheet
MSW, see Municipal solid waste
Municipal waste combustors (MWCs), 42,
    170–175
Municpal solid waste (MSW), 10, 40, 41
  combustion of, 170–175
  sludge management and, 143

Municpal solid waste (MSW) landfills, see
    Solid waste landfills
MWCs, see Municipal waste combustors

N

NAAQS, see National Ambient Air Quality
    Standards
National Ambient Air Quality Standards
    (NAAQS), 158–159, 164, 170, 175
National Contingency Plan, 88
National Emissions Standard for Hazardous
    Air Pollutants (NESHAPs), 116,
    118–121, 126, 161, 170, 175, 176
National Pollutant Discharge Elimination
    System (NPDES), 72, 131, see also
    Clean Water Act (CWA)
  penalties under, 140
  permits under
    applying for, 132–135, 137–138
    classifications of, 135–136
    modification of, 139
    operating under, 138–139
    reapplying for, 139–140
    requirements for, 135–136
    stormwater runoff, 135–138
  sludge management and, 141, 142
National Priorities List (NPL), 8, 43, 44, 214
National Resources Defense Counsel
    (NRDC), 23
National Response Center, 61, 62, 70, 71, 74,
    76–78, 111
"Navigable waters", 75, 76, 86
Negligence, 6
NESHAPs, see National Emissions Standard
    for Hazardous Air Pollutants
New source performance standards (NSPS),
    133, 159, 161, 165, 170, 175, 178
Nitrogen oxides, 159, 161, 165
"No-fault" liability, 6
NOI, see Notice of intent
Nonhazardous sludge, 45
Nonpoint source discharge, 50
Nonrestricted-use pesticides, 107
Notice of intent (NOI), 138
Notifications, see also Risk communication
  of claims, 213
  emergency, see Emergency notifications
  of insurance companies, 224–227
  of pesticide spills, 111
  real estate transactions and, 213
  under SDWA, 149–152
  of USTs, 92, 93

NPDES, see National Pollutant Discharge
    Elimination System
NPL, see National Priorities List
NRDC, see National Resources Defense
    Counsel
NSPS, see New source performance standards

O

Occupancy, 210
Occupational Safety and Health Act (OSHA),
    60
  air quality and, 159
  asbestos and, 116, 126
  Hazard Communications Standard of, 63,
    64
  inventory reporting and, 62–66
  oil management and, 81–82
Oil, 14, 39, 69, 72
  compliance programs and, 184
  CWA regulations on, 75
  discharge of, 132
  harmful quantities of, 85
  leaks of, 89
  management of, 81–89
  off-spec, 83
  on-spec, 83
  spills of, 83–89
  used, see Used oil
Oil filters, 84
Oil Pollution Act (OPA), 81, 85, 87
Oil Spill Response Plans, 85, 87–89
OPA, see Oil Pollution Act
Operating permits, 167, 169, 170
OSHA, see Occupational Safety and Health
    Act
Ownership concept, 210–213, 217
Ozone, 159, 167, 178

P

Paint, 69
PCBs, see Polychlorinated biphenyls
PCM, see Phase contrast microscopy
Permits, 30, 73, see also specific types
  applying for, 132–135, 137–138
  CAA, 73, 78, 167, 169, 170
  classifications of, 135–136
  CWA, 73, 78, 131, 133, 135
  facilities requiring, 132
  general, 132
  individual, 132
  for injection wells, 154

minor source, 164
modification of, 139
NPDES
    applying for, 132–135, 137–138
    classifications of, 135–136
    modification of, 139
    operating under, 138–139
    reapplying for, 139–140
    requirements for, 135–136
    stormwater runoff, 135–138
    operating, 167, 169, 170
    operating under, 138–139
    reapplying for, 139–140
    requirements for, 135–136
    stormwater runoff, 135–138
Pesticides, 105–113
    accidents with, 69, 107, 111, 113
    applicator certification for, 108–109, 111
    banning of, 106, 111
    bioaccumulation of, 107
    disposal of, 112–113
    emergency notifications of, 61, 72, 78
    identification of, 21, 22
    labeling of, 105–110, 112, 113
    nonrestricted-use, 107
    records on, 110–111
    restricted-use, 107–109, 111
    SDWA and, 147
    selection of, 106–107
    source reductions for, 106
    spills of, 107, 111, 113
    storage of, 109–110
    toxicity of, 107
Phase contrast microscopy (PCM), 124
Pits, 7
Point charge discharges, 131
Point sources, 50, 72, 135
Police departments, 177
Pollution exclusion clause, 222, 223
Polychlorinated biphenyls (PCBs), 42, 47, 69, 72, 76, 81, see also specific types
Ponds, 7
Potenially responsible parties (PRPs), 5–10, 44
    insurance and, 225
    real estate transactions and, 212
POTWs, see Publicly owned treatment works
Power generators, 91, 92, 178
Pretreatment plans, 134
Pretreatment standards, 27, 132, 134–135
Pretreatment standards for existing sources (PSES), 133
Pretreatment standards for new sources (PSNS), 133

Prevention of significant deterioration (PSD) program, 162–165, 170, 175, 178
Primary sludge, 142
Property acquisition, 14–17
Property management, 14
Property ownership, 210–213, 217
Property purchase audits, 15–17, 183
Property titles, 210
PRPs, see Potenially responsible parties
PSD, see Prevention of significant deterioration
PSES, see Pretreatment standards for existing sources
PSNS, see Pretreatment standards for new sources
Public consent, 201
Public education, 202–207
Public health, 201
Public information, 200, 202, see also Risk communication
Public involvement, 202–207
Publicly owned treatment works (POTWs), 72, 131–134, 136
    air quality and, 161
    sludge management and, 141–143
Public participation, 202–207
Public relations, 201, 204
Public resistance, 200
Public right-to-know, 11, 57, see also Emergency Planning and Community Right-to-Know Act (EPCRA); Risk communication
Public support, 202
Public trust, 201

Q

Quality-of-life issues, 199

R

RCRA, see Resource Conservation and Recovery Act
RDF, see Refuse-derived fuel
Reactivity, 23
Real estate transactions, 209–218
    as is clause in, 212
    data acquisition and, 214–215
    disclosure requirements in, 211
    dispute resolution mechanisms in, 213
    environmental compliance assessment and, 217–218
    indemnity clauses in, 213
    liability and, 209–211

site assessments in, 213–217
site contamination and, 209–210
site investigation and, 213–218
site visits and, 215–217
structuring of, 211–213
Record of Decision (ROD), 8
Records, 28, see also specific types
    emergency notification, 75
    emergency response planning, 58
    EPCRA requirements for, 67
    for large-quantity generators, 35
    on pesticides, 110–111
    under SDWA, 152
    for small-quantity generators, 31, 33
    on USTs, 96, 102–103
    waste shipment, 119
Recycling, 40, 41, 82, 83, 134, 170
Refrigeration, 178
Refuse-derived fuel (RDF) systems, 41
Regulated asbestos-containing material
    (RACM), 118–121
"Regulated waters", 85, 86
Remedial Investigation and Feasibility Study
    (RI/FS), 8
Remediation, 53
Remediation plans, 48, 49
Renovations, 116–121, 126
Reportable quantities (RQs), 59, 61
    CWA and, 75
    EPCRA and, 111
    of pesticides, 111
    RCRA and, 76
    Superfund and, 70, 71, 73–74, 76, 111
Reports, 28, see also specific types
    annual, 31
    biennial, 29, 31, 35
    CWA, 137
    emergency, see Emergency notifications
    exception, 29, 33
    inventory, 62–67
    for large-quantity generators, 35
    real estate transactions and, 216
    SDWA, 149–152
    for small-quantity generators, 31, 33
    Superfund, 137
    on USTs, 102–103
Request for proposals (RFPs), 11–13
Resource Conservation and Recovery Act
    (RCRA), 19, 22, 23, 26, 29, 30, 32,
    153
    emergency notifications under, 70, 72, 75–
    77
    hazardous substances covered under, 73
    oil management and, 81, 83

permits under, 30
pesticide regulation under, 105, 108
real estate transactions and, 210, 211
sludge management and, 144, 145
solid waste and, 39, 42, 47, 48
solid waste landfills and, 43
UST regulations under, 92
Restricted-use pesticides, 107–109, 111
RFP, see Request for proposals
RI/FS, see Remedial Investigation and Feasi-
    bility Study
Right-to-know, see Community right-to-know
Risk assessment, 201, 203
Risk communication, 197–207
    defined, 198
    effectiveness of, 198–202
    public education and, 202–207
Risk education programs, 203
Risk management, 203
Risk management plans, 165, 166, 170, 175–
    177
Risk reduction, 183
Risk retention group (RRG) coverage, 100
ROD, see Record of Decision
RQs, see Reportable quantities
RRG, see Risk retention group
Runoff, 49
    stormwater, 42, 131–140
        industrial, 136
        permit for, 135–138
    wastewater, 131–140

S

Safe Drinking Water Act (SDWA), 47, 72,
    147–155
    health advisories under, 149–152
    local government applicability of, 155
    notifications under, 149–152
    primary standards under, 147–149
    real estate transactions and, 211
    records under, 152
    reporting requirements under, 149–152
    secondary standards under, 152–153
    sludge management and, 141
    sole source aquifer protection under, 154
    underground injection control program un-
        der, 153–155
    Wellhead Protection Program under, 154–
        155
SDWA, see Safe Drinking Water Act
Secondary maximum contaminant levels
    (SMCLs), 150–152
Secondary sludge, 142

Self-insurance, 99
SERCs, see State emergency response com-
        mittees
Sewage sludge, 10, 45, 144, 165, 175–176
Sewer systems, 136, 137
SIPs, see State implementation plans
Site assessments, 212–217
Site contamination, 209–210
Site investigation in real estate transactions,
        213–218
Site visits, 215–217
Sludge
    CAA and, 175
    defined, 141–142
    dewatering of, 142, 143
    disposal of, 144
    generation of, 142–143
    incineration of, 143, 144, 165, 175–176
    land application of, 144, 145
    land disposal of, 144
    management of, 141–146
    nonhazardous, 45
    primary, 142
    quantity of, 142–143
    recycling of, 134
    regulation of, 143–145
    secondary, 142
    sewage, 10, 45, 144, 165
    stabilization of, 143
Small-quantity generators, 26, 28–30
    emergency notifications and, 76
    landfills and, 45
    requirements for, 31–33, 35
Small stationary engines, 169–170
SMCLs, see Secondary maximum contami-
        nant levels
Sole active ingredient rule, 22
Sole source aquifer protection, 154
Solid waste, 39–55, see also specific types
    ban on disposal of, 39
    CAA and, 170–175
    combustion of, 170–175
    commercial, 45
    composting of, 40, 41
    disposal of, 39, 170–175
    household, 14, 45, 47, 54
    incineration of, 40–42
    industrial, 45
    landfills for, see Solid waste landfills
    management alternatives for, 40–43
    management plans for, 40
    municpal, 10, 40, 41
        combustion of, 170–175
        sludge management and, 143

recycling of, 40, 41
reduction of, 39–41
source reduction of, 40–41
storage of, 170–175
treatment of, 170–175
Solid waste landfills, 39, 40, 42–43
    closure of, 43, 45, 50–52, 54
    corrective action for, 43, 45, 47
    coverage of existing and new, 44–45
    design of, 43, 45–47, 50, 51
    financial assurance for, 43, 50, 53–54
    legal requirements for, 43–54
    location of, 45–46
    monitoring of, 43, 45, 47, 50, 51
    operation of, 43, 47–50
    post-closure care of, 43, 50–52, 53
    sludge management and, 143
Source reduction, 40–41
SPCC, see Spill Prevention, Control, and
        Countermeasure
Spill Prevention, Control, and Countermea-
        sure (SPCC) Plans, 81, 84–87, 89
Spills, 57, 69–74, 79, see also specific types
    defined, 77
    oil, 83–89
    pesticide, 107, 111, 113
    prevention of, 94
    from USTs, 94, 95
State emergency response committees
        (SERCs), 57–60, 63–67
    emergency notifications and, 70, 74, 78,
        79
    pesticide spills and, 111
    Superfund and, 70, 74
State implementation plans (SIPs), 49, 158
Steering committees, 9
Storage tanks
    CAA and, 170, 178
    underground, see Underground storage tanks
        (USTs)
Storm sewer systems, 136, 137
Stormwater runoff, 42, 131–140
    industrial, 136
    permits for, 135–138
Sulfur dioxide, 157, 159, 161, 162, 164, 165,
        175
Superfund, 5–17, 19, 22, 33, 153
    cost recovery under, 7
    de minimis settlement under, 10
    disposal contracts under, 11–14
    emergency notifications under, 69, 70–75,
        77, 78
    emergency reporting and, 61
    hazardous substances covered under, 73

in-kind contributions under, 10
insurance and, 225
Interim Policy under, 10
landfills and, 43
liability under, 5–7
  disposal options and, 30
  protection from, 8–17
  real estate transactions and, 209
preventive steps to limit liability under, 10–
  11
procedures under, 7–8
property acquisition under, 14–17
property management under, 14
property purchase audits under, 15–17
real estate transactions and, 210, 211, 214,
  217
"releases" covered under, 71–73
reportable quantities and, 70, 71, 73–74
reporting requirements under, 137
settlement process under, 9–10
solid waste under, 14
steering committees under, 9
third-party defendants under, 10
Surety bonds, 100
Surface impoundments, 7
Surface water requirements, 49–50

T

TCLP, see Toxicity Characteristic Leaching
  Procedure
"Technical" hazardous waste, 22
TEM, see Transmission electron microscopy
Third-party defendants, 10
Third-party liability, 98
Threshold limit values (TLVs), 159
Threshold planning quantity (TPQ), 59, 60,
  66
Tires, 39
Titles, 210
TLVs, see Threshold limit values
Toxicity, 23, 107
Toxicity Characteristic Leaching Procedure
  (TCLP), 23
Toxic Substances Control Act (TSCA), 69,
  72, 76, 81, 116, 145, 211
Toxic Substances Hotline, 23
TPQ, see Threshold planning quantity
Training, 28–30, 33, 34, 63
  for compliance programs, 194, 195
  for oil management, 85, 89
Transfer stations, 41
Transmission electron microscopy (TEM),
  124

Treatment, storage, and disposal (TSD) fa-
  cilities, 24, 25, 29, 30, 32, 33, 35
Treatment standards, 24
Trust, 201
Trust funds, 100
TSCA, see Toxic Substances Control Act
TSD, see Treatment, storage, and disposal

U

UIC, see Underground injection control
Underground injection control (UIC) program,
  153–155
Underground storage tanks (USTs), 82, 85,
  91–103
  1988 rule on, 98–101
  1993 rule on, 101–103
  cathodic protection systems for, 93, 95, 98
  compliance programs and, 184
  corrective action requirements for, 97–98
  corrosion protection for, 93–96
  defined, 91
  existing, 92–95
  financial assurance for, 92, 98–103
  governmental guarantee of, 102
  guarantee of, 99–100, 102
  installation of, 93–94
  inventory control for, 95, 98
  leaks in, 95–96, 98
  monitoring of, 95
  new, 92–95, 98, 103
  notifications concerning, 92, 93
  prevention of spills and overflows from, 94
  real estate transactions and, 210
  records on, 96, 102–103
  reports on, 102–103
  spills and overflows from, 94, 95
  state regulation of, 100–101
  technical standards for, 92–96
Used oil, 14, 27, 39, 91
  aggregation points for, 83–84
  collection centers for, 84
  compliance programs and, 184
  management of, 81–84
  off-spec, 83
  on-spec, 83
Used oil filters, 84
USTs, see Underground storage tanks
Utility generating plants, 20, 57, 178

V

Vapor monitoring, 95
Vehicle maintencne garages, 57

W

Waste minimization, 25–29, 33, 35
Waste shipment records, 119
Waste-to-energy (WTE) systems, 40–42, 54,
    199
Wastewater recycling, 134
Wastewater runoff, 131–140
Wastewater treatment plants, 20, 57, 69, 72,
    131, 175–177

Wellhead Protection (WHP) Program, 154–
    155
WHP, see Wellhead Protection
Worker Protection Rule, 116, 119, 126–
    127
WTE, see Waste-to-energy
ment and, 143
  recycling of, 40, 41
  reduction of, 39–41
  source reduction of, 40–41